ANTHROPOLOGY AND THE ECONOMY OF SHARING

Thomas Widlok

Routledge
Taylor & Francis Group

LONDON AND NEW YORK

First published 2017 by Routledge
2 Park Square, Milton Park, Abingdon, Oxon OX14 4RN

and by Routledge
711 Third Avenue, New York, NY 10017

Routledge is an imprint of the Taylor & Francis Group, an informa business.

British Library Cataloguing-in-Publication Data
A catalogue record for this book is available from the British Library.

Library of Congress Cataloging-in-Publication Data
Names: Widlok, Thomas, author.
Title: Anthropology and the economy of sharing / Thomas Widlok.
Description: Abingdon, Oxon; New York, NY: Routledge is an imprint of
the Taylor & Francis Group, an Informa Business, [2017] |
Includes bibliographical references and index.
Identifiers: LCCN 2016012524 | ISBN 9781138945555 (hbk. : alk. paper) |
ISBN 9781138945548 (pbk. : alk. paper) | ISBN 9781315671291 (ebk)
Subjects: LCSH: Sharing–Economic aspects–Cross-cultural studies. |
Sharing–Social aspects–Cross-cultural studies. | Economic anthropology
Classification: LCC GN450.75 .W53 2017 | DDC 306.3–dc23LC record
available at https://lccn.loc.gov/2016012524

ISBN: 978-1-138-94555-5 (hbk)
ISBN: 978-1-138-94554-8 (pbk)
ISBN: 978-1-315-67129-1 (ebk)

Typeset in Times
by Cenveo Publisher Services

Printed and bound by CPI Group (UK) Ltd, Croydon, CR0 4YY

For my family and friends
and for the LSE MSc course of 1988/89

CONTENTS

LIST OF FIGURES AND TABLES

Figures

Tables

INTRODUCTION

Sharing – an alternative

You are about to begin reading a book on sharing. "You went to the bookshop and bought the volume. Good for you." (Calvino 1981:4) – at least this has been a reasonable expectation for authors, publishers and readers alike. We expect that most of you who read this book will have actually bought it – if you have not done so, as yet, I for one hope that you are considering doing so, since it is worthwhile to make it your own. However, a good number of readers may possess and read the book without having bought it themselves. You may have been given it as a gift or you may be borrowing it from a library or downloading it from somewhere. Still, we assume that the gift-giver, the library or the online site will have bought the volume or a license. Hence, among the many ways in which you can access this book, buying it directly is only one. We are nevertheless accustomed to the idea that "ultimately" a market-type purchase frames those other modes of transfer such as lending and borrowing, gift-giving, exchanging and sharing. Maybe things were different in the past but surely not today since commercialization now extends into many spheres of life that were previously exempted. However, there are reasons for rethinking this expectation.

Purchasing books and other things in market exchange requires an income: money which in turn is expected to come from selling one's labour on the job market. But for the majority of the human population, subsistence is not gained through market exchanges. In Germany only four out of ten citizens sustain themselves through selling their labour force on the market while the majority makes a living as family dependents, as pensioners or social benefit recipients (Duschek 2006: 14, see also Schäfers 2008). In countries with less developed welfare systems the situation is not radically different. In the United States only 60% of the adult (!) population is in employment (Ferguson 2015: 22). Among the other half, those who actively seek work form a minority. A very large proportion are not buying their necessities through a market exchange of their labour but on the basis of a variety of other transfers. This wide spectrum ranges from state-dependent prison inmates, across young people depending on their parents, old people depending on retirement funds to rich people who live off rent received from capital and real estate. As James Ferguson has recently pointed out, millions of students do not work for a living but "are supported by some combination of parental largesse and institutional grants and scholarships" (2015: 22). He has also suggested that in terms of reorganizing this redistribution, Africa and other regions of the global South are not lagging behind but are pioneers of innovation (2015: 192). Despite the importance of wage labour, many people in the global South realize that after leaving traditional subsistence economies behind they will not be able to feed themselves through selling their labour. The newly emerging jobs are chronically small in number and for an increasing proportion of the population jobs and market exchanges cannot ensure access to goods. Even where production intensifies it is a lack of access to land and waged employment that has led societies in the global South to experiment with new forms of distributive practices that are based on sharing. By demanding "a rightful share" they seek to ensure participation in the wealth of a country or region. The challenge that remains is how such a share in the national or global wealth can be realized. This is where the global search for more effective forms of distribution turns towards anthropology with its "inexhaustible record of inventiveness" (Ferguson 2015: 216). Anthropology has a track record of documenting and reflecting upon alternatives to market exchange. As this book aims to show, the emphasis in this endeavour has for too long been on gift-exchange theory. It is time to turn towards an anthropology of sharing. By tapping into the extensive evidence for human ways of successfully organizing sharing we can make anthropological knowledge fruitful for developing alternative ways of enabling access to services and goods, including things like the book in front of you.

Market exchanges foster a tendency, for instance with regard to books, to separate contents from transfer. Most authors, at least those of scholarly books with little or no royalty payments, usually care little about the way in which their readers have got hold of their books as long as they read them – just as many publishers or booksellers, not all of them, care little as to whether the buyers of a book are actually going to read it. Anthropology, by contrast, has long insisted that the mode of transfer does matter as much as what it is that is being transferred and to whom. Evaluating objects separately from those who possess, give, or receive them and from the context in which the transaction takes place is in itself the product of a particular type of market exchange that has entrenched this view. A book, for one, is not only a marketable product but it also has the potential to create a link between author and reader, or between readers, for instance when it is recommended to a student or a friend or when given as a present at a particular event. The fact that it can be easily shared sequentially by many readers without becoming "less" has implications for transfers as much as the recent development that costs of creating extra copies are diminishing once an electronic version exists. New technical possibilities of multiplication and storage fuel heated debates about copyright and copyleft, not only of books but also of music, artworks, patented goods, plant seeds, genes and so forth. Anthropology is also a good place to start when there is growing dissatisfaction with the dominant modes of distribution and access. Anthropological accounts of "the gift economy" have been read (and written) as a critique and a viable alternative to commodity exchange. But while the contrast between gift and commodity has been elaborately discussed, there is still a tendency to use gift-giving and sharing interchangeably and "there is little in the literature that explicitly compares gift-exchange to sharing" (Belk 2010: 719). This book sets out to change this situation. It deals with sharing at a point in time when sharing is subject to growing expectations as to how it may solve a host of current problems. As Belk noted: "Issues of social justice, consumer welfare, environmentalism, materialism, commoditization, global food security, sustainable environments, and much more, all stand to be vitally informed by work on sharing" (Belk 2010: 730). Movements in the contemporary "sharing economy" are fuelled by hopes that more people could get better access to more things through co-consumption. Similarly, there is widespread moral outrage when food is destroyed or wasted in some places while it could be transferred to those who need it – both at a local and a global level. The realm of market exchanges, transfer through buying and selling, is clearly not the whole spectrum of possibilities for allocating food or books. Moreover, it is likely that changing the ways in which things are allocated and distributed will also affect the social relationships that make up our lives. Anthropology provides a record of diverse modes of transfer and access in its ethnographic accounts from the past and from far away but also from close by. It can also give hints on how this human cultural heritage can help to design our future.

The contract that I have signed with the publisher for this book refers to the transfer of rights to publish the book "in all ways now known or yet to be invented". In other words, there is an assumption that market contracts will extend across all formats in which this text may be circulated. However, given that all texts now exist as digital files, there is an increasing number of ways – legal and illegal – in which readers can get access to books, or parts of them. While we are aware about the growing technical possibilities, our understanding of the socio-cultural dimensions of such transfers and modes of access deserves equal attention. What is socially required to enable transfers beyond buying and selling? Having grown up with an expectation that books and other things are usually sold (before they get lent out, are given away as a present or shared) we need to realize that our cultural baggage is influencing and at times obstructing our understanding of sharing and of other ways of gaining access to the things we value. As a consequence, this book uses many examples from a variety of societies in which people have grown up in different ways. Ethnographers around the world have described situations in which people share. These situations vary with regard to the degree to which people's lives depend on market exchanges, with regard to the size of a group, degree of cooperation between people in these groups, the degree to which their economic transactions are with kin or with anonymous others, and whether they are governed by complex corporate entities outside their personal sphere of control.[1]

Many of my examples are from hunter-gatherer societies in which sharing is the common way of allocating goods – and not market exchange, or gift exchange for that matter. This is not in order to portray these societies as idealized models from which one should or could easily copy ways of doing things. Just as detailed ethnographic accounts of gift-exchange work against a romanticization of "the gift economy", a closer look at sharing prevents similar idealizations. The ethnographic approach underlines that it is important to recognize differences while not overlooking continuities. We are not dealing with separate and self-contained economic worlds. Being aware of alternative modes of allocation and cultivating practices that shape them in different ways holds the potential for innovation. I argue in this book that this is not a new process but one that we can see in the making in the anthropological record, and which we see the more clearly the wider we cast our ethnographic net. Sharing, like every social practice, is integrated into the wider socio-economic settings so that it cannot be imported as an isolated cultural trait without considering the wider conditions and implications. Nevertheless, by looking more closely at a range of cases we can begin to understand which social and cultural conditions are beneficial for realizing and maintaining sharing practices – and which ones are not. Moreover, we can assess the conditions that are conducive to *imagining* alternatives, and those that allow us to realize ideas about alternative ways of allocating economic goods in practice. We can take advantage of the comparative perspective that anthropology provides and re-assess what seems natural to us.

Chapter 1 outlines the main theoretical advance of the book, namely emancipating the study of sharing from the paradigms of gift exchange and reciprocity. For a long time sharing was explicitly or implicitly subsumed under debates on "the gift", at least ever since Marcel Mauss' seminal text on gift exchange (2002 [1923-24]) and Marshall Sahlins' influential classification of sharing under the notion of reciprocity (1988). Over time there has been a growing ethnographic and theoretical reservation against subsuming sharing under gift giving. The reservations largely came out of hunter-gatherer studies, above all in the work of James Woodburn (1998) but there were also criticisms based on Melanesian ethnography (by Alfred Gell 1999) and from comparative economic anthropology (Price 1975, Hunt 2000). Economic anthropology has for a long time been characterized, some may say haunted, by the dualism between commercial market exchange and the gift economy. A fresh look at sharing also has the potential for breaking up that dualism and for opening up new perspectives in economic anthropology at large. The empirical basis for attempting this recalibration is primarily the ethnography of hunter-gatherers which is underrepresented in many of the recent important contributions of influential economic anthropologists such as Keith Hart, David Graeber, Chris Gregory, James Carrier or Stephen Gudeman. The aim is an outline of a theory of sharing that enables a systematical investigation of sharing on its own terms and not in terms of gift-giving or commodity exchange.

In Chapter 2 I summarize why sharing has for a considerable time played an important role in evolutionary anthropology. The preoccupation with sharing in evolutionary models is both a treasure and a problem. It is a treasure insofar as it has stimulated a lot of research on sharing, providing a sound empirical basis for our thinking about sharing as a mode of allocation and distribution. It is a problem insofar as evolutionary assumptions of various kinds saturate and at times over-shadow debates around sharing, its role today and for the future. The chapter therefore discusses some of the main evolutionary ideas connected to sharing. These primarily concern the study of hunter-gatherer groups worldwide and ideas surrounding hunters and their prey. Sharing, in this context, is considered to be, above all, an insurance against erratic hunting success and irregular food source reliability. More generally, evolutionary models link sharing with questions of original altruism and generosity which is ethnographically unwarranted. When confronted with the empirical ethnographic record, many of these models prove to be insufficient as a general explanation of sharing and they point towards the need to look more closely at the social practice of sharing.

Chapter 3 seeks to develop a theory of sharing from the "bottom up", that is, by looking at it as a bundle of concrete social practices. These are practices that create particular forms of co-presence, relatedness and communication and which are predicated on various kinds of demand sharing (Peterson 1993) and more pre-cisely on sharing demands. Accordingly, sharing is understood here as *the social practice of enabling access to what is valued on the basis of shared demands.*[2] While gift and commodity exchange may also be dealing with "access to what is valued" they do not require that all parties involved share one another's demands. Sharing practices have been recorded in considerable detail around the world and in a variety of social and political contexts. This allows insights into the role of sharing for the social order and in social change. It also allows us to see the implications for political power, group formation and individual social networks. The aim here is to develop a theory of sharing that is grounded in the social pro-cess of interaction in which the sense of self is extended but in which the sense of self is also limited through the demands of others and through the finiteness of human life. The patterns that emerge differ from what Mauss and others have identified for gift-exchange. Instead of the obligations to give, to receive and to return the ethnography of sharing suggests a pattern of opportunities to ask, to respond and to renounce.

Chapter 4 develops the view that sharing is a distributive process that is unlike what the theory of gift-giving with its focus on givers and receivers predicts. Beyond individual strategies of granting access to goods it is also the objects of sharing with their specific affordances that matter. Apart from the size of objects (their divisibility) it is the fact that they can generate commensality and that their materiality invites certain uses and excludes others. As the material objects of sharing change, so do the more ephemeral aspects of social life and the opportu-nity for innovation. The ways in which agents and objects form a community of practice not only explains the diversity of sharing practices but also how they are being learned and transmitted across situations and generations whether explicitly supported by an externally imposed moral code or not.

Chapter 5 tackles the question as to how to bridge the hunter-gatherer ethnography with debates and empirical cases from the current state of a complex and globalized society with its corporate agents, shareholders and internet users. Since hunter-gatherers themselves are now integrated into wider political and economic processes tracing the changes to the sharing practice in contemporary transformations provides a series of naturally occurring social experiments. People who have cultivated sharing for millennia face the challenge of coming to grips with an economic system and an ideology that banks on very different principles and very different strategies for allocating goods and for providing access. As I shall show in this chapter, the challenges in these settings are not all that different from what we all face when we seek to overcome the biases, tensions and limitations of present-day capitalist economies.

Chapter 6 looks at instances in which innovations have been introduced to the capitalist economic system under the label of "the sharing economy". Schemes under this label range from car sharing across music streaming and other internet platforms to the placing of "give boxes" in public spaces. These are presented as a moral solution to the current and future problems of human economic relations and for sustainable human-environment relationships. They appeal to ideas of human relations that are not solely governed by notions of utility, while they are at the same time to a large extent intertwined with increasing commercialization and accumulation. The chapter also looks at movements such as the campaign for a Basic Income Grant which do not use the label "sharing" but which seek to put some of the lessons learned from everyday sharing into the practice of large-scale societies on the basis of resource pooling and taxation.

Chapter 7 further explores analogues between patterns found in the sharing practices of small-scale societies and challenges for establishing new distributive systems at larger scales of complexity. Cases that may seem to be at opposite ends on the spectrum of scale can be made mutually informative and they help us to elucidate recurrent problems when integrating sharing with other modes of transfer. Such issues include the question of "oversharing" in electronic and in face-to-face settings, the problem of concentration that is found in storage regimes and that concern both the direct accumulation of material goods and the derived accumulation of knowledge in digital environments. The chapter also introduces the issue of timing in establishing the right time to share and the right time to keep which I elaborate on in the conclusions of the book.

The main thread that runs through all of these chapters is the anthropological project of exploring the ethnographic record for developing social alternatives. When we seek to change the unequal and dissatisfactory ways of distributing goods, the first step is to tap into the rich track record of comparative ethnography. Sharing has proven to be an effective way of opening up opportunities for humans who seek access to what they need. The anthropological uneasiness with policies that claim that "there is no alternative" is also found in economic anthropology where it is manifest in the critique against the large-scale commercialization of the ways in which things are distributed and against the tendency to turn everyone, everywhere into a consumer and a seller. So far, the critique has been harnessed primarily in terms of the ethnography of gift-exchange. Gifts and giving have been heralded as models for coping with industrialization and modernization, as in the writing of Mauss himself, but also with more recent phenomena such as the increasing commercialization of higher education (Cooper 2004). This book argues that this is not the full story. Given the sound empirical base that we now have on sharing practices we can explore a broader range of alternatives than before. We can also go beyond an inverted utopian counter-image based on gift exchange and collective ownership. The deficiencies of the present global economy are complex so that a simple inversion is not sufficient. Goods are distributed in extremely unequal ways and at very different scales. A small proportion of the population owns and controls a large part of all assets. Many of us are excluded from accessing what enables a dignified life despite strong ideologies that claim to foster equality of opportunity and equality of outcome. Getting to know the lived practice of people for whom sharing plays a major role is to better understand what is required when seeking to develop new modes of transfer and allocation that endorse the potentials of sharing.

Each chapter of this book comprises several text boxes in which case studies are presented in more detail. It is important to note that these are not illustrations of what is typical but indications of what is possible. These text boxes, just as the use of ethnography in the book at large, follow the logic of the practice approach that I have applied and they are part and parcel of an attempt to de-essentialize the debate on access, allocation, distribution, property and equality. The ethnographic accounts included in the text boxes and across these chapters are not "merely case material" but they are part of a theoretical approach that seeks to rehabilitate lived practice against other frames of reference. Although I deal with evolutionary questions (above all in Chapter 2) and with questions of historical changes (above all in Chapters 5 and 6), I refrain from presenting a "cultural history of sharing" or "the evolution of sharing". This is because I do not believe that these are the most appropriate frames for discussing the ethnographic evidence. Rather, I support the position that Wittgenstein held against the historical and evolutionary accounts of Frazer, namely that these constitute only one possible form of explanation (Wittgenstein 1993[1967]: 130). Wittgenstein maintained that an account of origins was not a privileged mode of investigating the problems of myth and ritual and focused on family resemblances instead, the "'perspicuous' representation" by means of arranging data along "factual content alone" "in their relation to one another" (1993[1967]: 131–33). I argue the same for issues related to the economy of sharing. The case studies in the text boxes are connected through such a family resemblance. They can be imagined to be like the portraits of members of an extended family that are assembled on a wall: they are not "hung up" on principles of genealogy and lineage but they allow us to see similarities and differences along a whole range of possible connections. Across the chapters I note how much sharing practices are tied to the historical and cultural situations and settings in which they occur. However, there are also considerable continuities and recurrent influences across long stretches of time and space. We are dealing with everyday "exemplars" of sharing as part of the ongoing generation of social life. As practices they form an important complement to the well-known narratives of sharing, for instance with regard to St. Martin and St. Nicolas that symbolize sharing in Christian traditions but also surrounding the Trickster stories of southern African San and many other hunter-gatherer groups. I argue that some of the recurring attractions of sharing, as well as some of its limitations, are implicated in the practice itself and are not confined to certain evolutionary stages, to particular cultural narratives or to particular historical eras. The continuities are therefore most appropriately shown and traced across a number of detailed case studies that cover a wide spectrum and that also reveal the social forces and the potentials for innovation in situated practice.

The ethnographic case studies are therefore not seeking representativeness in the behavioural science sense of the word (see Agar 2008, 2013). Rather they seek a better recognition of patterns that emerge as one moves from one instance to the next. As it happens, there are cases from all continents included in this book. But more importantly, the majority of ethnographic cases are from what is often called the periphery, from Africa in particular. This is important because the failure to fully acknowledge the potential of sharing is linked to the fact that cases from marginalized parts of the world and marginalized sections of the global society have not received appropriate attention outside anthropology. It is also important, however, that the examples comprise not only cases featuring the "usual anthropological suspects" in the global South but also cases that are from my home turf as an anthropologist living in Europe as well as in other parts of the world. If it is the task of anthropology to allow fellow humans to make sense of their actions, this extends not only to those whose sense of action has been appropriated from them by colonial domination (Bourdieu and Schultheis 2010: 184) but ultimately to all of us.

The cases in text boxes also underline the main theoretical thrust of this book, namely that it is the practice of sharing, and not its ideology, that is the key to a better understanding. It is the "essence" of the human condition that we never encounter humans in essence but always in their particular relational position of being younger or older, poorer or richer, with more or less power, healthy or sick, as member of this gendered group, that ethnic group, or a particular occupational group rather than another one. If there is an essence of being human it is that humans encounter and recognize one another always in terms of these particular relational properties, usually in combination and in reference to a particular stage in their lives, in a shared history, a particular situation of health, social status, gender and nationality (Marten 1987: 92).[3] As a consequence, any theory of sharing that seeks to be anthropologically adequate will have to make sure that these "contingencies" are adequately reflected. The use of text boxes with ethnographic cases is therefore an integral part of my argument and a step towards this aim.[4]

Preliminary versions of individual chapters have been presented at conferences and seminars at anthropology departments of the universities of Aberdeen,

Cologne, Edinburgh, Freiburg, Ghent, Vienna, Zürich, and at the Max-Planck Institutes in Nijmegen and Halle. I am thankful to students and colleagues who made helpful comments that allowed me to complete this manuscript. Particular thanks go to Akira Takada, Nicolas Peterson, David Nash, Yasmine Musharbash, Lye Tuck-Po, Sabine Klocke-Daffa, Stephan Henn, James Ferguson, Ute Dieckmann and Michael Casimir. Special thanks go to Peter Flach for creating the cover image and to Monika Feinen who provided assistance with the illustrations. The University of Cologne helped by granting a semester of sabbatical leave. The frequent references to my own field sites and to the places in which I have lived and worked also indicate that this book relies heavily on the support of those with whom I have shared my lifeworld, my native environment in Europe and my adopted environments in Namibia and Australia and elsewhere. I am especially grateful to my close family, Dagmar, Lorna and Merle, who had to cope with my movements between these environments, and the "reduced presence" that comes with this mobility.

Notes

1 The conditions just listed (settlement size and amount of cooperation, market integration, privacy and anonymity, social complexity) are, not coincidentally, the type of group-level variables that recent comparative anthropological projects in economic anthropology have applied (Henrich *et al.* 2005: 808), but it should be kept in mind that this is not a complete list of how variation is constituted.

2 This advances the notion that sharing is "allowing others to take what is valued" (Widlok 2013). The specification "on the basis of shared demands" underlines that the main prerequisite for successful sharing is the human ability to respond to demands towards one another and towards the world we share. Anthropologically, the basic sharing of "language, place of birth, or set of experiences" are not just "simple coincidences" with regard to the volitional sharing in the form of transfer or allocation (Belk 2007: 127) because the former is the basis of the latter.

3 In Marten's words: "Being human, disclosing oneself to others as a human, means to live *as a woman* among women and men, *as a young* person among young and old, *as a sick* person among the healthy and sick, *as a Walloon* among Walloons and Flamings." (1987: 29, my translation).

4 Bourdieu has noted the problems of exemplification in any argument that deals with sociological and anthropological issues. He pointed out that whatever binds people in a social field unfolds through the "apparently contingency" of the personal particulars (Bourdieu 1992: 33).

1

THIS IS NOT A GIFT

Introduction

One of the central messages of this book is that sharing phenomena are inadequately understood when they are considered as cases of reciprocal gift-giving. I shall also point out the repercussions that this change of perspective has for what we think humans are and what culture and society is all about. However, reconceptualizing sharing in a negative way, with regard to what it is not, is not good enough. As Strathern (1988: 11) has pointed out, there is an unfortunate tendency in anthropology to build theory largely out of negativities, emphasizing when and where existing concepts and ideas do not apply. I do not want to entrench this trend and therefore will also be pointing out what is important to take in, positively speaking, from the substantive results of the anthropology of gift-giving and of other modes of transfer to date. One possibility of condensing the contents of the book into one positive sentence is as follows: *Sharing, defined as enabling others to access what is valued, provides a conceptual and practical alternative to market exchange and to gift-exchange.* The social practice of sharing is therefore a fundamental and independent part of the human repertoire of making a living. Sharing continues to have important repercussions for what humans are and what they can become. Aspects of sharing in this technical sense are to be found in all societies. However, a necessary first step towards such a positive reconceptualization is nevertheless a critical assessment of what has been blocking our understanding of sharing and its role in human relations. A major intellectual obstacle that is in the way, is the assumption that sharing is a form of reciprocal gift-exchange and that it can be expected to follow the same logic that we find in gifts or other reciprocal exchanges. The goal of this chapter is to get this obstacle out of the way and to prepare the ground for a more productive view of what sharing is all about.

Ceci n'est pas un don

"Reciprocal gift-exchange" sounds innocent enough for anyone with even basic anthropological training because its constituent parts "reciprocity" and "gift-exchange" are the bread and butter of many social science theories and ethnographic descriptions. It is difficult to find any current introduction to anthropology that does not contain these terms, or some derivatives thereof. In economic anthropology, probably within the first thousand words or so of any introductory chapter or article, there will be some reference to reciprocity and gift-exchange. And there are good reasons for this since in many ways these have been productive terms for generating anthropological knowledge. However, as I will try to point out below, in conjunction with phenomena of sharing, the phrase "reciprocal gift-giving" is not only misplaced or misapplied but it seriously hampers new insights. If we look at it in more detail, "reciprocal gift-giving" in fact enshrines a forceful coalition of approaches that are in many other ways at loggerheads with one another, namely a scientistic notion of universal and law-like "reciprocity" and a cultural-relativist notion of "gift giving", two sides of a complementary antagonism that I shall discuss in turn in this chapter.

Over the last three decades considerable effort has been spent to clarify that sharing is not adequately represented by the image of reciprocal exchange, or to slightly modify René Magritte: This is not a gift (*Ceci n'est pas un don*). Rather it is a form of transfer *sui generis*, "an important transactional mode in its own right" (Gell 1999: 77). The discussion was first started by specialists working in hunter-gatherer studies (Price 1975, Woodburn 1998, Wenzel *et al.* 2000) and other small-scale societies (see Gell 1999) who argued that the sharing phenomena observed had to be stretched beyond recognition in order to make them fit the theory of reciprocal exchange. Since then the argument has been picked up in more general accounts (Hunt 2000, Widlok and Tadesse 2005, Ferguson 2015) that show how, in turn, the notion of exchange would have to be stretched beyond recognition if it was to cover sharing as well. The conceptual point in this debate is that reciprocal exchange has mutuality as its defining property, usually combined with some sense of transactions that "even out" and that are connected to one another. The binary distinction between one-way and reciprocal transactions may seem simple at first but quickly becomes problematic and blurred since it is often difficult to ascertain whether something is equivalent when the items exchanged are not exactly the same. Similarly it is a matter of debate whether an act of giving and an act of receiving should still be considered connected if the "return" is only received indirectly or after a long time lag, for instance in the next generation. In principle, any unreciprocated transfer may be counted as an instance of incomplete exchange of which we simply have not seen, as yet, the return transaction. However, there are serious doubts as to whether we can or should assume reciprocity across all of these cases. Thus, when Woodburn (1998) underlined that "sharing is not a form of exchange" he invoked the ethnography of East African foragers (see Box 1) to voice the emerging critique against the tendency of understanding all transfers in terms of reciprocal gift-exchange. That tendency was, and in some ways still is,

BOX 1 NO GIFT INTENDED: SHARING GAME MEAT
IN A HADZA HUNTING CAMP

The Hadza are a small group of hunter-gatherers in Tanzania but they have served as a test case for a number of anthropological theories – including those related to sharing. They have been the focus of much anthropological atten- tion, partly because they live today as foragers in the region where modern humans are thought to have originated. Therefore, it has been argued, they may represent better than any other group the life of early humans. In the spec- trum between egalitarianism and sharing on the one hand and hierarchy and exchange on the other hand they mark the egalitarian end of the spectrum that is opposed to the ways of life in most societies, including those of their immedi- ate neighbours. However, it is important to note that the Hadza, as far as we know, have always recognized personal property and have objects that are not shared (for instance, their hunting bows). As Woodburn (1998) has pointed out, it is not the case that material objects in Hadza society would circulate because of collective ownership but rather because of social practices such as continuous gambling and continuous asking and demanding. Gathered food is also considered to be personally owned but with large game meat in particular, less so with gathered food or small animals, there is considerable emphasis put on the sharing of the meat. The initial sharing at the killing site ensures that the larger part of the meat is earmarked for all Hadza who live in a camp (25 to 30 individuals on average). Only a small proportion, the *epeme* meat, is reserved for initiated men. The second stage of sharing takes place when the meat is transported back to camp where it is cooked by the hearth groups before it then enters a third round of sharing among everyone who is present. Ways of storing meat are known but hoarding is socially unacceptable so that sharing will continue if some still have meat while others are still hungry. Everyone in the camp will get a share but needs to claim it. Correspondingly, those who make weak claims, for instance the old and frail, will receive less than those who can make forceful claims, for instance pregnant women. The amount of meat available for sharing to some extent determines the size of the camp since large kills attract more people who come to acquire shares. Although the sharing ethic is strong, this does not imply generosity. Marlowe (2004: 85) confirmed in experimental settings that Hadza offer *less* food than members of other groups *unless* it is claimed from them but at the same time they are much *more* likely to readily reject small offers just as they would readily split from people whom they consider to be stingy. Woodburn and Marlowe observed frequent attempts to hide and to evade sharing but also noted that chances for this to succeed are slim in small camps. Moreover, the social pressure through demands is such that tolerating others to take from what one has is the most rational and the most common strategy in Hadza everyday life.

prevalent not only in economic anthropology but also in kinship studies and other fields of anthropological enquiry. Woodburn emphasized that sharing is character-ized precisely by contexts in which transfer is not based on specific kin obligations and in which it is not about creating specific long-term commitments. It is exactly this ability of exchange to create social continuity and commitments and to main-tain social order that became the core of gift theory when it was first formulated and that has since fuelled the anthropological imagination.

In the early 1920s Marcel Mauss compiled the then available ethnographic sources on phenomena that he collected under the heading of "the gift" (Mauss 2002). These include examples from a very broad spectrum, back in time to European antiquity and Roman law and across all continents with many examples from the indigenous groups of North America and of the Pacific. The purpose of this comparative view was not primarily ethnographic, a better understanding of "exotic" peoples, but instead a critique of the dominant modes of exchange that had come to characterize European modernity at the time. The endeavour was risky because Mauss' appeal to social and economic reform was based on the life of people who were then considered pre-modern and primitive. His main contention was that gifts may appear to be voluntary but that they in fact structure and secure social order because gift-exchange is governed by obligations, the obligation to give, to receive, and to return a gift. These obligations, in his view, are foundational for the social order more generally. In the language of the Maori, a gift had a *"hau"*, it contained some of the essence of the giver, which produced a force that would ultimately force recipients to return the gift and to comply with the obligations.

Mauss was subsequently criticized for basing an anthropological theory of society and the social contract on the mythical worldview of pre-modern people. This critique was expressed in very pronounced ways by Lévi-Strauss. Lévi-Strauss took on board the importance of exchange for social order and any form of human culture but tried to purify the theory of mythical contents by placing the driving force not within exchanged objects but instead in ultimately mental and universal structures of duality that saturate all fields of life (Lévi-Strauss 1949, 1965). It therefore took until the end of the twentieth century for Mauss' theory of the gift to gain ground, eventually in an unprecedented and sweeping way.

"The anthropology of gift-giving" is more than a rather specific subfield of a subdomain of economic anthropology. I think it is fair to say that the opposite is true since the anthropology of gift-giving has in a way become one of the key theories in anthropology, in some sense even the most dominant theory of the discipline at large that influences anthropological thinking in many fields.[1] Its standing may be com-pared to that of econometrics in economics as a discipline in the sense that although there are many more theories and methods around, this is the one to which much of the discipline boils down to in the "real life" of teaching it to undergraduates and when applying shared ideas in research. Here are some indicators why this is true for anthropology today. The theory of gift-giving, in particular in the tradition of Marcel Mauss, is found in all subfields of the discipline, far beyond economic anthropology, from the anthropology of religion (e.g. Morris 1987: 266) to the anthropology of kinship (e.g. Fox 1967: 202). It has been picked up by virtually all of anthropology's neighbouring disciplines. *The Gift* is one of the few books that have made it into the general canon of the humanities (see Leggewie et al. 2012). It has now got a key position in most Anthropology 101 course materials. Almost a century after it was written, Marcel Mauss slowly emerges as champion among other "founding fathers" of the discipline. Bronislaw Malinowski is usually credited for bringing in participant observation as a methodological innovation but he is disregarded and indeed belittled for his weak theoretical impact. However, the fact that his introduction into ethnographic method was bound up in one volume with his celebrated case study of the Trobriand *kula* cycle helped to fuel interests in gift-exchange. Franz Boas may be credited for establishing the culture concept in the discipline, but not for a productive and comprehensive theory of culture. Both Malinowskian-type ethnography as a representation of "the other" and the Boasian culture concept have been severely critiqued over the last decades, allowing Marcel Mauss to eventually outrun other contenders from this early generation that helped to establish the discipline of anthropology. This is made quite explicit in some of the introductory textbooks of anthropology which praise Mauss as "the most important" anthropological "ancestor" (Eriksen 2004: 16) and *The Gift* as "the single most important text in twentieth-century anthropology" (Eriksen 1995: 19). Throughout the anthropological literature of today there are many references to the book (and to Mauss' other work).

The second half of the twentieth century saw many theoretical innovations emerging from Melanesian anthropology where systems of gift-giving are rampant and where neither religion nor politics, nor basically any other aspect of life can easily be described without reference to gift-giving. Consequently, Mauss' theory of gift-giving was used in a variety of productive ways. In fact, one may argue that a good proportion of the recent most celebrated findings and theorems in anthropology can be more or less directly connected to the context of gift-giving. The concepts of "dividuals" (Strathern 1988), "inalienable objects" (Weiner 1992) and "fractal" person (Wagner 1991), for instance, are direct descendants of theories and ethnographies of the gift. "Cargo cults" are not only a celebrated phenomenon with which anthropology has made its mark on the social sciences but the notion of cargo itself has been presented as the main contender of an inverse anthropology (Wagner 1975) of the way in which "the others" see "the West" and which challenges Western philosophical ideas (Därmann 2005). Wagner (1975) pointed out that Europeans use the notion of culture strategically to make sense of the differences that they have confronted since the colonial encounter but that for many non-Europeans the notion of "cargo", of eliciting counter-gifts, was the preferred strategy for dealing with this encounter. Thereby, the notion of gift-exchange has become a key template for understanding non-European reactions to the colonial encounter. Ideas surrounding gift-exchange provided the richest source for attempting to create a dialogical or reverse anthropology in which the concepts of non-Western "ontologies" are brought in as a critique of Western philosophy and the sciences that descended from it. Därmann (2005) has undertaken an elaborate review of this process, suggesting that basically each and every direction of Western philosophy is being challenged by the theory of the gift as it was initiated by Mauss.[2] In this view, the theory of gift-giving questions the major philosophical traditions of the West, including Anglo-Saxon utilitarianism, French existentialism and German phenomenology.

The gift has not only been used in relativizing Western thought but also more concretely in outlining alternatives to the capitalist system of commodities. The separation between "us" and "them", or "the West" and "the Rest" has been systematically established with reference to two diametrically opposed ways of conceiving the world and of managing social relations in the world, under the labels of "gifts" and "commodities" (Gregory 1982). Notions from gift-exchange permeate anthropological self-images and profiles at all levels, whether as the title of a German student journal (www.cargo-zeitschrift.de), a French social science school of thought (www.revuedumauss.com and www.journaldumauss.net) or one of the most recent successful start-ups among the English disciplinary journals in anthropology (http://www.haujournal.org/) published with a focus on open access. They all orient themselves towards concepts arising from "The Gift", taking theory since Mauss as their dominant intellectual heritage and inspiration.

If this analysis provides a correct image of the sociology of knowledge of modern anthropology, then it no longer comes as a surprise that many phenomena were read, and continue to be read, against a gift-exchange template. This is certainly the case for "sharing", a phenomenon that after all is situated in close neighbourhood to gift-giving and in some instances overlaps with it. It also becomes clear why it took such a long time to emancipate research on sharing from gift-exchange, despite the fact that many ethnographic accounts have been insisting on separating the two (see below). At the same time it underlines why it is particularly necessary to show the differences between gift-giving and sharing and to emphasize these distinctions in theoretical rather than only in descriptive terms. In analogy to what I will point out below with regard to the notion of "reciprocity", this emphasis is not to denigrate or belittle what has been achieved in and through the theory of the gift and gift-giving. Rather, the goal is to sharpen the view as to what exactly we mean by gift-exchange and what does not fall under that category. I shall do this in the remainder of this chapter, necessarily in an outline manner, with no attempt to cover gift-theory in any sense of completion or with the systematicity that this would deserve. Instead, I will focus on some basic points in which gift theory is misleading the study of sharing, while not underrating the positive contribution that gift-theory has made.

The core of gift-giving theory since Mauss is the tripartite obligation to give a gift, to receive it and to give a return gift, as already mentioned above. The time lapse between receiving and returning a gift is of central theoretical importance and will be discussed at some length below. The inapplicability of the concept and theory of the gift with regard to sharing has been discussed primarily with regard to the lack of a return gift. Sharing often has no recognizable return, certainly not in the way in which gift and counter-gift are connected in the theory of exchange. However, there is more to it. While gifts are often accompanied by displays of generosity and power, sharing acts are not – and indeed often explicitly should not be. The obligation to share typically only emerges when and if a demand is being made and attempts are often made to refuse or diffuse the demand (see Chapter 2).

Moreover, it is the link between the three elements, the connection between them, which typically gets dispensed within acts of sharing. As the ethnography shows, acts of giving are "downgraded" to acts of "leaving things for others to take", intercepting the movement between giving and receiving. This is achieved by either sending intermediaries (often children) with shares, or with demands for a share, or by allowing others to simply take without any direct offer being made. In either case, acts of receiving are disconnected from acts of giving either through intermediaries or other means so that it is not really valid to talk about a "return" even when there is sharing in various directions (see Figure 1.1). When children are sent out to provide shares or when there are several waves of sharing, the giving becomes diffused so that those who receive game meat, for instance, often do not receive it from the hunter but from someone else. In practice, an effort is made to erase the path of what is being shared, thereby even turning shares that do go in two directions into independent events that are not connected by the same path.

FIGURE 1.1   ≠Akhoe Hai//om children are often intermediaries in sharing, here taking a tobacco pipe from one adult to another. Photo: Th. Widlok

Elsewhere (Widlok 2010, 2012, 2013) I have pointed out that sharing is in itself a complex practice, a point to which I shall return in Chapter 3. Here it should suffice to outline briefly how acts of sharing are made as part of a wider process with a number of interrelated dimensions. There is a horizontal complexity in terms of a time scale as sharing often takes place in waves of primary, secondary and further sharing. Lorna Marshall (1961, 1976) has documented the various waves of sharing that take place among the !Kung (San) of southern Africa. In the case of hunted meat, the sharing begins early on with mutual swapping or "borrowing" of arrows for the hunt. This allows the arrow makers to participate in the hunts of fellow hunters who carry and use arrows in their quiver belonging to several co-resident men. The maker of the arrow that strikes the game animal explicitly participates in the hunting success although he may not have participated in the hunt himself. There is primary sharing at the killing site, secondary sharing upon returning from the site of the kill to the camp, and tertiary sharing after food has been prepared at various fireplaces (see Figure 1.2). Complementary to this complex time horizon of sharing is what may be called the "vertical" dimension of complexity. Marshall (1976) and Lee (1993) have pointed at the gossip, talk and commentary that surrounds sharing, again beginning long before there is anything to share, then while the sharing is taking place and long after the event. Sharing is demanded and commented upon; people claim that it does not take place frequently enough and when it takes place the provider or the share may even be ridiculed in a way that is generally explained in terms of a levelling device to underwrite equality. Hence the acts *of* sharing and the comments *about* sharing are far from being in unison and language adds a separate dimension of complexity to the sharing phenomenon; it is not merely a mirror of action (see Aikhenvald 2013). Acts and the way they are presented and commented upon not only differ, they may also be purposely in contrast with one another because comments on sharing are at the same time also themselves (speech) acts that may be intended to prompt acts of sharing or to prevent their political exploitation. The vertical complexity includes the meta-comments involved which also connect to a third, lateral axis of complexity to the extent that previous experiences and actions constitute reliable expectations about future acts of sharing that cannot be derived solely from the horizontal timeline or the vertical gradient between explicitness and implicitness. Thus, sharing is complex because its outcome is in many ways open while being influenced by the past (see Widlok 2013). While details may vary, the overall picture of sharing as a complex phenomenon holds across regions. Figure 1.2 summarizes the process of sharing as Bahuchet (1990) has provided it for Central African forest foragers, with striking parallels to the southern African cases just described.

Let me reiterate that none of the above invalidates Mauss' theory of the gift – when it is applied to gift exchange. But sharing and gifting are processes that are clearly distinct and the argument is about refuting the applicability of gift theory to sharing. At least in some cases the departure from the gift sequence is so marked in sharing events that one does get the impression that those involved in sharing are indeed very much aware about the obligations that gift exchange creates. They subscribe to gift theory, as it were, but actively seek to create or maintain

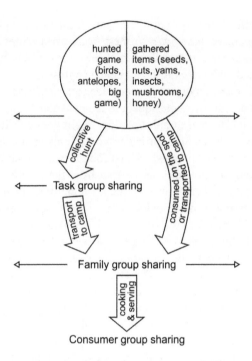

FIGURE 1.2 The waves of the sharing process among foragers in tropical Africa (Graphics: M. Feinen, adapted from Bahuchet 1990). The Aka terms match the sharing at the various levels (see Bahuchet 1990:39): To give (*kab-*) at the task group level, to divide (*nangam-*) at the family group level, and to serve (*teleng-*) at the consumer group level. All of these are in turn distinguished from forms of selling and exchanging with the villagers that are categorized. Whereas the former is considered in terms of one's due (*mo.bando*) to someone, the latter are conceptualized as one's debt (*mbusa*). All terms fall into three semantic fields associated with a distinct social sphere, that Bahuchet labels "calculated exchange" (buy and sell, barter), "uncalculated exchange" (reciprocal gift-giving) and "keep giving" (uncalculated sharing)

something different, a mode of transfer that can take the sting out of gifting so that no specific obligations between specific recipients and to specific donors are created through specific objects of exchange. Given that sharing and gift-giving often occur side by side in many societies, the need for marking a transaction as either a gift or a share in order to specify its expected social implications may indeed occur – but so may be the interest to leave the transaction in its ambiguity and to tweak a transfer according to one's needs. Conversely, people like the San who are very versatile in their sharing practices also entertain gift-exchange systems that can cater for different purposes such as creating specific obligations for specific partners – something that is hard to achieve through sharing. The best-known example is the !Kung *hxaro* exchange (Wiessner 1982). It allows individuals to maintain specific partnerships across space and time (even transgenerationally) and to channel gifts, mostly of non-food items, through these partners. Although they are not competitive like a *potlatch*, these *hxaro* partnerships are in many ways more similar to *kula* partners than they are to the everyday sharing that takes place among the San and with which it should not be confused.

Apart from the question of how to recognize and categorize acts of sharing and of gift-giving when one encounters them in the field and in the literature, there is a more fundamental challenge (and attraction) to gift theory. Gift-exchange theory not only provides a schema for a particular type of transfer but also a more general theory of how social obligation and a social contract and something that we recognize as society and social order can emerge from the practice level. In Mauss' dealing with the subject there is an evolutionary dimension since he seeks to establish a sequence starting from an oldest form of gift (largely speculative), on to a non-antagonistic form of giving (e.g. in Polynesia) to an antagonistic form of giving (for which the North-West Coast term *potlatch* has become the technical term) and finally to the individual contract as we see it in commercial buyer–seller transactions (Därmann 2005: 95). The attraction for theory is to account for the origin of society without oversimplified notions of utilitarianism and voluntarism. Since Mauss we are able to see how the various forms of gift exchange have led to social forms that were neither inevitable nor planned responses to problems of material survival. Moreover, his account shows how very different social systems can emerge from a fairly small set of practices surrounding gift exchange – potentially also pointing at alternatives to what he criticized as the accepted dichotomy of "pure gifts" and entirely contractual trade.

This is also where much of the attraction of gift theory continues to rest for anthropologists who follow Mauss in his critique of transactions in twentieth-century Europe. Mauss lamented that Europe was troubled by a bifurcation into purely economic (utilitarian) transactions on the one hand and "pure gifts" of generosity on the other hand, a problematic separation of the public life of economy, politics, law and religion from the private life of morality (see Därmann 2005: 171). He recognized (fading) traces of gift-giving in Europe and was advocating a return to systems of group solidarity, for instance in the social schemes that benefitted the industrial workers (Mauss 2007: 92). Gift theory, based on the indigenous theories of non-Europeans, thereby provided an alternative account of how societies could work without facing an abyss between egoistically economizing individuals and an abstract and largely disconnected legal system of social contracts and duties. In this account gifts created social bonds and obligations effectively because they appear to be based on voluntariness, which in fact disguises a coercion; they are the "social lie" par excellence (Mauss 2002: 7). Mauss' theory provides the foundation for a whole strand of anti-utilitarian research (see the work of the *Mouvement anti-utilitariste dans les sciences sociales*, M.A.U.S.S., already mentioned) and, most recently, of policy-orientation under the label "*convivialisme*" (www.lesconvivialistes.org) and "*Konvivalismus*" (Adloff and Heins 2015). However, as I shall point out in more detail (in Chapter 3), sharing provides an empirical basis for yet another alternative scenario of how society can emerge and can be maintained: A scenario that highlights opportunities instead of obligations and that replaces the tripartite scheme of giving, accepting and returning with one of requesting, responding and renouncing. This is an account that provides an alternative to both the logic of utilitarian means–ends categories *and* to the "convivialist" concept of society based on imposed obligations and abstract collective bonds.

Anthropologists tend to look upon Mauss as someone who achieved what many consider to be the ultimate anthropological feat, namely to be able to challenge European concepts on the basis of comparative ethnography. In this particular case what he challenged is the strict separation of generosity from utility and its alignment with wasting versus saving, disinterestedness versus interest (Mauss 2002: 99, see Därmann 2005: 171). The means for spelling out the challenge is provided by non-European concepts such as *hau* and *mana*, which bring together what Western philosophy erroneously separates as Mauss saw it. In these alternative systems, Mauss maintained, there is no rigid separation of persons and things, since the obligation to receive and to reciprocate is justified through an element of the person that is part of a thing given (its *hau*) so that giving things between people unavoidably creates personal bonds between them (Mauss 2002: 15). By implication, gift-exchange theory also suggests that unless societies attempt to create social bonds by forcing individuals into contractual obligations (as in the commodified "West"), they do need social institutions of gift-giving which create social solidarity by fusing people and things (as in the gift-giving "Rest"). Correspondingly, gift theory was systematically read also into ethnographic accounts of sharing as yet another manifestation of this alternative, non-Western way of achieving social order. The point of an anthropology of sharing is that there are not only those alternatives to voluntaristic ideas of the social contract that gift-exchange theory picked up on. Sharing provides yet another mode of establishing and maintaining social relatedness which is practically and conceptually distinct.

There have been (and in many ways still are) doubts about whether societies could work in which sharing relations dominate. What would a social formation look like that does not follow the logic of gift giving, or of commodity exchange for that matter? It was argued, for instance, that such systems of sharing would produce very fragile and inherently unstable societies, at best (see Brunton 1989). Alternatively, any groups which are not based on exchange obligations should not be called societies (see Ingold 1999: 408) or indeed social (Dentan 2011: 90) if we take power and externally imposed obligations as defining criteria for the social. Those who study sharing insist that any specific obligations of indebtedness that are so characteristic of commodity exchange *and* gift exchange are not implicated in social relationships of sharing (see Woodburn 1998). The chapters of this book outline such a theory of sharing and thereby also provide an alternative account as to how social order and commitment can emerge – namely in a social setting characterized by sharing instead of gift-giving and legal contract.

A number of important features may be appropriated from exchange theory when developing a theory of sharing. The foremost virtue of gift theory is that it has shown a consistent outline of a mode of exchange that is distinct from commodity exchange. Mauss and others have shown that the concepts of commercial exchange, contractual sociality, centralized polities and so forth, that emerge from conditions in European modernity at a particular point in time are not necessarily suitable for describing and understanding what is going on at other places and other times. They have shown how diversity at the level of the social practices of allocation and transfer, and the social implications that come with it, force us to take a broader view of the ways in which social bonds and social order are created. This view now needs to be opened up even further. Moreover, gift theory has illustrated how inverse anthropology can help to distil concepts from distant cultural frameworks. It can also provide a fresh and enlightening perspective of the social institutions of modernity that are so familiar to us that they are hard to fully grasp and criticize from within. These general points can be incorporated when developing a new theory of sharing that is distinct from both the conceptual framework of commoditization and the framework of gift-giving.

A seemingly specialized debate on what constitutes sharing in contrast to gift-giving therefore takes us to much bigger questions of the constitution of social relations and the social order. The liberal theory of the social contract was formulated in Europe after experiencing protracted wars and devastating conflicts to which commercial exchange and externally enforced contractual obligations seemed the only solution (Michea 2007). Gift-exchange theory formulated in dialogue with non-European and with pre-modern sources provided an alternative to this contractual liberal mode of integration, one that could do without a centralized or external authority ("regulated anarchy", see Sigrist 1979) by fusing objects with subjects. What would constitute an alternative to both modes of integration, liberal-contractual and exchange, an alternative based on sharing? The following chapters provide an answer to this question. Before engaging in this account, however, the ground has to be cleared with regard to another key assumption, that of reciprocity, often implied in accounts of gift-exchange but much broader in scope.

The myth of reciprocity

Built into the notion of reciprocity is the idea of a balance of comparable mutual sacrifices, as the late Alfred Gell (1999: 88) has pointed out. When we subsume sharing under reciprocity we overstretch the term since mutuality is lost as the defining property. For instance, when a child receives food and support from its parents, this may or may not be considered to even out later when the parents grow old. Apart from the fact that the quality (and often the quantity, too) of what is being shared is likely to be very different, there are children who receive without returning and parents who give without receiving back, and it is difficult to establish a link between every act of provisioning for young children and the specific acts of provisioning for old parents. The relation and transfer is often not one between interacting contemporary individuals, or necessarily between adjacent generations during their lifetimes. To consider it to be mutual, we would need to stretch it further by equating the parent who provides for today's children with the children of tomorrow's parents, i.e. conceiving of the grandchildren as receiving back from their own parents what their grandparents have provided to these parents when they were bringing them up. Moreover, to stretch reciprocity in this way we need to entertain a transcendental notion of generation since it is not necessarily the case that any one person at the level of grandparent generation is directly linked with any particular other person at the level of grandchild generation.[3]

Despite these problems, the notion of "reciprocity" has featured in a number of theoretical strands in anthropology. As I will show in more detail in the following chapter, it has been employed extensively by evolutionary anthropologists, human behavioural ecologists and evolutionary psychologists, as well as by scholars in neighbouring disciplines such as ethology, primatology, evolutionary economics and so forth. For these "scientistic" approaches, reciprocity as a rule promises to reconcile ideas about the selfish nature of humans (and their genes) with observations of marked sociability among humans. If humans do things for others, it is argued, they ultimately do it because there will be some reciprocation so that even apparently altruistic acts do in fact benefit those who perform them. The net result of such behaviour would be explicable in terms of return benefits for the individual, or at least for the kin group or the species as a whole. This allows us to do away with idealistic images of mankind (whether religiously, utopian or romantically inspired), while acknowledging that humans indeed sometimes do things for one another. The notion of reciprocity allows the accommodation of such prosocial acts in a closed universe of material survival pressures, and as an expression of mechanical processes of selection. Humans thereby become seamlessly integrated into the wider animal kingdom and into a universe that is made up of self-interested organisms and that requires no distinct theoretical account of the social and cultural dimension of human action. I am not suggesting that everyone who uses the notion of "reciprocity" necessarily subscribes to all these underlying assumptions just mentioned, but that taken together these underlying assumptions explain the tenacity with which many researchers insist to see reciprocity where there is no evidence for it. It is extraordinary to see how persistently the notion of reciprocity has been applied *as the defining aspect* of sharing practices despite the fact that those who produced first-hand data on sharing have again and again pointed out that sharing is *not* a matter of reciprocity. Take ethnographic accounts from anywhere around the world and they convey a clear message: ethnographers working in South America (Rival 2000), in East Africa (Woodburn 1998), southern Africa (Kent 1993), the Arctic (Damas 1972), southeast Asia (Lye 2004:14), South Asia (Bird-David 2005), Australia (MacDonald 2000), Island Oceania (Gell 1999), and Europe (Layton 2000: 192) all insist that the sharing that they have observed is not in the first instance a matter of reciprocity, it may in fact not be reciprocal at all. Pryor and Graburns' study of Inuit sharing in northern Canada (see Box 2) was one of the first to test reciprocity effects in sharing on a quantitative basis. Their overall result across a large body of data collected over several months of field research was that sharing is *not* reciprocal. Instead, there were net receivers (the men, the disabled, and members of the group who were single and had low income) and there were net providers (women, the able-bodied and members who were married and who had a high income). Moreover, they were able to identify the variables that structure the non-reciprocal sharing of time and of objects. Against prevalent assumptions the variables that had no significant effect included the prestige of the partners, the status of the family concerned and the political power (relative closeness to the political leader) of those engaged in the transactions. Correlations were calculated separately for the entire community and for the adult (married) members only. The results did show an imbalance of transfers according to individual income, house size and, at times, belonging to a particular band of foragers. These factors prevented sharing going both ways in a reciprocal fashion. On the whole, food transactions among the Arctic people of Sugluk seem less clearly patterned than visits for which it was easier to pinpoint non-reciprocal efforts. Both gifts and visits are characterized by imbalances so that reciprocity cannot be considered the defining factor in these transactions. It is not that there were no reciprocal exchanges at all at Sugluk, but rather that these were clearly outweighed by unilateral transactions, flows in one direction only.

BOX 2 BEYOND RECIPROCITY: SHARING FOOD AND VISITS IN AN ARCTIC VILLAGE

One of the first systematic studies of sharing was carried out in the Takamiut Eskimo/Inuit settlement of Sugluk at the Hudson Strait in Canada in 1959. At the time the local population lived on hunting, fishing and occasional wage labour. Whoever hunted successfully was expected to share not only with immediate family members but also with the larger household, the band or the whole community (Pryor and Graburn 1980: 234-5). Especially in the event of large kills, the whole community might be invited to the hearth of a hosting family to receive their share but visitors were also allowed to take shares on an everyday basis. Generosity was highly valued but it was often people of low status who were generous in their giving (without thereby raising their status) while others maintained a generous reputation even though they only provided occasional conspicuous giveaways. The ethnographer N. Graburn made over 300 visits to every household in the community of 254 inhabitants and recorded 1,250 instances of different types of "distributional transactions" including transfers within the dwellings of visitors and between dwellings within the village. Recorded but excluded from further analysis were transactions with outsiders, e.g. with fur traders, government welfare offices and employees. Sharing in this study included "sharing time" (i.e. visiting one another) and "sharing objects" (mostly food) and it is one of the first studies that tested by using quantitative methods how much, or rather how little, reciprocity there is in sharing. A regression analysis was run to see which social predictor would explain imbalances in transactions. Some 30 variables were tested which refer to the social, political and economic characteristics of the transaction partners involved, aspects such as marital status, the prestige of a family, its size and income, its distance to the group leader and so forth. The "net exchange index" was calculated by establishing how many outward gifts/visits there were in relation to inward gifts/visits, using the following formula:

$$\text{Net exchange index:} \quad \frac{\text{gifts/visits TO others} - \text{gifts/visits FROM others}}{\text{gifts/visits FROM others} - \text{gifts/visit TO others}}$$

In other words the index value for anyone who gave as much as he or she received would be 0, for anyone who only gave visits/gifts without receiving, it would be -1 and for anyone who was only given/visited, the index would be 1. When correlating these indexes, the "visit index" and the "gift index", with the above mentioned variables that characterize a transaction partner, the overall result showed that transactions did not even out reciprocally at all, but that there were net receivers and net providers (see Table 1). Consequently, the authors presented their results under the title "the myth of reciprocity" (Pryor and Graburn 1980).

TABLE 1 Net receivers and net providers in the Arctic case study (following Pryor and Graburn 1980)

Net receivers	Net providers
men	women
single	married
low-income	high-income
disabled (for visits)	able-bodied (for visits)

Taken together, the ethnographic record of sharing and the numerous (wo)man years of field experience that they represent strongly point away from reciprocity. Therefore, the forces of inertia that continue to insist on calling sharing a reciprocal transfer indicate not a mere oversight or sloppiness in terminology but a more deeply rooted ideological dimension. Take for instance Winterhalder's definition (1996: 47) of sharing as either being a "two-way transfer of portions of a like resource or service […] as in reciprocity-based food sharing" or a "one-way transfer among kin without equivalent return in kind". According to this view either sharing is reciprocity (i.e. reciprocal and producing equivalent returns) or it is nothing. The second type of sharing (one-way transfer among kin) is not strictly speaking an exemption from the first (two-way transfer), due to the hedges "among kin", "in kind" and "equivalent". It is implied that one-way transfers among non-kin never occur by definition and that among kin these transfers should be expected to have a return, maybe not quite equivalent and maybe not in kind but in a way that they will eventually even out and therefore have some reciprocity to them. The important limitation to kin that Winterhalder points out already contains reciprocity in the evolutionary framework of inclusive fitness (i.e. I help my kin because they help me reproducing a good proportion of my genes, see Chapter 2). A definition of this sort therefore leaves no room for sharing outside reciprocity. As a consequence, the larger part of the cases of sharing that I will be presenting in this book should not exist according to such a reciprocity-driven definition. At the same time, such a definition leaves no room for distinguishing clearly between various forms of sharing, gift-giving, exchange, barter and so forth. Or, to put it differently, such a conceptual frame that is predicated on reciprocity fails to cover the majority of cases of sharing that we are looking at in the ethnographic record; it conflates them with many non-sharing transfers and it is therefore not very helpful.

The Inuit case study from Sugluk is a case in point. The imbalanced transactions recorded were not random but they show a clear pattern as they were related to some specific social features (e.g. marital status and income) but not by others (e.g. prestige and power). The "immunity" of transfers to prestige and power does not support the view that food transfers are reciprocated by invisible "returns" such as followership and admiration as they are sometimes claimed when no visible reciprocal flows of material goods ("in kind") are to be found. The case also does not support the proposition that transfers between closer kin tend to be more imbalanced than those between more distant kin, which is one of the claims in Sahlins' influential model of reciprocal exchange (Sahlins 1988). Both visits and things were transferred among non-kin, near kin and far kin (Pryor and Graburn 1980: 232). The authors of the study still phrase their findings primarily in terms of exchange rather than sharing, but they do explicitly critique what was then called "the theory of reciprocal exchange". The constellations that they describe closely match what we would be calling a sharing system rather than an exchange system.

It is instructive to see how the broad claims of reciprocity as a universal of all transfers among humans have been falsified in a piecemeal fashion and with them the associated claims that have become less and less defensible in the light of emerging evidence. The first feature that had to be given up was that of equivalence. Sahlins' (1988) much reiterated distinction of negative, generalized and balanced reciprocity was an attempt to maintain the notion of reciprocity despite the fact that two out of three types were in fact not exchanges of equivalences at all. Although widely quoted, this was an attempt to keep sharing in the framework of reciprocity at the cost of watering down the concept beyond recognition. As Gell (1999) and others have pointed out "re-ciprocity" without a forward and return movement makes little sense. One of the reasons why this model nevertheless continues to be popular, especially outside economic anthropology, is that it proposes a forceful correlation between modes of economic transaction ("negative", "balanced" and "generalized" reciprocity) and modes of social organization (house, lineage, village, tribal, intertribal). Sahlins' well-known diagram (Sahlins 1988: 199) even suggested that the modes of transaction could be mapped onto the living arrangements of transfer partners in a single two-dimensional graph of concentric circles with "house" and "generalized reciprocity" at its centre, "negative reciprocity" at the outside and "balanced reciprocity" in between. As with all simple models this represents some features of reality better than others. The model rings true only insofar as it suggests that very close and very distant relationships are not necessarily those of balanced reciprocal transfers in actual fact but also in terms of the moral expectations involved. The happiness of the commodity trader, positioned at a social distance from his customers, is based on the fact that he has received a *more* valued item for a *less* valued one (Gell 1999: 85). Similarly, the pride of those in close "popular" neighbourhood environments is that they do not need (nor expect) a "thank you" for acknowledging the value of the service they provide (Graeber 2011:124). As a whole, however, Sahlins' model is flawed conceptually and almost from the start it has been criticized on two counts: firstly, it overstretches the notion of "reciprocity" to cover transactions that are clearly not reciprocal at all, namely "generalized reciprocity" for sharing and "negative reciprocity" for stealing (see Damas 1972, a summary is provided by Hunt 2000); secondly, it assumes that "generalized reciprocity" always implies close kinship relations. This does not stand up to the fact that sharing has been observed to be at times indiscriminate with regard to specific kin relations, since it may include everyone present, even "distant" visitors or anthropologists who are not treated as close kin in other contexts (see Woodburn 1998).

The next axiom to fall was that reciprocity was a fundamental *norm* of behaviour (as Lévi-Strauss1949 claimed) since it had to be accepted that in many normative systems that include sharing there is an emphasis on giving that is supposed to be unconditional and disconnected from previous or anticipated transfers (Woodburn 1998). We have already seen in the Inuit case (see Box 2) that some reciprocal effects can emerge from sharing even though sharing norms insist on *non*-reciprocity. In a network analysis study of sharing in the African settlement of Fransfontein in Namibia, Michael Schnegg (2006, 2015) found that his informants continually emphasized that giving should take place indiscriminately ("If you are asked, you have to give"). However, the study also showed that these events are conditioned in a regular way by things such as living in close proximity with one another, by being able to observe what others have got to eat (through checking on the number of pots on the open fireplaces), by observing the forms of behaviour by those who demand and so forth. In other words sharing as a norm may be "unconditiona*l*" but sharing as a practice is not "unconditione*d*". The question is what conditions sharing if it is not a simple law of reciprocity.

From the perspective of network analysis the Fransfontein case illustrates the contrast between indiscriminate, undirected sharing and reciprocal practices (see Box 3). In my view the data suggests that reciprocal effects are not precluded as a consequence of sharing, without, however, being the overall principle that causally structures these events. Moreover, a loose sense of mutual recognition is to be distinguished from calculable reciprocal returns. As in many other places around the world (see Chapter 3), the cultural conditions that generate sharing at Fransfontein include spatial proximity, kin links, the particular material setup of the houses, various recognized modes of demand but also sufficient knowledge

BOX 3 NOT RANDOM GIVING: SHARING AMONG RURAL POOR IN A MARGINAL AFRICAN SETTLEMENT

What is sharing like in a contemporary African settlement in which the majority of the population has a daily income below one Euro? Fransfontein in north-western Namibia is such a place. When Schnegg and Pauli conducted their anthropological field research among the 137 households of this settlement of Khoekhoe-speaking Damara and Nama people between 2003 and 2014, sharing was a daily occurrence. Children were regularly sent out to neighbours when there was a shortage of staples such as milk or sugar and their demands were usually met. Cooking took place outside on open fireplaces and it was very hard not to give to passersby who stopped at one's hearth and waited until the meal is cooked and was ready to be eaten. The researchers covered 1,740 sharing transactions over a complete period of 10 days covering almost half of all the households in the area and then tested for reciprocity (see Schnegg 2006: 13). Out of all possible dyads (every single household in relation to every other household) there were 80 asymmetrical pairs and 58 reciprocal pairs (as well as 1,753 pairs of households between whom there was no transfer during the research period). The analysis shows a cohesively connected and robust network which is "decentralized and egalitarian" and which differs from both a random network and from a centralized network in which one or several hubs would dominate (Schnegg 2006: 16). Together with some simulations extrapolated from this data, it appears that although the local norm says that sharing has to take place indiscriminately, the circumstances are such that patterns emerge which also involve reciprocity. In other words, although reciprocity was explicitly not the normative rule, this does not exclude that some reciprocal side-effects occur over time. In an analysis of the data (Schnegg 2015) a number of transactions were later excluded from analysis, importantly the 144 events in which a sharing demand was made but not met, and another 400 that were classified by locals as "lending/borrowing" and involve non-food items. In turn, out of the remaining 1,087 transactions 46.7 % were carried out within the circle of 62 households for which data was collected. Out of those 508 transfers within the sample, 44% occurred in dyads in which there was a two-directional flow. In other words, again it is not the majority of transfers that occur in reciprocal pairs, but about eight times more than what mere chance would suggest. The network analysis contrasts the norm of indiscriminate sharing with reciprocity effects although the informants emphasize that sharing should take place indiscriminately ("If you are asked, you have to give") they are also not blind to the fact that sharing events are conditioned in a number of regular ways. The regularities are not explicable with reference to reciprocity alone, rather they involve other facts of the practical conditions of which local people are acutely aware, for instance living and being in close proximity with one another.

about who currently has something to give and who previously has been giving and receiving. One of the effects of these conditions all taken together is that sharing creates a non-random pattern and some reciprocal effects may be generated as part of this pattern in the course of many transfers across time. However, this is a far cry from characterizing these transfers as "reciprocal exchange" in the way outlined at the beginning of this section. It lacks the calculation and the direct back-and-forth coupling that is so characteristic of gift-exchange systems. Depending on other conditions in the cultural setting a sharing system may produce some reciprocal effects in the long run without this being its guiding principle. In his Fransfontein study, Schnegg (2006, 2015) highlights reciprocity, since he contrasts it with idealized views of sharing as being indiscriminate and random. However, the constellation that he describes closely matches what we know about the conditions for sharing practices elsewhere.

A full account of the uses and misuses of the notion of reciprocity in anthropology and its neighbouring disciplines is beyond what I can discuss here in the context of sharing. Occasionally, "reciprocity" is applied as a shortcut key to invoke an image of human cooperative rather than competitive transactions but, as we have seen, it can also be used to implicitly cement a utilitarian view of all transfers as quasi-market exchanges. In sum, Pryor and Graburn (1980) speak of the "myth of reciprocity" and Graeber (2001: 217) points to the fact that the notion is so widely used today that it has become "very near to meaningless". Here, I am only concerned with the problems that the notion of reciprocity generates in the context of sharing phenomena. It is important to note that reciprocity is not only a notion that has been bent and debated among academics. There is also an ideology of reciprocity (and, at times, an ideology of rejected reciprocity) among those who practice sharing and gift giving. Relying on local terms instead of technical terms is therefore no ready solution to the problem. In some instances local terminology matches closely an analytical separation into market, gift-exchange and sharing. Grinker (1994: 133) reports that the Lese of Central Africa distinguish lexically between dividing/sharing (*oki*), purchasing (*oka*) and exchanging (*iregi*), and Bahuchet found a similar set of distinctions among the Aka (see caption Figure 1.2). Stotz (2015) maintains that Walbiri never speak of "sharing" but only of "asking". Bird-David (2005: 203) underlines that despite a high incidence of sharing among the Nayaka, they do not have a single word "corresponding neatly to 'sharing'" but instead distinguish more concrete actions like giving, receiving, begging, distributing and so forth. Similarly, in ≠Akhoe Hai//om, the African language that I know best, selling (*//amaxu*) is distinguished from giving (*ma*) but is then further divided into a number of more specific practices such as to divide (*/gora*), to supply with (*≠hũi*), to give away (*au*), to lend (*//khubi*) and a host of other expressions for sharing food from a single dish, sharing a drink, sharing assets, sharing a dwelling and such like. As Damas (1972) has shown, there are often a whole set of local terms that get glossed over by the researchers into "sharing" or "exchange", although local terms do not neatly match these distinctions (see Box 2). With regard to reciprocity, it is noteworthy that many languages, including that of the ≠Akhoe

Hai//om, who are (former) hunter-gatherers in Namibia and who practise a lot of sharing, have reciprocal particles that can attach the meaning of mutuality to any verb. Thus, "giving" (*ma*) can easily be transformed into "giving to one another" (*magu*) or "sharing out" (≠*hũi*) into "sharing in with one another" (≠*hũigu*). Moreover, not only verbs can receive reciprocal meaning but also some nouns, for instance "/*aigun*" ("those being cross-cousins to one another") and triadic relations, too, can be covered with the reciprocal form (see Rapold 2011). Moreover, meanings shift not only across situations but also in the long term. While the English "sharing" is related to terms denoting cutting in neighbouring languages, the German/Dutch forms "*teilen/deelen*" denote apportioning and are related to English "deal" that today has business connotations (see Widlok forthcoming). Finally, a term like the English "sharing" can bridge the quite distinct meanings of "dividing things between individuals" (sharing out) and "joining individuals in a common use action" (sharing in) in a single word (Bird-David 2005: 203). Whether languages clearly or diffusely distinguish sharing in from sharing out, sharing from giving, non-reciprocal from reciprocal modes or not – this does not mean that there is no analytical need to separate these dimensions (see next section below). We also need to distinguish representations from practices, including representations of reciprocity from effects of reciprocity (as has been noted earlier by Pryor and Graburn 1980). We have ethnographic accounts that testify a gap or even a contradiction between the claims of reciprocity and the effects – and in diametrically opposed ways.

Pryor and Graburn were dealing with Arctic foragers who insisted that their giving would be highly reciprocal but this was not borne out by their quantitative analysis of transactions (see Box 2). Schnegg and Pauli were dealing with a group of Khoekhoe-speakers who insisted that their giving would be indiscriminate with regard to anyone in need and that it was not premised on reciprocity – but their detailed network analysis suggests that many of their transfers are in fact reciprocal (see Box 3). This is not a matter of locals misrepresenting or even "deceiving" themselves but rather a matter of acknowledging that the ways in which people conceive their transactions may have an immediate effect on these transactions but are not to be confused with it. In the Arctic case, Pryor and Graburn (1980: 235) note that "what people said about the rules of sharing sometimes counted for more than what people did". The high-prestige persons in this community held up the notion of generosity which was, however, questioned among some of the poorer members – but the latter then turned out to be giving more frequently than the former.[4] Throughout the community there was a strong and unquestioned notion that social equals enjoyed a roughly balanced exchange which, Pryor and Graburn suggest, in fact made them feel little need to keep an exact mental account of who gave what to whom. In other words, their ideology of reciprocal exchange effectively fostered imbalanced sharing. It is easy to imagine that conversely a society with an ideology of unequal exchange may, for analogous reasons, make people more alert towards imbalance, ensuring that records are kept and inequities are balanced out. The relation between representation and behaviour is therefore not a simple matter of one matching the other, or of one contradicting the other. Rather the two can be dynamically linked into one complex practice. Pryor and Graburn conclude that what people think about reciprocity or non-reciprocity may be "the most important causal factor" in bringing about the *reverse* situation in actual behaviour. As I shall point out in Chapter 3, which outlines the ethnography of sharing as a social practice, I think there are many more causal factors to be considered, but the general point they make is well taken: When we discuss the presence or absence of reciprocity and distinctions between sharing and gift giving, we are not simply retracing the judgements and rationalizations that agents make. Rather we seek to establish a conceptual framework that allows us to understand social practices across different settings. In other words, anthropological arguments about these terms are not a matter of establishing "correct translations" for vernacular concepts but a matter of understanding the statements made about transfers and allocations as actions by themselves in the dynamic processes that constitute sharing or giving as social practices. They are not ideological statements independent of "behaviour" but part and parcel of the process at large. As I have pointed out elsewhere (Widlok 2013), the fact that social agents have strategic reasons for stretching terms such as sharing, borrowing or gift giving does not imply that our analytic understanding is best served by blurring terms and by being vague. As Belk (2010: 719) has observed for consumer research, some authors continue to use sharing and reciprocal gift-exchange interchangeably while for others sharing is defined by being non-reciprocal (see Benkler 2004). Therefore, considerable effort is necessary to separate ideas that are often confounded and to establish more precise terms. The emergence of "sharing" as a technical term that is not to be confused with reciprocal giving is a case in point. An elegant way of dealing with the problem is provided by Belk (2010: 721) who elaborates a polythetic definition of sharing, gift giving and commodity exchange. This allows us to list characteristics for each of these modes which co-occur in prototypical examples but without any one characteristic being essential in itself. The list for sharing would include characteristics such as non-reciprocity, creating links to others, inclusion, caring, which are often (but not always) associated with sharing and there are "counterindications" such as reciprocal expectations, two-way exchanges, debts etc. which we find among the characteristics of gift giving and commodity exchange. Some characteristics (such as inclusion) may link gift giving to sharing, while others (like reciprocity) link it to commodity exchange. It also allows us to clearly identify borderline cases such as borrowing/lending (between sharing and gift giving) or money gifts, secondhand goods, and business friends (between gift giving and commodity exchange) that have several characteristics associated with different prototypes.

The realities of sharing

A definition based on family resemblances (see Belk 2010) is productive because it allows us to name distinctions and ambiguities in a coherent way. More work is needed to discuss what the best prototypes for each category are and whether or not the existing lists of characteristics are sufficient. As I will show in more detail, mothering and pooling, the prototypes of current consumer research, are somewhat biased from an anthropological perspective.[5] However, they are an important step forward insofar as these are both cases where there is little, if any, reciprocity. As Belk (2010) rightly points out, much of the everyday sharing that goes on in families and in the bringing up of children has been ignored because of a bias in Western economics to focus on public (versus private) exchanges.[6] Sharing in these contexts is unnoticed and unappreciated because it goes without saying, whereas gifts are marked by ceremonial exchanges of thanks and ceremonial actions of wrapping (Belk 2010: 717). It only becomes a matter of attention and debate when it disappears, for instance when families no longer share meals or time in front of a family television but eat and watch separately. The differences also become visible in a comparative perspective, when contrasting the prototypical cases of sharing in a family, of wrapped Christmas gifts, and of purchases in a store. Still, attempts have been made to re-phrase family sharing in the terms of reciprocal exchange and therefore ultimately in terms of self-interested commodity-type exchanges (see Ruskola 2005). This is only possible when reciprocity is made the common denominator of gift and commodity exchange and if no other alternative to commodity exchange than gift giving is thought to be possible. It is therefore important to underline that not only are there exchanges that are non-reciprocal but moreover there are transfers which are not exchanges. This is why Hunt (2000) has suggested the more neutral term "transfer". "Transfer", he suggested, could serve as a cover term that could then be split into one-way transfers (sharing) and two-way transfers (reciprocal gift-exchange). This nicely avoids the conceptual fusion sketched above but it does not solve all underlying problems.

To distinguish one-way from two-way transfers does not tackle the underlying problem that insisting on "reciprocity" and "exchange" disregards the perspective of the practitioners and instead privileges a perspective that is usually called "bird's eye view", or "view from nowhere" or "perspective of structure". For gift giving this has been discussed by Bourdieu (1977) who pointed out that what motivates and drives the actions of those engaged in gift giving is the fact that they do not know when and where and how a gift may be reciprocated or not. It is exactly that tension which excites participants in these exchanges and which explains the extraordinary energy that, for instance, *kula* participants invest. When seen from a bird's eye view, the gifts from A to B may in fact be reciprocated by gifts from B to A. However, a major error occurs when this perspective is then planted – as causal motives and strategies – back into the agents who are involved in the exchange. Their concerted and sustained efforts to elicit a counter-gift from partners, to be able to return a gift to them, and to make the best out of the period in which gifts have not yet arrived or are not yet given, exactly works on the crucial time lag and the uncertainty that surrounds it. This uncertainty is lost in the distanced view "from above". By calling the exchange "reciprocal" the critical uncertainty is wiped out which makes the whole practice (and the people involved) look ridiculous and irrationally convoluted. If the purpose of the practice is to provide reciprocal benefits and an even distribution of resources through two-way transfers, then gift giving seems like a "ceremonial" and deficient mode of barter. This impression of irrational action is the product of an ultimately redistributive perspective from above, superimposed over the perspective of the practitioners. From their perspective the suspense of being uncertain about whether, when and what will be given in return is what constitutes the excitement and driving force underlying gift giving.

The critique that Bourdieu has formulated with regard to structural accounts of gift giving needs to be taken several steps further. Typically, in the case of sharing we are not only dealing with two different perspectives (that of the agent and that of the aloof observer) but with a multiplicity of perspectives. People who may rapidly shift from being a recipient to becoming a provider may also shift their views, even in the course of a single event (Widlok 2004). What agents (or observers for that matter) expect to be a two-way exchange may turn out to be a one-way transfer (and vice versa). There are many examples (see Widlok 2013) illustrating how the person who is providing a share may expect either the same object to return eventually (as in lending) or as an equivalent being returned (as in swapping) but where for whatever reason the return transfer never happens, either because the item was destroyed or lost or because the opportunity never arises. Consequently, an intended two-way transfer may turn out to be one way. Also, one and the same transfer may be conceived of as a reciprocal two-way transfer by some and as a one-way transfer by others, as typically happens across ethnic boundaries. I have discussed this elsewhere with regard to the phenomenon of "paying tribute" between hunter-gatherers and their agro-pastoralist neighbours (Widlok 1999: 30-32). The former may provide provisions as "shares" that the latter conceive of as a tribute, an acknowledgement of overlordship. The foragers may also take provisions from their neighbours as free "shares" while the latter may see it as an investment that creates obligations. Conflicts easily ensue, especially in cases of "first contact" when those who "exchange" items have little previous experience with one another and little mutual understanding. Testimony for such conflicts abound as many European explorers (and researchers) have resorted to giving without knowing whether these transfers were seen in the same way by all parties involved, often with disastrous results for both the locals and the visitors involved (see Sahlins 1985 and Obeyesekere 1992).[7]

Bourdieu's insistence on a perspective that arises out of practice thus leads us to recognize the divergence of perspectives and the possible confusions that occur about what a transfer constitutes (or even about what constitutes a transfer). But there is more to it than that. Despite perspectival divergence, the shared practice usually generates sufficient overlap to enable interaction so that allocation and transfers can proceed more or less successfully. What is inevitable, though, is that transfers and transactions affect the positions that are taken in social relationships which in turn affect the interaction. Note that "interaction" is conceived of very broadly here, covering planned strategic action as much as intuitive spontaneous action that in more phenomenologically oriented approaches would be called "intercorporeality" (see Csordas 2005). There is no mastermind or cognitive understanding necessary for interaction to take place, it can also be routine interaction below the level of conscious decision and awareness. The degree to which agents reflect on their position and develop clear perspectives for themselves is likely to vary. They cannot help but be endowed with a social position as soon as they engage in transfer practices. Minimally, their position may change from having no access to a good to having access to it (and back again), from granting access to denying access (or the other way round), from demanding access to being granted access (or vice versa). Positions are relational so that any change that affects those with whom we interact also affects us. For example, as the others become hungry, we become potential providers and, as others gain food, that puts them in a position of potential providers towards us. Personal biographies and human sociality embedded in a living environment make constant re-positioning the normal state of affairs. This focus on the inevitable positionality that comes with human social practice is therefore a useful empirical starting point for approaching sharing theory "bottom up". As I will show in more detail below, interaction never takes place in a vacuum, free of social or other environmental context. An exclusive focus on interaction as "behaviour" is misleading since the transfers not only involve those who take action but also the conditions that enable this action in the first place. Although there has been an unfortunate tendency for research on reciprocity to look at agents in isolation, in the interests of a "controlled" experimental setting (see Chapter 2), the notion itself points towards the fact that without a particular positionality of the agents it is actually difficult to conceive of "reciprocity" or any other form of transfer. The temporal, spatial and social distance between agents in practice is highly relevant. For research with humans it is particularly important that this distance, including the social and political setting, is explored ethnographically because it is always the product of previous interactions of agents who are involved in a social situation.

The first suggestions for a non-egocentric theory of sharing include what Bird-David (2005: 207) has called "entangled identities" or "joined lives" and what Belk (2010: 724) calls "extended self". These notions are built on "sharing in" rather than "sharing out", as mentioned above, not on dispersing property but on uniting people. Or, as I have put it elsewhere (Widlok 2004: 61), the focus is not on giving and receiving but on "extending the circle of people who can enjoy the benefits of the shared resource". The key to sharing, in Belk's view, is that those who are close to us are "part of our extended self" so that "sharing with them is like sharing with self" (2010: 724).[8] This is why sharing takes place within the immediate family circle even in highly commercialized societies. When children take food that their parents have bought and placed in the fridge, when they use the facilities of their family home etc. it would be wrong to consider this reciprocity because there is no movement between two units. Rather, it is a single (family) unit feeding itself, the "aggregate extended self" (Belk 2010: 725). Research about sharing is then all about tracing the ways in which agents succeed to extend their selves (or not). What works in most immediate families can work more or less among peers in an age-set (see Box 9 in Chapter 5) or in new emerging settings among co-consumers sharing a brand of clothes (Belk 2010: 726) or those sharing files on the internet (see Chapter 6). Thus, the extension of aggregate selves is likely to change over time and across cultures. Schmidt (2014) has analyzed west Kenyan political ideas and practices in similar terms. Here the Luo notion of "*chamo*" is translated as "feating" (feeding and eating at the same time) following the multiple local metaphors that morally approve of co-utilization of food, land and other resources as long as it takes place in one "gastromoral body", prototypically the kinship group as a corporeal entity in which there is no exchange of food but which in a sense feeds itself (Schmidt 2014: 9). If politician and followers are conceived of as being part of the same extended body, then transfers between them are not considered "corruption", in contrast to those cases in which leaders and followers are part of different "gastromoral" bodies or when they violate these socially bounded bodies, for instance when trying to sell ancestral land.

The notion of an extended self is useful in many ways and will resurface repeatedly in the course of this book. For instance, it provides a useful critique of current processes of the so-called "sharing economy" (see Chapter 6) in which there is an increasing privatization and atomization of selves with more independent budgets and assets and with less joint ownership and communities of accrued gain even among married couples and core families.[9] However, on the basis of the ethnography on which I develop an emerging new theory of sharing I shall depart from the model of extended self in an important way: among people who share a lot and routinely, as in hunter-gatherer societies, there is less "collectivism" or "a common sense of self, even a common body" (Belk 2010: 724). Instead, we find a strong sense of personal autonomy. As we shall see, sharing relations that extend situationally in many ways do not create strong corporate groups but sharing is also an important practice for establishing a separate self in the first place. This requires a theory of "limited self" (rather than simply an "extended self"), a self that is limited by the demands of others and by the opportunities to access goods through others. The "desire for connection" (Belk 2010: 715) or "desire for unity" (Belk 2010: 729) may be more of a product of advanced industrial society than the driving force behind sharing more generally if we consider that demand sharing and attempts to avoid sharing are in fact prototypical manifestations (see Chapter 3). What is special about sharing in comparison with most other modes of transfer is not that it would create a sense of unity which allows us to merge our separate identities into collectives. Gift exchange with specific obligations is more likely to achieve this. Rather, what is special about sharing is that it allows people to bear with inevitable distinctions and to deal with inequalities that continuously arise since each and everyone is positioned in particular ways. Sharing realizes intrinsic goods, above all access to resources, which only become available through sharing (see Widlok 2004). It is not an instrument to strive for some derived goal or abstract community but it deals practically with the particulars of personal limitations, a self limited by the others with whom we share our lives. This is an aspect that will resurface in a number of the chapters in this book but it deserves some clarification in this introductory chapter.

Sharing is usually associated with egalitarian societies (Woodburn 1982a, Widlok and Tadesse 2005), that is to say with societies in which equality of outcome is actively pursued and in which levelling mechanisms are being employed to achieve that goal. Many of these societies have achieved a remarkable level of equality for all members of society – and not only a far more limited equality, for instance, among adult men or among recognized household heads. At the same time there are inequalities also within hunter-gatherer societies. The more important theoretical point is this: sharing is also training for accepting unevenness! To feed everyone, for instance, requires uneven input from those who are involved. Young hunters doing the kill may risk more, senior men may contribute better arrows due to their experienced craftsmanship, women may contribute more caloric input with what they gather than men, children and the old have their specific contributions and requests. With sharing, strict meritocratic principles are often dispensed with or violated as those who have contributed less can still demand their share.[10] Sharing therefore involves preparedness to live with such specific forms of imbalance.

It is thus misleading to associate sharing exclusively with symmetry (as, again, implied in the notion of reciprocity) or communion. Similarly, the other forms of transfer are also not exclusively associated with asymmetry. Each of these modes of transfer, including sharing, has specific articulations of both. In a sense both gift giving and market transactions require a much stronger sense of symmetry. It is less the amounts of asymmetry that would distinguish them than the acceptable rhythms of creating and levelling unevenness. In barter, lending, debt giving and receiving there is often an obsession with symmetry in the sense of cultivated equity as things are supposed to "even out". In a market setting this tendency gets aggravated by combining the notion of debt with accounting practices which allows people to keep exact track and equalize the stakes (Graeber 2011). Although the goal of getting "an exceptionally good deal" – receiving a lot having paid very little – may be widespread among many market participants, the idea ultimately requires a substantial notion of "coming out even" if only in order to measure the "good deal" that one is striving for. Those who have received little for their product hope for better deals in the future, and indeed require some counterbalancing to recompense for their efforts in order to stay in the game. Moreover, today a lot of concern is placed on "equality of opportunity" as in equal access to markets. In the practice of gift exchange, as discussed above, reciprocation may become a norm. At the same time, the asymmetry of a gift invites future gifts creating a new asymmetry, this time tipped in the other direction. While specific inequalities are provoked, the gift-exchange practices train participants to be evenly engaged and to strive for symmetry. The gifts themselves may never even out but they typically still alternate across an equilibrium baseline.

Sharing, by contrast, cultivates some disregard for unevenness with regard to the contributions made and with regard to what people may have – unless others take action to demand a share from them. After all, there would not be any need for sharing if life did not regularly produce unevenness due to many factors that are beyond human control in general and, in any case, beyond the control of individual persons in their specific circumstances. Life is inherently a source of unevenness given the growth and aging of our bodies, an unevenness that cannot be eliminated for good for as long as one lives, a point to which I will return towards the end of this book. Moreover, in many situations temporary unevenness is unavoidable. Think of a new cap or some other singular item that at any one time can only be worn by one person. Even if an item is shared, unevenness does not disappear. Food that is eaten is gone, unavailable for others. All that sharing does is to effectively intercept given asymmetries and to challenge them. Sharing is a possibility for preventing asymmetries from saturating into fossilized inequalities of outcome.

Despite this "destabilizing" force of sharing, most evolutionary accounts highlight its adaptiveness and the role it plays for the functional integration of human social relationships, as we shall see in the next chapter. In fact, sharing is not a revolutionary force as it does not lead to a wholesale and permanent shift, like when Marxists envisage the transfer of the means of production from one class to another. This would require a redistributive agent and break with the rhythms of having and losing. I would argue that sharing is more likely to support a kind of "conservative anarchism" (see Michea 2007). It recognizes the realities of life; it has a levelling effect but does not initiate fundamental changes. These are more likely to occur with competitive gift giving in which surplus resources can be converted into political capital of followership (see Hayden 1994). As we shall see in the following chapter, turning sharing into an everyday social practice, its integration into the routine behavioural repertoire of humans, has enabled *Homo Sapiens* to emerge as a being that is very different from its primate relatives in its social practice. As we shall see, since its emergence sharing has not only helped to keep humans in existence, it has also helped keeping human existence in shape.

Conclusion

This chapter has shown that we are far too quick to label transactions as "reciprocal" and as exchange. As a consequence we also misconstrue what the social implications of sharing practices are. Although many insights have been generated under the notion of reciprocity and exchange, I have pointed out that it has also imposed serious limitations. Following the work of Woodburn (1998) and others I have argued that it is empirically and conceptually wrong to cover sharing under reciprocity or exchange as a structurating principle. The attempt to rescue the notion of reciprocity by qualifying sharing as "asymmetrical reciprocity" (Peterson 2013) or "generalized reciprocity" (Sahlins 1988) bypasses the central question because the problem is not only that these transfers are uneven but also that we are dealing with transfers that seem more like several one-way transfers going in different directions rather than a single two-way transfer linked into a single exchange. Trying to see it otherwise makes it necessary to maintain that exchanges take place between abstractly conceived and identified entities that are shifted onto a level that is spatially and temporally removed from practice and from what can be observed empirically. At that level almost every transfer can be linked to any other transfer to construct reciprocity of sorts but at the cost of considerable arbitrariness. One and the same person may be involved in many parallel sharing events, sometimes as provider and sometimes as receiver. The point is that these events are not connected to one another in the same way as they are in reciprocal gift giving. Rather, they are loosely linked to one another in the same way that we would also talk of individuals "working for one another" in a society organized by a division of labour. The social system depends on (more or less) everyone contributing (more or less regularly) by providing shares and providing labour (at some stage, to someone), but this is a far cry from saying that labour or shares were offered "reciprocally".

As we have seen, this does not mean that there is no mutuality involved at all, either in orientation or in effect. Furthermore, although it may seem banal to many today, it is worth pointing out that any interaction involves some reciprocity in the sense of a vague mutual engagement, as for instance manifest in conversational turn taking or communicative feedback. It is hard to think of any transaction that would *not* need to be investigated in that weak sense of reciprocity as is interaction. To avoid further confusion I suggest that we speak of mutual recognition rather than reciprocity. A generous intention, for instance, would not constitute sharing (or any other mode of transfer for that matter) unless there is some action that can be perceived by others – their perception being a minimal form of feedback. Such action includes – and as we shall see in Chapter 3 this is important – the action of refraining from interfering with someone who is about to take something. What this chapter has highlighted is the importance of looking more closely at the actions that make up the social practice of sharing. We now turn to evolutionary debates which deserve critical discussion but also careful attention because they have contributed to an impressive amount of detailed empirical data on the actions that make up sharing.

Notes

1 A likely second in terms theoretical schemas that got also extremely widespread is van Gennep's model of the rites of passage which has also been picked up in numerous ways (see Turner 1969, Bloch 1992).

2 The reactions by philosophers were largely defensive and negative, see for example Mechlenburg's critique (2006).

3 A similar problem arises when we consider the accounts of indigenous hunters across the world who frequently see the game animal as offering itself to the hunter (Duerr 2010: 85-88) or the image of foragers that the environment is "giving" food to them (Bird-David 1990). When trying to characterize these phenomena as instances of reciprocity one would have to go as far as stretching mutuality into a notion of "cosmic" returns whereby some reciprocity is assumed to occur not only across some generations down the line but in some diffuse way across species whereby species A may receive from species B but may "reciprocate" by feeding species C, at best, or by feeding into a notion of cosmic exchanges whereby everything is somehow connected to everything else.

4 Ziker (2014: 354) found a similar effect in a post-socialist Siberian community with strong norms of mutual assistance where wealth indicators were negatively correlated with generous offers in experimental economic games, while (as predicted) disposable income was positively correlated with generous offers.

5 One of the biases concerns the type of family and household that is presented as a prototype insofar as there are very different ways of conceiving "a relative" or "a family" of which the inward-oriented "bourgeois" nuclear family is but one. Cross-culturally households not only differ in composition and size but also in terms of their permeability and stability. Many societies allow membership in more than one household, giving members considerable room for manoeuver. Another critical point concerns Belk's contention that "sharing involves joint ownership" in contrast to transfers of ownership in gift giving and commodity exchange (2010: 720) since there seem to be too many anthropological counter-examples to include this criterion.

6 He also points at the connected gender bias since "traditionally women have been associated with the interior of home and men with the exterior world", the former being characterized by many acts of sharing but the latter being more readily recognized economic transactions (Belk 2010: 716).

7 In other words, what is considered a simple transfer from one perspective may be considered an exchange from the perspective of another participant and as a consequence different expectations may emerge. Similarly, there are also cases of conscious euphemism or unintended "bending" of terms, especially in contexts of unprecedented encounter or rapid change. Strathern (2011) provides an example from the Pacific where the notion of "lending" emerged as a compromise term for transfer events that the European missionaries considered "stealing" and the local children read as "exchange". This process of bending terms continues today in the so-called "sharing economy" as I shall point out in Chapter 6.

8 Note that there is a difference between Belk's notion of "extended self" (i.e. a person extending his or her own self) and anthropological notions of "extending selves" as for instance in the literature of hunting and gathering people who attribute agency and other aspects of personhood to animals, effectively turning hunting into an exchange relationship (Nadasdy 2007, see also Duerr 2010).

9 Although Belk (2010: 728) characterizes these new forms in terms of "what appears to be sharing [but] is actually more of a self-interested commodity exchange" he also embraces the idea that consumers in the new settings "can extend themselves through possessions" (2010: 726), i.e. not only through "sharing in" but also through "sharing out".

10 See Schäfer (2014) who has experimentally supported the ethnographic finding that children in hunter-gatherer societies are much less likely to apply meritocratic rules than other children. Note that agro-pastoralists are known to have harsh reactions against such an apparent "unfairness" (The Parable of the Vineyard Workers in Matthew 20:16).

2

SHARING THE PREY

Evolutionary assumptions

Introduction

In the previous chapter I outlined why it has taken some time before sharing became accepted as a distinct category, a phenomenon that needed an explanation in its own right. Interpreting sharing events as if they were commercial transactions or gift exchanges is to misread these events. The message from comparative anthropology is that sharing events are different enough to require a distinct theoretical account. The following chapters address the question of *which* theoretical account in particular might be appropriate to shed more light on sharing. A literature search on "sharing" as a key word quickly shows that a lot of scholarly texts about the subject are written from a perspective of evolutionary theory. Explaining things on the basis of their origin is the dominant explanatory blueprint in science and the humanities. Moreover, sharing is also frequently referred to in debates about the evolution of *other* aspects of human culture and sociality. In this chapter I discuss these two links between sharing and evolutionary thought in turn. I then turn to an alternative, practice-oriented approach, to be developed in detail in the chapters to follow, that looks at the temporal dimension of sharing in a very different way than evolutionary approaches.

Origins of sharing

Evolutionary and historical modes of thought are both fuelled by a deeply engrained cultural view according to which knowing the origin of things is to be able to explain their essential nature. Note that this preoccupation with historical origins is neither shared by all cultural systems (see Lévi-Strauss 1965) nor do philosophers of science agree that an explanation in terms of origins is necessarily superior to other explanations (Wittgenstein 1993 [1967]). "Evolutionary thought" is here conceived of very broadly as the study of "change of culture over time" (Richerson and Christiansen 2013: 3). It is therefore not limited to the Darwinian branch of evolutionary theory and even less to the sociobiological adaptations of that theory which have met with considerable resistance from the social sciences and the humanities. In fact, I maintain that evolutionary theory shares some fundamental assumptions with historical-diffusionist accounts in the widest sense (see Bloch 2005) to which it is often set in fierce opposition.

The cultivation of (and sometimes fixation on) historical and evolutionary accounts typically takes place in societies in which genealogical models are important for establishing social groups, for determining the succession to office and power positions, for reckoning kinship, inheritance and legitimacy. This applies not only to societies in Europe and the colonial settler cultures that they have established around the world, but also to most societies of Asia and to many social formations in Africa and other parts of the world. In other words, there are folk theories outside scholarly research that continue to fuel both historical and evolutionary explanations. For the most part, however, there is a deep divide between historical-diffusionist accounts and evolutionary accounts of culture, a divide that has led to a bifurcated landscape of knowledge in which approaches with an evolutionary focus and those that have a historical-cultural focus are incubated from one another or are at best in more or less peaceful coexistence with one another.[1]

In this arranged coexistence, evolutionary theory typically covers the development of features up to the point at which *Homo sapiens* appears (or "anatomically modern human" as it is commonly phrased). Culture history goes on from there to explain the changes and distribution of features since then. In Ingold's critical depiction of the problem, "walking", for instance, is considered evolution while "cycling" belongs to culture history, just as "speaking" is seen as a part of evolution while "writing" is part of culture history and so forth (Ingold 2000). With regard to sharing this means that evolutionists establish theorems like "kin selection", "costly signaling", "reciprocity" and "tolerated scrounging" (see p. 42) which are expected to explain the first emergence of sharing among primates and, usually by combining some of these theorems, also "in humans". What is left to the culture history approach is to explain how the occurrence of sharing and other modes of transfer is distributed across cultural groups, e.g. by showing that the Nayaka (Bird-David 1990) have a cultural cosmology of a "giving environment" (and most of their Indian neighbours do not), that the Hadza (Woodburn 1982a) have a strong "cultural obligation" to share (and the neighbouring African farmers do not), or that indigenous Australians (but not other Australians) have a "relational ontology" about persons, an ontology that reproduces sharing even in the contemporary welfare economy (Macdonald 2000, Peterson 2013). Such an academic division of labour between proximate (historical) and ultimate (evolutionary) explanations is unsatisfactory on several accounts. To begin with, it implies a human being made up of two components, a dual human existence that is split between a natural and a cultural component which seem disconnected and difficult to reconcile (see Ingold 2000). Furthermore, it tends to superficially cover up fundamental disagreements between the two explanatory accounts where they should be put into a productive dialogue with one another. Since the two approaches, even within anthropology as a discipline, constitute two largely separate discourse worlds, each with its own journals and peer audiences, we can only occasionally see the underlying conflict flaring up.

This is the case when evolutionists insist that their evidence provides the "ultimate" (Jaeggi and Gurven 2013) explanation, suggesting that the forces that have been "selected for" a certain practice are responsible for all instances of sharing at all levels of complexity. Correspondingly, culture historians may insist that sharing is established or maintained "well beyond utilitarian need" in an economy that is a "moral economy" (Peterson 2013: 167) suggesting that with culture and morality enforcing sharing, all other effects can be assumed to have lost their relevance. That is to say, for the most part, the proponents of evolutionary and culture history accounts ignore one another and their results are hardly combined. While this is true for many topics in anthropology (e.g. mobility, kinship, violence, ritual, medicine), it is certainly particularly visible with regard to sharing because it is a key concept for both approaches.

Hence, where evolutionary and cultural-historical theory part ways is their assessment as to whether the observed phenomena are due to unified mechanisms and "natural laws" or whether they are due to culture-specific ontologies, rules and norms. Cultural-historical theories underline that it is due to the peculiarity of human development that ideas and practices are transferred, mixed and copied "culturally", i.e. within a relatively short time-frame and without being materially inherited. This effectively decouples the cultural history from any changes in the underlying genetic or biological make-up of human beings. It also excludes the possibility of establishing unilinear trajectories or universal "mechanisms". Evolutionary theory, by contrast, insists that there are such mechanisms that can be recognized in the long-term processes of adaptation. It also insists that such mechanisms allow us to understand how a feature such as sharing is generated in the social and cultural world as it is today and how it can be predicted to continue to be generated in the future. In other words, evolutionary theories are attractive to many because they promise to explain social institutions not in correlation with some short-term cultural transfer but in reference to some "external" underlying principle such as "natural selection". In this view, the practice of sharing among humans may be associated with strong cultural rules that help to enforce it, but these cultural rules would only count as a proximate cause. They require in turn a more long-term explanation reaching back to the "material conditions" before cultural diffusion started to play a role. Before I suggest an alternative "third way" that takes us beyond this apparent impasse between what appear to be irreconcilable alternatives, I want to briefly summarize some of the results gained through evolutionary studies of sharing.

Assessing the primate heritage

Animal behaviour research, including work in primatology, shows that rather little sharing takes place among non-humans. The incidences that can be interpreted as sharing are limited in a number of ways: among most so-called social animals (for instance insects or bats) the pro-social behaviour consists of co-consumption, tolerating that others feed themselves in the same patch, or is, at best, to be described as support. It does not involve the transfer of food or other valued provisions that we recognize as sharing. With birds, the feeding of the young is usually grouped together with hatching and other forms of assisting offspring under the notion of "care of the brood" rather than under "sharing". Cooperative mammals such as lions do share but only in the sense that they allow others to drive them off and to take from a carcass ("tolerated theft"), a behaviour that is similar to the more widely spread co-foraging or co-consumption already mentioned (see Packer and Pusey 1997). Sharing of food also occurs among a number of other mammals (e.g. wild dogs) but is usually limited to one's own offspring or direct partner and it occurs only among a very small number of species even within the order of primates. It is, for instance, "conspicuously absent" among many Old World monkeys (Jaeggi and Gurven 2013: 188). Capuchin monkeys (belonging to the New World monkeys) have been observed to assist one another in gaining food and to drop pieces so that a fellow monkey can take them ("facilitated taking", see de Waal and Berger 2000) but it has been remarked that that this occurs far less outside captivity, away from experimental setups (Jaeggi and Gurven 2013: 192). Among the apes, chimpanzees have been observed to occasionally share with fellow chimpanzees who either reach for food or "beg" for it by stretching out their hands (Mitani and Watts 2000) but, as with the other cases mentioned, these are rather rare events accounting for a very small proportion of the nutrition of an individual and of the group as a whole.

There are two conclusions to be drawn from this evidence: firstly, the zoological record provides us with proof that human sharing did not "start from scratch" so that there was no need to create it out of nothing.[2] At least some of the constituent actions contained in human sharing are also part of the behavioural repertoire of mammals and in particular of primates. However, what looks similar in terms of outward behaviour may not necessarily follow the same logic or the same origin. Not caring to chase away others while accidently dropping some food may also be interpreted as carelessness but also as facilitation. Secondly, the zoological record does not explain why and how human foragers developed sharing into an elaborate and dominant practice. After all, among humans only very few food items are *not* shared. On the contrary, the apparent success of subsistence procurement by other means among all other species poses the question even more sharply as to why humans opted for sharing in such a big way since many related species cope perfectly well without it.

Ethnographic case studies show that among human foragers sharing in the mean increased the nutritional status of all group members by 80 percent across different foods procured in a variety of ways (Kaplan and Hill 1985: 233). When considered against this prevalence of sharing among human foragers, the instances among non-human primates are negligible. Therefore, whatever leads animals to share, when they share is likely to have other reasons than what motivates humans to share and vice versa. A simple transposition of motives or techniques across these very different cases seems very weak as a model of reality and very unlikely as a general developmental theory.

Unfortunately, that does not preclude that such an explanatory "short-cut" has not been attempted. There are (still) sociobiologists who consider sharing as a manifestation of altruism that can be traced "across all phyla of the animal kingdom" (Voland 2007: 15), drawing a straight and short line from "social amoeba" across chimpanzees, stone age hunters, present-day hunter-gatherers and modern day neighbourhood assistance. In such accounts all these mentioned instances are thought to be premised on the inclusive fitness of biological kinship and its reproductive strategies that are ultimately in compliance with "selfish gene-programmes" (Voland 2007: 25) and their maximal distribution, a single biological imperative that explains world history in its entirety. Drawing such a direct line is not just a matter of using a broad brush that necessarily creates a caricature of reality. Rather, it is unempirical and unsound since it conveniently ignores ethnographic evidence and replaces it with the plausibility of metaphoric analogy. When Voland (2007: 23) writes "the simple and plausible formula food for sex regulates already pre-human social transactions and is still the business foundation of the oldest profession in the world" he misrepresents the results that biologists have gained about primates (see Mitani and Watts 2000: 922) as much as the knowledge that anthropologists have about prostitution (see Day 1999) – and about any possible links between these two fields. There is a serious mismatch between the presumption to write an evolutive universal history on the one hand and explanations that do not seriously consider variation and complexity beyond early hominid phenomena on the other hand (see Lüdke 2009). To be fair to sociobiology, it should be mentioned that there are also other more cautious voices in this approach that criticize such a swift move between animal and human examples. Instead they recognize that neither do genes determine human social life in its complexity, nor are cultural practices geared towards a wider distribution of genes (see for instance, Weber 2003).

The sharing curve

As we shall see in the second half of this book, the notion of sharing has wide currency (and attraction) today in public life as well as in science. This, however, is a fairly recent development. Originally, it was not its ubiquity but the relative absence of sharing in social life that made it an important topic for scholarly debate. As we have seen, sharing is underdeveloped among animals, including non-human primates and other social animals that may occasionally help each other but very rarely share food or other items. Similarly, sharing has also been considered to be decreasing in human society under conditions of growing social complexity since the Neolithic introduction of animal and plant domestication (see Marlowe 2004). Sharing is therefore considered the dominant mode of allocating goods only under the rather specialized conditions of egalitarian societies that are relatively few in the overall record to date. Consequently, the study of sharing was for a long time part of a rather specialized branch of anthropological research, namely the evolutionary ecology of foragers.

Even though human sharing cannot, as we have seen, be explained simply by mapping it on non-human sharing, it is nevertheless intriguing to see what the evolutionary (in the sense of "long-term") trends and dynamics of this practice might be. In this context it is important to realize that there are contrastive positions held also within evolutionary thought. For the purposes of a quick orientation we may distinguish the approaches associated with Herbert Spencer from those associated with Charles Darwin. Spencer is usually attributed with progressivist ideas of unilinear evolution as the dominant form of evolutionary thought that entered anthropology first. These ideas have influenced anthropology through a number of routes, largely through the work of Taylor and Morgan, who in turn influenced Marx and Engels. All of these authors would have associated sharing with an early stage of human evolution for which the label "primitive communism" had been coined (see Lee 1988). In fact the large influence of this particular strand of evolutionary thought on social theory has been identified as a main reason for a hiatus in evolutionary thinking in the social sciences of the twentieth century (see Richerson and Christiansen 2013: 8). Put in very brief terms, Spencer and those who developed his ideas assumed that all phenomena of the present could be sorted into an invariant sequence encompassing organic and social change directed from imperfect simplicity to adapted complexity. This account failed in many ways as many supposedly simple systems of organization turned out to be rather complex and show great within-variation. This is certainly true with regard to hunter-gatherer societies which, despite apparently simple technical tools, can have very complex kinship or mythological systems – and an unexpected variability. As a consequence the unilinear progressivist schemas are now denounced by most anthropologists including those who today maintain an interest in cultural evolution (see Richerson and Christiansen 2013).

However, the notion of increasing complexity has some intuitive support and some related ideas continue to resurface also in the current discussion of sharing practices. Jaeggi and Gurven's graphic summary of the evolution of food sharing is a case in point (see Jaeggi and Gurven 2013: 188). The schema (see Figure 2.1) suggests a correlation between different types of sharing and the phylogenetic evolution of primates (plus some co-evolved conditions). Out of 69 primate species in their sample, 30 do not share at all, 39 share only with their offspring, in 15 species there is also sharing among adults, and only in one species (*Homo sapiens*) do we find widespread sharing. Although there are exceptions (see Jaeggi and van Schaik 2011: 2130) the linear path from "non-sharing" to "widespread sharing" in this account largely follows the phylogenetic tree, starting with prosimians (lemurs etc., mostly non-sharing) on to monkeys (sharing with offspring), to apes (sharing among adults), and to humans (widespread sharing). The unilinearity that the graph suggests is in fact deceptive in two ways. Firstly, the correlations are only borne out at a statistical level. The accompanying data shows that even very closely related species may differ considerably in their sharing behaviour just as

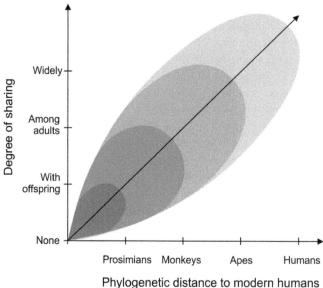

FIGURE 2.1 Mapping sharing onto a phylogenetic tree. Graphics: M. Feinen, redrawn from Jaeggi & van Schaik 2011 and Jaeggi & Gurven 2013

distant species may have similarities in sharing patterns. It is therefore hard to establish from this record any causation based exclusively on genetic inheritance. Secondly, the inbuilt implicit assumption is that the occurrence of sharing has the same cause or implication across these cases, although observed sharing can in fact be motivated and enabled in quite different ways.[3]

The only categorical distinction that the primate sample allows us to draw is that between human sharing (widespread) and non-human sharing (rare and only with offspring or close kin). It is a categorical distinction insofar as there is only one species of humans in the sample. Interestingly, humans were not included in the original version of the graph (Jaeggi and van Schaik 2011: 2136) and we may wonder what a graph would look like if we include all humanoid cases. From an anthropological point of view humans could in fact be placed in *all* categories (compare Figure 2.1 and 2.2). After all, it is easy to find human subcultures where there is no food sharing or where sharing is rejected and very rare. Typically, these are situations of extreme famine, but one could also think of hospital wards for infectious diseases, posh restaurants or repressive detention camps – all of which effectively exclude sharing. Similarly, there are social groups where sharing is limited to the core family, within each sex or within other socially demarcated groups – think of monastic communities for instance. And if we accept, for the sake of the argument, as most evolutionists are likely to do, that the high incidence of sharing among contemporary hunter-gatherers reflects sharing among Palaeolithic hunters, just as the more limited sharing among farmers reflects limited sharing during the Neolithic, then a non-linear image emerges (see Figure 2.2). If we were to plot the

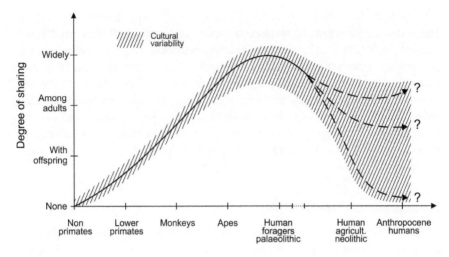

FIGURE 2.2 Mapping sharing onto social complexity. Graphics: M. Feinen

importance of sharing for social relations and subsistence onto an evolutionary timeline that included the various economic systems that humans have developed up to today we would not get a linear cline or a line of growth. Instead we would probably arrive at a (sinoid) curve that illustrates how sharing is less common in animal societies (including non-human primates) *and* less common in the flows of goods and services in state-capitalist or state-socialist societies. The provisional peak of the curve seems to be reached among small-scale societies, in particular hunter-gatherer societies, which are positioned in between the two extremes. It would also be appropriate to qualify the peak as "provisional" given the openness of human history (see Chapter 6 and Chapter 7). This sinoid distribution follows the incidence of egalitarian societies observed so far which, again, is very pronounced among many hunter-gatherers but not among apes, and not in agriculturalist, feudal or state-based societies. For present-day complex societies the evidence seems inconclusive since sharing is seen to be declining due to "possessive individualism" (Belk 2010: 727) but also as being boosted by the internet as "a new era of sharing that has quickly been embraced by millions" (Belk 2010: 715).[4] Neither the incidence of sharing nor that of egalitarian social organization can be forced into a linear trajectory of growth or decline. Rather, sharing seems to be functionally related to a larger bundle of practices that ethnographers call "levelling mechanisms" (Widlok and Tadesse 2005) including those that primatologists cover under "reverse dominance hierarchy" (Boehm 1999). The bundle consists of social strategies for countering aspirations to create social dominance and hierarchy and we shall look at the ethnographic details of these levelling practices in the following chapters. Social groups tend to become hierarchical if they are not successful in establishing such practices as is the case among non-human primates and in modern societies with accumulated wealth and coercive power in the hands of a few (see Gintis and van Schaik 2013: 43).

Although the relation between ideas of progressing complexity and of Darwinian evolutionism remains problematic, and was ambivalent for Darwin himself (Ingold 2007: 113), explanatory schemes that build exclusively on unilinear progressivism are now less common in science but continue to be frequently entertained as part of simplistic arguments in some public debates. Given that unilinear scenarios have proved to be problematic, evolutionary anthropologists have recently turned away from a Spencerian type of progressivism and towards more genuine Darwinian ideas in an attempt to establish correlations between the various types of allocation and transfers and the political structure of a social group.

From origin to function

A more strictly Darwinian version of evolutionary thought that highlights co-evolution and selection is increasingly gaining ground in the social sciences and this is also reflected in research on sharing. Above all, sharing continues to constitute a puzzle for theories of natural selection that premise the evolutive process on selective mechanisms in which "selfish genes" are competing with one another. In such a setting sharing should not occur, certainly not with non-kin. Providing other organisms, with other genes, the means of survival or improving their reproduction by sharing resources with them, seems to undermine Darwinian arguments. Part of the problem is that sharing tends to get equated with a particular image of altruistic behaviour. The expectation here is that carriers of genes producing "altruism" would need to die out because they were to be outcompeted by others, making altruistic practices disappear quickly across generations. Since this has apparently not been the case, a number of attempts have been made to accommodate sharing into the Darwinian evolutionary paradigm. In this context it has been argued that altruism was not only beneficial to gene-reproduction within a group of close blood relatives but that reciprocal altruism enabled human cooperation in a way that gave humanity as a whole a reproductive edge over other species – at least as long as the between-species advantages would outweigh the possible negative effects of altruistic individuals at within-group level of competition (Marlowe 2004). Decoupling the behaviour of individuals from group effects thereby solves some of these issues. Furthermore, the puzzle of sharing is less of a problem for evolutionary approaches that are no longer centred exclusively on the gene, as an agent in itself, the homunculus in genetic models, as Deacon (2012) has pointed out. If we accept that both sharing and altruism are enabled through institutionalized social practice that cannot be reduced to the genetic level, the problem largely disappears. The frameworks of cultural conventions and institutions may overlap with processes at other levels, including the level of organic processes, but they are not identical with these. Consequently, the more recent approaches in cultural evolution that are less gene-centred try to depict a more complex idea of co-evolution in which genes are but one element in a wider epigenetic landscape just as social institutions are part of a historical landscape that they shape and which they are in turn shaped by (see Whitehouse 2013: 358). The general Darwinian argument is that similar forces and processes are at work with regard to genetic and cultural selection but without direct or immediate links between organic and the superorganic scales. Sharing is still of interest here because it seems to be on the edge between cultural changes with clear reproductive effects (e.g. subsistence technology) and cultural features such as language and religion which are often considered to be largely "adaptively neutral" since, arguably, their variation has no direct consequences for reproduction (see Richerson and Christiansen 2013: 12). However, the Darwinian project is still hampered by the fact that the links between genetic and cultural change are far from clear and how the central idea of natural selection should be understood when dealing with cultural evolution. Moreover, in both domains there is a rather restrictive notion of what social relations entail in practice.

Although culture is clearly a social process, many evolutionists have been adamant that methodological individualism is the only acceptable way into understanding cultural dynamics (see Smith 1988: 225). The prominent assumption has been that it is those practices that will be selected for in the long run of evolution which provide the largest payoff to the individual (see Kelly 1995: 171). The preferred method of choice for establishing what constitutes the largest payoff has been game theory, either in the form of Optimal Foraging Theory or related experiments of ultimatum games and prisoner dilemmas (see Marlowe 2004). Game theory experiments pose a choice between hoarding (or not sharing) and sharing (or giving up hoarding) but also prompt subjects to react to more or less uneven shares offered by others and to tune one's own offers according to what they have given. Given the variability of food sources (seasonality etc.) and given the variability of foraging success, especially for high-risk activities such as hunting, sharing provides – in principle - an unbeatable strategy of effective resource use across all participants. However, as soon as there is even one individual who defects from sharing and begins to hoard, that individual – game theory assumes – will fare better but the rest will fare worse. Consequently, the game model assumes that "hoarding will eventually become the dominant strategy" – despite the principal advantages of sharing (Kelly 1995: 172). Or, as Smith (1988: 239) puts it: "[O]ur exercise in game theory predicts it will never pay to share!" But what can explain sharing if we are not willing to assume that everyone who shares acts irrationally? Since apparently perfectly rational members of many societies chose sharing as a strategy, the proponents of these models would probably defend the model by saying that it directs our attention to search for complementary strategies that allow the sharers to have their cake and eat it, to enjoy the benefits of sharing at group level without forfeiting their rationality at individual level. As a consequence, a lot of research effort has been put into questions asking how sharing may be hedged so that free riders are excluded. For instance, how can territoriality be institutionalized to avoid the blanket exploitation of shared resources that would lead to the breakdown of the system? Game theory models have sought to identify factors that individuals take into account that go beyond the allocation of food and other goods. With no room to summarize the extensive (and growing) literature on this topic it should suffice to say that, maybe ironically, game theory points to the fact that sharing events need to be placed in a wider context (see Schäfer 2014).[5] This is ironic insofar as the experimental paradigm systematically cuts out the everyday context of sharing practices in the first place.

Sharing "behaviour", I suggest, is only understandable as part of a larger sharing "practice" with at least informally institutionalized forms of trust and expectations, with a time depth that allows for memory and experience as important effects and with recognition of the social setting in which it takes place. In all social settings we are not dealing with an isolated giver facing an isolated recipient but with a situation in which the two have a history with one another and in which, typically, there are onlookers and other "third parties" involved. There are, unfortunately, no good examples in which game theory has integrated these dimensions in a satisfying way. This is not coincidental because the limitations of the experimental approach effectively prevent this.[6] In the reminder of this book I shall explore an alternative to these models which takes in a wider range of more ethnographic details but also seeks to establish patterns in the ethnography of sharing, bottom up as it were. Unless we understand sharing as a complex social practice, it will continue to be a puzzling fact for social theory.

Questions of evolutionary origins therefore remain problematic but this research can still be instructive for understanding long-term impacts of sharing once it has entered the repertoire of human practices. While it is generally accepted that sharing practices contribute to the ability of humans to survive, there has been considerable debate to find out what the specific consequences of sharing are when humans get involved in sharing, be it as men or women, as children, adults or the old, as hunters or non-hunters, as close kin or non-kin. The hypotheses that have been generated in this context are ultimately still premised on ideas of natural selection. They have been tested with regard to quantitative data on naturally occurring human sharing among foragers and, more recently, there is an increasing body of cross-cultural experimental data. In both instances there is a rather narrow probabilistic logic that is applied with the result that only quantitative case studies are seriously considered which comply with the disciplinary conventions of evolutionary psychology and primatology. The celebrated test case is that of the Ache hunter-gatherers in Paraguay (see Box 4).

In the Ache case, as in many forager cases around the world, sharing is the dominant mode of accessing resources. This is in contrast to many stratified societies in which gift giving and the giving of alms, often (misleadingly) considered instances of sharing, only make up a small proportion of all transactions, with limited impact to a small proportion of the population. In the Ache case, by contrast, sharing in this instance saturates the whole society. It has an impact on everyone in the group and for most resources it is the main mode of access. Interestingly, confronting the common evolutionary hypotheses with the Ache data produces very sobering results for adherents of simplistic sociobiological assumptions. Most prominently, the Ache case does not support "inclusive fitness"

BOX 4 SHARING BEYOND KIN AMONG THE ACHE FORAGERS OF PARAGUAY

Research on sharing among the Ache of the lowland subtropical forest in Eastern Paraguay includes quantitative data that registers with the probabilistic models of evolutionary anthropology and has therefore had considerable impact in this field. In the early 1980s, the Ache still lived to a very large extent on a foraging diet of game meat, honey, and gathered bushfood such as insect larvae, fruit and other plant items. Kim Hill and his collaborators went along on nine foraging trips lasting between 7 and 15 days in bands of 15 to 28 individuals, men, women and children (see Kaplan and Hill 1985 for details). The data they collected represents 81 days of full forest subsistence with elaborate sampling techniques to make sure that the collected foodstuffs that they recorded had no bias with regard to what was collected and by whom. They not only focused on individuals, what they collected and what they ate in the course of an entire day, they also "followed" a particular resource that reached the camp, recording who acquired it and how it was shared. As a research team, they were also able to check what was consumed by everyone in the camp at selected points in time (usually in the mornings and evenings) and in regular intervals across the day for everyone who was in sight. The 5,500 entries in their database show some very clear patterns. All Ache in these foraging bands received the larger part of their diet from food that was acquired by others in the group. This proportion was particularly high for meat (between 80 and 90 percent acquired by others) and honey (calorically second in importance, around 80 percent) and still high for other gathered food items (between 50 and 70 percent). The amount only dropped with regard to resources that were brought from the forest into the mission station (less than 1 percent in total). There was virtually no storing of the food, which was usually consumed within 24 hours of its procurement.

The high incidence of sharing collected food is underlined by the fact that the hunters actually ate *less* of the meat that they killed themselves than what would be predicted if all meat was pooled at random. Only with honey did men and women acquire more than chance would predict. Moreover, with regard to the meat shared, there was no bias towards specific individuals, i.e. a hunter did not favour his direct kin in the distribution of meat. Similarly honey was not received more often from close kin than random pooling would suggest. Only with other foodstuffs there was a probability above the level of chance that individuals would get shared food from immediate close family (parents, children, siblings, spouses) instead of more distant kin (affines, distant kin and non-related persons). The amount of food shared, and the proportion that is shared beyond close kin, came as a surprise to many researchers who had not conducted ethnographic field research and who had been suspicious about previous non-quantitative accounts that arrived at similar conclusions.

arguments according to which sharing should only occur with close kin (see Box 4). When a systematic attempt was made to test a range of predictions developed in sociobiology against the ethnography of sharing among the Ache of South America the following results emerged (see Kaplan and Hill 1985):

- Kin selection (privileging close kin in sharing) was not supported by the data. It is not the case that sharing and kin distance were inversely related, i.e. hunters did not share less with distant kin than with close kin. Sharing, it appears, is not a mechanism that would select for the close kin of successful hunters. Rather, sharing improves the survival condition of everyone within the network at large.
- Reward for labour (cooperative acquisition, greater shares for those who cooperated in acquisition) was not supported as a hypothesis. It is not the case that things that were procured collectively were also shared more often. Sharing is not a mechanism that amplifies the fitness of those who (are able to) invest their labour. Rather, sharing can even out inequalities based on investments and the ability to make such investments.
- Tit for tat reciprocity (reciprocal altruism, those who give more should get more in return) was not supported. It is not the case that those who give more also received more in sharing events. Sharing is not a mechanism that supports only those who can make claims on previous acts of provision, cashing in on obligation and debt. Rather, sharing is well suited to even out entrenched inequalities and to (re)create a level playing field.
- Tolerated theft (sharing only when defence is too costly) was not supported. It is not the case that resources were only shared when it was no longer worth defending them. Sharing is not limited to situations in which the provider has no choice or where the providers cannot be bothered with defending what they have. Rather, sharing also occurs with items that are considered valuable by both provider and receiver and when defending these items would pay out.
- Ecological pressure (sharing what is scarcest) was not supported. It is not the case that those resources that were particularly scarce or suffering from over-exploitation were shared. Sharing is therefore not a measure of last resort, conditioned by extreme scarcity. Rather, sharing seems to occur largely independently of the overall availability of the resources in question.[7]

The only two features tested for positively against the Ache data is that (1) resources that come in larger packets, prototypically a large game animal, are significantly more often subject to sharing; and that (2) resources that are "synchronously accessible" by many group members, prototypically the small amounts of fruit and tuber collected on everyday foraging trips, are significantly less subject to sharing. In other words, while it is not the essential type of resource that is decisive, it is the manner in which the resource becomes available that seems to matter. In Chapter 4 I shall pursue further this question of the affordances of the things that are being shared.

The largely negative evidence of the Ache case notwithstanding, a similar set of hypotheses is still on the agenda today, as a summary account (Gurven 2004) of current evolutionary research shows: "kin selection-based nepotism", "reciprocal altruism" and "tolerated scrounging and theft" match closely what was investigated in the Ache test case, complemented by a new hypothesis labelled "costly signalling" (Gurven 2004: 545-6). The latter seeks to explain men's sharing of game meat that requires particular skill and courage as an indication which potential partners could read as an "honest signal" for identifying partners with such skill and courage.[8] On the whole, recent work using this approach is much more cautious and advocates a "multicausal analysis of food transfers", recognizing that the predictive power of current models "is still qualitative rather than quantitative" because there is a lot of empirical evidence that remains unaccounted for in regression analysis (Gurven et al. 2000: 214). There is also a shift in emphasis insofar as these hypotheses are now no longer discussed primarily in terms of origins, or as a fixed sequence of evolutionary steps. Rather they are seen as functions in behavioural ecology, behaviours that have been brought about, and continue to be brought about, in a particular way because they fulfil important functions in enabling humans to survive in their ecological niche. As such they can complement one another or substitute one another, but none of these features is considered necessarily to apply to any particular case, a point to which I shall return shortly.

One of the points of critique against the testing of evolutionary hypotheses against the Ache material is that it proceeds purely along the lines of quantitative evidence, more specifically along the lines of the amounts of calories generated and distributed through various modes of transfer. Thereby it ignores many relevant factors from the context that ethnographers consider to be important for individuals' decision making and for the social dynamics involved (Hyndman 1985). In other words, the research is somewhat skewed towards behavioural features at the cost of motives and evaluation. In effect, it makes the human beings look more similar to animals in this comparison. The researchers who conducted the Ache research were generally in support of the sociobiological agenda in their assumptions and in their approach. That makes it ever more noteworthy that in effect most of the sociobiological hypotheses about sharing derived from animal behaviour turned out to be unsupported and untenable in the light of systematic empirical research with human foragers. Each of the findings summarized above responds to particular sociobiological assumption and in effect discounts them. As Cadelina (1985: 240) pointed out, it is rather astonishing that the authors of the study see their own results as generally supporting the application of sociobiological theory to the ethnography of human culture. In his view, by contrast, it rather points at the "inappropriateness of using empirical generalizations derived from the study of other animal taxa to explain the complex human behavior of food sharing".

It has also been pointed out that not every ethnographic instance fits the Ache pattern (Kelly 1995: 180). The attention of evolutionary modelling has focused on the Ache case (and a handful of others) partly because there were very few quantitative cases. Moreover, the rather bold versions of evolutionary theory tried to explain many different and complex practices on the basis of "similar selective pressures" and "within the same theoretical framework" (Kelly 1995: 164). In the meantime the presumption that the proposed evolutionary framework could provide a unitary explanation of all cases across the board has been seriously weakened. The proponents of an evolutionary approach to sharing themselves point out that "we should not expect to find *one* explanation for sharing" (Kelly 1995: 180, my emphasis) since sharing even within the circle of hunter-gatherer societies "appear to be related to a number of variables and motivated by different factors" (1995: 181). Occasionally, the evolutionary paradigm is defended by arguing that we simply do not have enough data (Kelly 1995: 180) and that more data would explain what now may be considered exceptions to otherwise unavoidable predictions and implications generated from the framework. I think there is a fundamental problem with this position. The ethnographic input not only produces exceptions from behavioural rules that could be ironed out by having more precise rules. As long as evolutionary principles are formulated by excluding "abnormality conditions" (see Widlok and Stenning forthcoming) they will not be able to provide a satisfactory account in answer to this question. Since all things are never equal, the possible impact of abnormality conditions has to be included from the start since they are an integral part of human (inter)action. This requires, however, that we pay more attention to the social institutions that comparative ethnography has shown to be relevant for explaining the diversity of sharing across cases and include this in our explanatory framework, a point to which I shall return in the following chapters.

Even through many evolutionary hypotheses were not supported by the Ache data, it is not as if the Ache case suggests that ecology or material conditions do not matter. What it does provide, however, is a refutation of some of the simplistic assumptions from sociobiology, namely that sharing is always governed by a tit-for-tat rule, that it only occurs when it supports one's own kin group or when there is a benefit to oneself that could be cashed in.[9] On the positive side, the evidence did show that sharing increased under certain conditions: when the shared resource came in large quantities and when not everyone was involved in the procurement, which is typically the case in game hunting. Or to put it the other way round: small quantities that everyone could procure simultaneously were shared less. The fact that large game successfully hunted by a few members is shared more often than the nuts that everyone can get access to at any time is not surprising. It also does not prove in any way that human sharing practices as they are observed today are the direct product of general processes of natural selection. If there are selection mechanisms at work in other parts of the natural world, simply projecting and upscaling these selection processes cannot explain the scale of human sharing, let alone its particular shape. This, in effect, has led many anthropologists to conclude that any evolutionary effects can reasonably be excluded from consideration altogether. However, what I want to point out in the remainder of this chapter is that although a framework of selective pressures may not be good enough, it may still hold some interesting results.

We have arrived at an important turning point when considering sharing from an evolutionary perspective. Instead of starting off with unitary evolutionary mechanisms that are assumed to have necessarily produced the sharing phenomena of today as a consequence of an animal heritage, we are now beginning to look at a number of long-term evolutionary consequences of sharing as it is practised in the human cultural heritage. There is a considerable literature that gives evidence about the evolutionary implications of sharing: independently of the question as to how sharing came into being among human foragers, it is safe to say that sharing practices have been beneficial to humans at the level of the individual, the social group and the species. The argument is now shifting gear from questions of origins to that of social functions. The functions of sharing that are debated most are, firstly, those that refer to nutritional benefits, to sharing being insurance against crises and a means of its risk-reduction, and secondly those that refer to issues of raising prestige, of attracting partners and of levelling differences.

The risk-reduction function

As individuals practise sharing, they enhance the nutritional status of all members in the group, rather than the reproductive success of a few, including those who share (see Kaplan and Hill 1985). In the course of time, sharing became an important feature in what we now recognize as "the human ecological niche" (Gintis and van Schaik 2013: 35). The "willingness to provide others with resources, the occasional, but critical, reliance on resources produced by others, and procedures of the fair sharing of meat" (Gintis and van Schaik 2013: 43) were important ingredients in the construction of that human niche. Note that we have now moved from an argument about origins and selection to an argument about functions with evolutionary, in the sense of long-term, implications. A functional argument need not accept that every social practice can be traced back to a particular "fitness benefit" (Kelly 1995: 177) that can be identified or that there is a simple mechanism by which practices are "selected for" when their fitness benefits are higher than others. In other words, if sharing has observable positive effects it is likely that humans have often selected sharing strategies but not that humans with a certain sharing practice were selected against humans without one, or with a different one.

There is a danger of circularity in both functionalist and evolutionist arguments. What determines the spread of a practice? Its fitness benefit. How do we establish a fitness benefit? By looking at the spread of a practice. Moreover, as evolutionists tirelessly remind us (Smith 1988: 240, Kelly 1995: 171) many functionalist arguments highlight the importance of sharing as a device for creating social cohesion and for having an insurance effect at a group level. They in effect assume that this result generates the choices of individuals which have led to this result in the first place as if individuals will necessarily choose to do what is best for the group. This would make the consequence of behaviour the cause of behaviour (Kelly 1995: 199). Moreover, it disregards intragroup variability and the fact that sharing is both part of individual strategizing and of patterns of preferred choices.

What we need, therefore, is a discussion of sharing strategies in the light of alternative but separate strategies that fulfil similar evolutionary functions, for instance strategies of storing.

Sharing is one of the three main strategies that humans have at their disposal for dealing with unreliable food supply in their environment due to seasonal or other change. The other two strategies, mobility and storage, can be combined with sharing in complex ways; all three strategies have their specific benefits and costs. As I have argued elsewhere, scholarly analysis faces a cultural bias in favour of storage and against sharing and mobility (Widlok forthcoming). Ever since the emergence of territorial states, mobile people have been looked upon with suspicion since they seem to evade state control. Sedentariness is often considered a value in itself and mobile peoples are marginalized and discriminated against in many societies. Ever since the emergence of capitalist economizing, sharing has also been looked upon with suspicion since it seems to counteract accumulation and property which are considered to be essential prerequisites in a capitalist economic system. European observers were often struck by the high incidence of sharing in many settings they encountered at faraway places. This is not surprising since the imperial expansion of Europe that facilitated early ethnographic accounts during European exploration and colonization coincided with a situation of feudal overlordship, beginning industrialization and continuing patrimonial family regimes in Europe that was not conducive to sharing outside the realm of tightly-knit core families. The first ethnographers, informed by their own cultural background, were genuinely surprised by what they saw. While some were appalled by a sharing ethic that seemed to undermine the bourgeois values of accumulation and austerity, others took what they saw as evidence of a primitive communism that supported their romantic or primitivist (inverse progressivist) version of evolutionary thinking. For both groups, it became a common theme to "explain" the widespread sharing on the basis of a lack of opportunity for storing. This was in turn often attributed to high mobility and the long shadow of these assumptions are still with us today as many governments seek to sedentarize mobile populations with the expectation that this would eventually also lead to more opportunity to store, to less need for sharing and eventually to the accumulation of property often considered to be the unquestioned prerequisite for successful economizing (see Chapter 5). In this light, the re-labelling of sharing as "social storage", i.e. storing surplus in fellow humans instead of storing it in hollow containers, seems like a more benign attempt to accommodate, or even rehabilitate, sharing in a world of storage ideologies – if at the price of reducing sharing to only one of its possible functions.

There is indeed an inverse correlation between storage and sharing in many reported cases but disentangling causes and effects is not quite so easy. To begin with, it seems that the knowledge about storage and opportunities for storing are widespread, even among hunter-gatherers (see Box 1) but knowing how to store does not immediately lead to storing being practised to a high degree. Storing practices are known from all human societies. Desert hunters successfully dry some of their game meat and collect rain water, for instance in ostrich eggs.

FIGURE 2.3 Storing gathered *!no-e* under ground in northern Namibia. Photo: Th. Widlok

Coastal and inland fishers dry fish and produce fish oil that can be used as a food ingredient or to provide candlelight. Gatherers bury fruit in underground storage burrows to let it ripen, to prevent animals from eating it and to preserve it for future use (see Figure 2.3). What differs cross-culturally is the amount of practised storage and whether it involves ecological, social or practical forms of storage (Ingold 1983). In many hunter-gatherer societies, sharing seems to be the preferred option for dealing with risk and the variability of resources across seasons and lean periods. Ichikawa (2005) has hypothesized that storage is more difficult to adopt as a social strategy because it has a number of serious social implications. Sharing as "social storage", by contrast, can circumvent some of the problems associated with other forms of storage (see the section below).

In the dualist Western conceptualization of culture versus nature, storage technology is a prototypical cultural achievement since it appears to provide human society with some independence from natural processes. Storage promises to secure continual subsistence in the face of an organic environment in which animals die, plant products decay and conditions may change unfavourably. However, this nature concept is not universal and storage is not only a bundle of methods to overcome seasonal or irregular shortages of food and other resources. Its social functions include the ability to mobilize and invest purposes and mechanisms of control (see Earle 2002). As such, the ability to store, to keep for later and to combine resources for larger endeavours is connected to a number of key features of human cognition and morality: the willingness to postpone the gratification of needs and desires involves the mobilization of social and moral forces that protect storage. Apparently simple tools like a bow-and-arrow set require the production of intermediate objects such as arrow tips, shafts, adhesives, poison and so forth that are stored in order to be integrated at a later stage (see Chapter 4). Similarly, an increasing complexity of social organization in many ways involves increasing storage. In the most immediate sense any larger gathering, for instance an Aboriginal ritual in which youth are initiated, marriage relations arranged, and foundational mythic events re-enacted, requires a certain amount of stored food that is shared among the aggregated people. The ability to store goods, in particular food, has for a long time played an important role in evolutionary accounts of human adaptation and risk reduction. The cultural means to keep food items and other resources across seasons and lean periods has enabled humans to occupy all parts of the globe. Complex technology requires that semi-finished items are kept available so that they can be integrated at a later stage. Complex social organization depends on the accumulation of goods to maintain high population densities and to ensure that places can be occupied without interruption. However, setting things aside for future use also incurs costs and is often inefficient due to loss in the process. Storage therefore involves social questions of how to deal with accumulated resources and that invite inequalities of property and power. Agriculture, industrialization and urbanization amplify the need for storage in many respects. Above all they amplify the need to deal with the social implications of accumulation and attempts to utilize surplus for control, coercion and domination. The discussion about storing and sharing as a means of risk reduction and security against nutritional crisis has therefore led us to functions which may be much more critical, namely the capacity to establish and shape social relationships. In the first instance, this is the function that sharing can hold as a levelling mechanism. It provides, as it were, a "conservative" alternative against other modes of transfer (such as storing and redistribution) that require and boost hierarchical relations. With storing being effective for mobilizing control, sharing is an effective means of coping with the social implications of hoarding and accumulation.

The levelling function

While earlier research considered storage and sharing predominantly in terms of human dependency from natural resources, more recent research has focused on the role of storage and sharing as crucial social institutions in the emergence of hierarchy and socio-economic complexity. Ethnoarchaeologists distinguish two models that explain the emergence of human competition and hierarchy (Hayden 1994). Models derived from analogies with non-human species suggest that scarcity is driving human competition and diversification. The alternative "prosperity model" of competition suggests that the availability of surplus is a key driving force. In this scenario, excess food was distributed and invested in ways that allowed the conversion of surplus food into social capital, obligations and political followership – the ingredients for complex societies. In both scenarios storage is critical, it has the potential for coping with occasional shortage but it also invites accumulation and problems of redistribution.

A far-reaching implication of storage is that it requires a certain degree of social hierarchy and it provides the means to establish, maintain and extend inequality and hierarchy. In the first respect social sanctions, social order and continuity are required in order to protect stored wealth. As soon as there are not only immediate returns for invested labour but delayed returns (see Woodburn 1982a) there is a need to protect investments and to regulate access to goods, for instance between the point in time when gardens are cleared and seedlings planted and the time of harvest, but also between a harvest and the next planting season. Property relations, social sanction and obligation, political authority and dependency on a larger group are therefore social side-effects of storage when it is practised to a sizable degree. In the second instance, the stored items are a form of capital that can be pooled and invested for a variety of purposes. Accordingly, the social challenges that come with storage are also two-fold: on the one hand, the expenses necessary for keeping things available (from dried meat to modern digital formats) so that they can be retrieved at a future stage; on the other hand the questions of access to stored items that may become the source of domination and conflicts. Sharing incurs less cost in this regard because it provides a levelling mechanism to prevent the monopolization of goods. After all, the distribution of food and the retention of stored information can be monopolized in a way that allows not only for the concentration of wealth but also of power. Privileged and uneven access to stored goods may undermine other important principles of the social order, for instance the functioning of exchange, peaceful social relations, social equality and individual autonomy.

In the face of such difficulties connected to storage, sharing becomes an option that promises to solve some of the very same problems at less social cost. The unquestioned positive image of storage, and farming as its associated subsistence technique, that dominates social theory, therefore needs to be placed into perspective. From the point of view of many foragers, farming is considered "a last resort for people who did not have game to hunt" (Lye 2004: 90). And many hunter-gatherers who were forced to resort to farming attempted to do so without storing seed or other forms of hoarding implied in it (Widlok 1999). The fact that sharing has been with humanity for much of its evolution, points at the material function of buffering resources. In this regard, sharing continues to complement storage – and in some cases almost completely substitutes it. The possibility of storing does not erase the necessity of sharing. Most of the ethnographic cases mentioned so far are cases in which storage opportunities are combined with sharing. It also points at social functions of sharing, beyond that of risk reduction, and that is the levelling function which counteracts the control implicated in storage.

The commonly invoked image of sharing is that of large-game hunts which produce more food than can be consumed by the hunters themselves. Such hunts are seen to serve as an insurance policy against the uncertainties of hunting if those who are successful today provide a share to those who are not and vice versa. Complementary to an explanation that is ultimately based on the distribution of resources and people in the environment, sharing as a practice of successful hunters has also been attributed to the prestige that these hunters may gain from their success. Since the ethnography shows that successful hunters in many cases do not receive a larger amount of meat than the non-hunters (or non-successful hunters), other – more indirect – benefits have been suggested. In many foraging societies hunters do not receive open admiration. On the contrary, the well-known Ju'/hoan case (Lee 1993) is one in which the successful hunters, and the game meat that they have provided, are scolded and ridiculed. But that does not exclude that the other members of the society do recognize (and remember) good performances. They may not become outspoken and dependent followers as in more hierarchical societies, but in their movements they may seek the proximity of successful hunters. In particular, it has been suggested that women are attracted by such hunters, again not necessarily providing successful hunters with more offspring but possibly with more chances of extramarital affairs (see Kelly 1995).[10]

Although the insurance aspect of sharing applies to all foods, the type of food does matter insofar as there is a greater likelihood of sharing when big game is hunted, for instance giraffe in Africa or whales by Nordic hunters – the "large packages which are non-synchronously acquired" as evolutionary ecologists (Kaplan and Hill 1985) would phrase it. However, the ability to store does not do away with the need to share but it may even aggravate such a need under conditions of unequal opportunities. What motivates the sharing of big game other than ensuring access under the condition that one is unable to consume it all at once? As Blurton Jones (1987: 41) has pointed out with regard to his model of "tolerated theft", even when some storage is possible it would rather increase than decrease the pressure and the preparedness to share if only some have been able to acquire and eat food. Storage makes sharing even more pressing under the premise that fending off others who want to take from a big kill becomes ever more costly the more desperate the others are for food (and the more one has been able to satisfy one's own most pressing need for it). After all, at day two after the hunt the stored food will be even more precious to those who already went hungry on day one which in turn will make it more costly and difficult for the successful hunter to defend hoarding. And the temptation to use the stored items to control others is omnipresent.

More generally, it is important to note that sharing not only hinges on what the successful hunter has available but on what the non-hunters (or unsuccessful hunters) need. As has been pointed out before (Marlowe 2004, Widlok forthcoming), African hunters do know how to dry meat and they do eat a lot of meat even when it has reached its best before date. In this setting sharing does not mean "giving away valueless surplus" (see Widlok 2013). In other words when considering the "non-synchronously acquired large package" it is not so much the size of the package but the synchrony between the people involved that matters. If the variation of returns is likely to be high across days due to the nature of the resource (high intra-forager variation) and we can expect some foragers to do well on a day that others do not (inter-forager correlations), individuals will often depend on the support of their neighbours and sharing is to be expected (see Kelly 1995: 179). At a group level this may lead to foragers allowing their neighbours access to their resources since the chances are that a group suffers ups and downs in resource provision, intragroup variance, for instance due to erratic rainfall or the movement of herds, while some groups are under ecological stress and others are not (intragroup variance, see Kelly [1995: 198]).[11]

With regard to the gender dimension of sharing it has often been assumed that hunting big game implies that the hunting men share out the meat. In actual practice, however, men and women typically both contribute to such hunts and they both play a role when the gain is shared out. Even the hunting versus gathering distinction which has stirred considerable debate with regard to the division of labour along gender lines (see Lee and DeVore 1968, Dahlberg 1981) is much less distinct than previously thought. In many foraging groups women are much more involved in hunting than the stereotypes suggest. They are either indirectly involved because they provide information about the whereabouts of game animals (Biesele and Barclay 2001) or directly because they engage in some small game hunts themselves (Kästner 2012). Some instances of foraging wild resources, for instance collecting swarming termites at nights or climbing trees to gain wild honey may be categorized as a "hunt" because of the uncertainty and effort involved – and both wild honey and termites are subject to widespread sharing. The differentiation is blurred further by the fact that men who routinely take hunting weapons along on their daily foraging journeys frequently return with gathered food but often without meat. Everyone depends on access to gathered food because, with few exceptions, much of the caloric intake of foragers is made up of gathered items (in the widest sense) and does not rely on the success of big game hunting. In other words, in practice the "insurance" aspect of sharing applies across the board, not only to big game. When a high premium is placed on big game meat, it does not directly translate into dependency of the group as a whole from a few individual hunters.

The versatility of sharing

There is now wide agreement that "we should be prepared for variability in sharing and in the reasons for sharing" since "the degree and kind of sharing […] appears to be related to a number of variables and motivated by different factors"

(Kelly 1995: 181). But what is the best way to prepare us for this variability? The main strategy of evolutionary approaches, which I have summarized in this chapter, is to begin by identifying the various adaptive functions of sharing behaviour, each of which may be considered as a distinct model of sharing. Any particular ethnographic case of sharing found may thereby be represented more or less well in terms of these various models as it is mapped onto these functions. An alternative strategy, which I will develop in the remaining chapters of this book, is to begin with sharing events as complex practices. These sharing events all have their specific trajectory and they are open-ended but they also show some recurrent patterns. As I shall explain in more detail in the next chapter, we may reasonably place the practices prior to the functions that they fulfill. Practices may be taken from one social and ecological constellation to the next and they may fulfill several functions in the course of this process. This is reflected in the fact that the agents themselves often highlight distinctions that relate to the practice itself. Many emic classifications have more than one term that may then be glossed as "sharing" by the ethnographer. A regional comparative Inuit example is instructive here (see Box 5). The impression that we get is that Inuit may not have one hundred words for sharing but they certainly have an elaborate lexicon associated with sharing and other forms of transfer (see Wenzel 2000: 65, see also Damas 1972 and Kishigami 2004). To begin with, some groups lexically distinguish exchange partnerships for every part of the ringed seal that they hunt (ranging from "stomach meat companions" and "hind quarter companions" to "four lower ribs companions"). Across the region they also distinguish between these more regulated and codified forms of transfers on the one hand, and more "voluntary" forms of sharing on the other hand. The latter is in turn distinguished from commensality when hosts feed guests at their house, or when they allow others to snatch meat from their sledge when they bring in resources from caches. With regard to the actual terms used, it seems that Inuit distinguish "waiting to get a share" (Damas 1972: 223) from "going to fetch food" or "carrying meat to other houses" and "gathering for communal meals" (Damas 1972: 230–232) where anthropologists have been limiting themselves to distinguishing one-way transfers from two-way transfers (see Hunt 2000). In other words, the emic terminology may not only *not* match the distinctions of the analyst, it may in fact have quite a different logic, in this case a focus on *how* the meat moves and where it is eaten rather than whether transfers are equitable, one-sided, two-sided or multiple-sided.[12]

Much of the emic classification focuses on the position of the potential receiver rather than that of the provider. The detailed study that Damas conducted among three Arctic foraging groups can illustrate this point. His summary of the ethnography leaves no doubt that the actual modalities of sharing are critical for its trajectory and outcome. Retaining a "personal store" was permissible for every family unless the need of others was such that it required the distribution of all meat in the camp. The amount shared depended not so much on the amount of game that an individual hunter was able to catch but rather on the meat available to others in a camp at any given moment (Damas 1972: 227). Starving was prevented in all

BOX 5 ALTERNATING BETWEEN SHARING PARTNERS, VOLUNTARY SHARING AND COMMENSALITY IN THREE INUIT COMMUNITIES

Following Damas' (1972) pioneering work, a regional comparison of Arctic foragers exemplifies the complexity of transfer and allocation modes that can get combined in particular societies. It also shows how practices are modified as they are employed across neighbouring groups. Table 2 is a summary of local terms and practices.

TABLE 2 A summary of transfers practiced by Inuit groups in Canada (following Damas 1972)

Copper Inuit	Netsilik Inuit	Iglulik Inuit	Suggested comparative nomenclature
piqatigiit (seal partners)	niqaiturvigiit (seal partners)	umiaqqatigiit (boat crew members)	gift exchange
payuktuq (voluntary sharing)	payuktuq (voluntary sharing)	payuktalik (voluntary sharing)	sharing
communal eating	minnak (giving visitors access to caches) ningiq (distrib. of large game)	nirriyaktuqtuq (communal meals) akpaallugit (invited visitors) ningiq (division of large game)	redistribution

Copper Inuit

Piqatigiit were structured along the lines of permanent preferred seal partnerships with kin and non-kin (separately named companions for exchange of parts of the ringed seal: stomach meat, heart, liver, flipper, lower back, hind quarter, shoulder, sides of breast, fat, lower spine, neck, large intestine, four lower ribs, stomach).

Payuktuq were complementary acts of "voluntary sharing" within houses and between houses after some period of storage.

Commensal eating, especially caribou and fish, took place among outdoor hearth groups during the summer season when no seals were available.

Netsilik Inuit

Niqaiturvigiit were preferred seal partners with some close kin explicitly excluded. Individually named companions refer to the hindquarters with one flipper, all ribs on the right side, shoulder and ribs on the left side excluding the last five, last four ribs on left side, right side of the belly, left side of the belly, neck and upper spinal column, two vertebra and rib above the last four ribs on left side, head, intestines, breast bone, last vertebra on left side, slice from the flank.

Payuktuq were less structured transfers of meat to people outside the seal partners.

Minnak includes distribution of meat to visitors and competitive taking from previously cached food.

Ningiq communal eating of meat of large game brought back to camp.

Iglulik Inuit

Umiaqqatigiit refers to sharing among crew members of whaling boats.

Payuktalik refers to voluntary sharing within the house and outside.

Nirriyaktuqtuq refers to communal meals that were held especially at time of shortage and under supervision of communal leaders.

groups using a variety of sharing practices. Sharing was flexible both in terms of the amounts that went out and with regard to the type of transfer and allocation that was taking place. The extended family was the basic unit of sharing but the interlocking sharing practices catered for a variety of kin ties as well as for residential ties or ties to do with free association based on age or collaboration. The different transfers running in parallel meant that if there were inequalities or shortages emerging as a consequence of one practice, then one of the complementary practices would kick in. Across the region there were distinctly named (and distinctly patterned) modes of transfer (see Box 5) some of which comply with our technical notion of sharing, others being more akin to gift exchange or redistribution.

Damas uses a culture area comparison between the three groups of arctic hunters and he speculates whether ecological conditions can account for how the variation is patterned. The more marginal environments of the Copper and Netsilik groups made use of the more structured, more obligatory (and, arguably, more reliable) seal partnerships whereas the Iglulik could rely on better provisioning due to access to caribou and fish on the one hand and large sea mammals on the other hand. There is no conclusive evidence that there is a causal relation here. However, there are good reasons to look at the region as a whole since there were not only overlaps in terminology and practices but also in terms of movement of people between these groups. If we look at it as one integrated system it presents itself as a cultural repertoire in which emphases shifted according to requirements that have to do with seasonal or situational shifts but also with internal social conditions (what Damas calls "internal adaptation").

Although Damas glosses the whole Inuit repertoire as "sharing" across all cases, there is in practice an emerging pattern of three very different modes that deserve distinct technical terms to distinguish them. The individual partnerships in which designated parts of a seal are reserved for specific named partners is very much like the gift-exchange systems that are also found among other foragers, the *hxaro* of the Ju/'hoan being the most prominent example (Wiessner 1982, see Barnard 2011: 78). The commensual meals in which hosts cater for their visitors, or boat owners cater for their collaborators, are, by contrast, a mode of redistribution, not surprisingly associated with leadership positions. This leaves a more narrow technical term of sharing for those systems which Damas (1972) calls "voluntary sharing" which is typically extended to everyone who does not benefit from gift-exchange partnerships. The Inuit case thereby allows us to see how sharing practices can coexist with other forms of transfer, with gift exchange and redistribution. In the next chapter I shall provide more arguments as to why I think it is useful to restrict the term "sharing" to those practices that Damas subsumes under "less structured forms" of giving, that is the tolerated taking (among the Netsilik) and the voluntary giving outside partnerships (found in all three groups). The common denominator of transfers that fits this more narrow, technical understanding of sharing is that possessions are divided into pieces and freely given (or allowed to be taken) when demanded. By contrast, the seal-partnerships create specific obligations with specific people, namely with chosen associates and they are strictly reciprocated. They therefore constitute a system of gift giving which allows individuals to engage in strategic partnerships tied to specific demands.[13] At the other end of the spectrum the sharing practices lean towards pooling and redistribution during communal meals in which emerging leaders (in the Iglulik case), the outdoor hearth group (in the Netsilik case) and snow assembly houses (in the Copper case) provide the base for such an emerging redistribution pattern.[14]

It may be tempting to emulate local categorizations (in this case that of the Inuit) in our analytical typology (see Kishigami (2004) who suggested a matrix of nine different types of sharing based on Inuit ethnography). I suggest that there are in fact recognizable patterns in social practice that can account for emic classifications without mimicking them. One of these patterns is a marked orientation towards the receivers, as was mentioned above. Another recurrent feature is that sharing reduces not only the risks of erratic production but also the risks inherent in other modes of transfer. From an ecological and evolutionary perspective the terminology we apply (whether emic or etic) is less important than the fact that the terminologies can account for changes in social practice that impact internal social relations and relations with the external environment. While all modes of transfer in this spectrum (gift exchange, sharing and redistribution) may be regarded as insurances in response to seasonal changes or other forms of food insecurity, the Arctic example indicates that sharing practice in the narrow, technical sense is in itself an insurance that can curb the possible failure of risk reduction institutions (such as gift partnerships). In other words, when gift partnerships fail or are unevenly distributed, when collective whaling ships or village-wide commensal consumption sites are not available for redistribution, sharing comes in to make sure that no one starves. In the Arctic case, both gift giving and redistribution seem to hinge on social and ecological conditions that are different from those that foster sharing. Gift giving is tied to particular species, and even more narrowly to particular body parts of that species, to recognized social ties of a particular type, to previous exchanges or previous engagements as in the case of whaling boats. Redistribution is in turn tied to sites or persons that form the pool from which redistribution takes place as much as the successfully hunted large game provides a corresponding ecological pool. Sharing is not tied to any of these requirements but provides a versatile part of a larger repertoire of forms of transfer and allocation.

Conclusion

Mechanisms of evolution do not provide the answer that would explain the way that sharing works. Reflective evolutionary thinkers have recently cautioned not to "impose external categories on ethnographic data" and to generate patterns from the bottom up instead (Jordan *et al.* 2013: 115). With regard to sharing, the externally imposed categories include "altruism" and "generosity" but also "selection" and "inherited trait". Sharing seems to be a key for understanding why human groups can live the way they did during their hunter-gatherer past and, to some extent, continue to use this option in organizing their economic life and their social order today. Evolutionary research triggered a lot of systematic and comparative ethnography which provides the foundation for our understanding of sharing and its social implications. Rejecting simplistic evolutionary assumptions does not exclude but rather invites a fresh look at the questions posed in these debates. The patterns that emerge "bottom up" are likely to point towards considerable complexity in which processes at the micro-, meso- and macro-level are not mutually reducible. Applying a perspective of transgenerational change to sharing suggests that the practice itself is the product of a number of constitutive interlocking elements such as regular co-presence, collective hunting, communicative skills and some degree of coordinated norms and values (see Mathew *et al.* 2013: 49). As this chapter has shown, it is rather futile to look at these practices in isolation since their effectiveness is largely due to their co-occurrence and successful combination in social practice.

Sharing out meat and other food creates bonds of trust and cooperation that are important ingredients for cooperative social life more generally. Beyond hunter-gatherer society, sharing is considered key in understanding close personal relationships. Sharing among close kin seems to be a cultural universal and the argument has been made that sharing in effect creates kinship in societies in which to be kin is not premised on genetic or genealogical links. The focus here is on how residence and nurture, or more concretely the practices of sharing of shelter and food, in turn create relatedness and social bonding.[15] These are issues that are inadequately covered by evolutionary models but to which I will turn in the next chapter.

Sharing is therefore not an archaic and primitive given, from early evolution. It is a cultural practice that is also a cultural innovation, even though one that has been around for a long time, that is closely related to other cultural innovations.

The prerequisite of advances in our understanding of these complex developmental and evolutionary processes is that we build up a thorough ethnographic understanding of sharing practices and the way in which they can be observed to interact with other cultural practices as modes of social relatedness. The following chapter therefore turns to the details of ethnographic record that we have of sharing practices around the world.

Notes

1 This bifurcation seems more pronounced in the United States with its "science wars" and a radicalization of evolutionist and anti-evolutionist thinking and less so in continental Europe where the notion of "science" (as "Wissenschaft") covers all natural sciences as much as social sciences and the humanities, as it refers to any form of critical and systematic research. Nevertheless, the dualism between "hard" and "soft" sciences exists here, as well, which has unfortunate consequences for anthropology in that an image of humans as dual beings is maintained.

2 This is true, of course, for basically everything that humans do since – unsurprisingly – precursive elements can be found in any current human behaviour without the latter being reducible to the former. Note that this does also not necessarily imply that there is an uninterrupted genetically-based inheritance of these features "down the taxonomic tree". There is also the possibility of humans observing and learning from other species and of "independent invention" when members of different species face similar kinds of environmental challenges.

3 There is also the problem of scant data for some species, an issue that is best left to the specialists to resolve. The same applies to the question of how many observations should suffice to reclassify a whole species as sharing or non-sharing. What if individuals in captivity do share but not in the wild, as seems to be the case among some monkeys?

4 It would be very hard, if not futile, to attempt to arrive at a quantitative assessment. Contemporary consumer studies, for instance, give no clear picture as to whether sharing is in fact growing or declining. It seems to be declining in the everyday lives of families in which less space, fewer material items and less time (at meals for instance) are being shared (see Belk 2007: 135; Belk 2010: 725). At the same time the internet is seen as allowing us to "access nearly infinite shared contents thanks to others' contributions" (Belk 2010: 727). These problems notwithstanding, it is possible to point out social changes that foster or impede sharing as spelled out in the following chapters.

5 This is the conclusion of a PhD project on sharing that was predicated on experimental design and methodological individualism (Schäfer 2014); it is also the starting point for most anthropological contributions to this research field.

6 Some anthropologists working on problems related to access to communal resources have turned to institutional economics, and in particular to critical institutionalism which considers the subjects to be *bricoleurs* who adapt their strategies continually as situations unfold in history. However, these approaches focus on the management of common pool resources, i.e. the distribution and maintenance of collective property regimes and not on sharing what is individually owned (see Menestrey-Schwieger 2015 for a recent contribution).

7 Evidence from elsewhere (Pryor and Graburn 1980) suggests that sharing actually breaks down in situations of extreme scarcity (i.e. during famines).

8 New in this context seems to be the realization that choosing such hunters as mates is not done as a form of reciprocal payback for the meat that the men have provided and that it is not only the material object (the "big package" of meat) that is relevant. Rather, it might be the intrinsic quality of being able to provide access to a good that would otherwise remain inaccessible altogether (Gurven 2014: 546).

9 It is noteworthy that more recent studies of food sharing under the evolutionary paradigm are considerably more cautious in their judgements. Nolin (2010, 2012), for instance, found evidence for reciprocity in food sharing but underlines that there are good reasons for cautious interpretations since there are a number of explanatory factors involved (notably spatial distance) and since there are also methodological problems related to evidence based on recall self-reporting (Nolin 2010: 263). He concludes that food sharing in his Indonesian case is not all about risk reduction but also functions "as an affirmation of relationships of mutual aid that go far beyond the exchange of food" (2010: 264). For related work see Hames and McCabe (2007) on Ye'kwana meal sharing and Koster (2011) and Koster and Leckie (2014) for work on horticulturalists in Nicaragua.

10 So far there is no proof that successful hunters indeed have more offspring than others, and it will be difficult to establish, but Kelly (1995: 355) notes that this may not matter if both the foragers (in this case the Ache) and the anthropologists believe that this is the case. I think it is likely that this belief is due to an expectation that hunting prowess and sexual potency coincide and not due to an exchange of "meat for sex" as has been suggested.

11 Group-based models of risk reduction have a tendency to under-problematize group boundaries – which are not given but which are made. This is because they tend to be modelled along the lines of "given" boundaries between animal species competing over resources. Human group boundaries, however, have very different properties since they are (more or less) permeable and since individuals may successfully claim (more or less) membership in several groups. Sharing is affected not so much by group boundaries as sharing practice in turn forges these boundaries.

12 This is in parallel to some of the anthropological debates about the classification of colours, smells and so forth (see Widlok and Burenhult 2014). Diane Young (2011) has argued that lexical distinctions made by Aboriginal groups of the Australian desert may translate as "green" what in fact is not a colour descriptor but denotes a quality of "sticking out" as green regrowth does after a fire or a long dry period.

13 In the Iglulik case where there are no such seal-partnerships the partnership of crew members who form a whaling boat is very similar in structure, providing specific individuals specific entitlements based on past exchanges. In contrast to both, seal associates and whaleboats, the complementary "voluntary" sharing in all three groups responds to the general demand of granting access to those who fall outside the preferred partnerships.

14 Another result of the regional comparison of transactions among Arctic foragers is that it is not the overall size of the game animal but its relative size and reliability in relation to whatever other resources the group has available that influences the modes of transfer. Hence the fact that the ringed seal was subject to specific exchange partners whereas the caribou and the fish were subject to broader voluntary sharing or commensal eating seems to have less to do with the animal itself than with its seasonality and the overall availability of food at the time when these animals were being brought into camp. Among the groups that relied on one species of seal for much of the year each hunter had a stock of partners who could make very specific claims to a specific part of the animal (Damas 1972: 235). Rarely hunted species were hunted without fixed rules and in those cases where there were a number of alternative resources the partnerships were less important and instead large sea mammals were shared village-wide.

15 In this context sharing receives critical importance as part of the attempt to redefine kinship and sociality on the basis of performative, constitutive acts of sharing, suggesting that the notion of kinship based on genetic or otherwise narrow biologically conceived links is a Eurocentric bias (see Holland 2012).

3

THE ETHNOGRAPHY OF
SHARING DEMAND

Introduction

The previous chapters indicated that human sharing goes beyond the primate heritage. Evolutionary pressures can neither explain why sharing is so pronounced and wide among humans, nor the various forms in which it takes place. Rather, human sharing is in itself a complex phenomenon, more complex than usually imagined by those who are not participating in the economy of sharing on a daily basis. From the point of view of behavioural ecology, sharing is all about strategic individual decisions about how to allocate things. In Gurven's view (2004: 543) this is what modelling sharing is all about:

> Imagine a male forager with a fresh kill, or a female forager with a basket of fruits or roots. Each must decide (or have decided for them): (1) How much to give to others (depth); (2) How many families should receive a share (breadth), and (3) How much should be given to each of n other locally available individuals (equality)? Each model [...] predict[s] when sharing should occur. These differ in the kinds of benefits returned to donors, and the manner in which these benefits are paid.

It is one of the great assets of the anthropology of the economy of sharing that we do not actually need to *imagine* what hunters and gatherers do once they have made a kill or collected fruits – we do have good ethnography that allows us to see the complexity of the sharing process as it unfolds in everyday human life. And the first lesson of that ethnography is to realize that the actual sharing event is not one of an individual who must make up his or her mind in isolation as to what to do with a resource. Neither is it a question of how to appropriate a common good that is free to take for everyone. Instead, we encounter a host of social practices that prepare and enable sharing, intertwined with a host of practices of trying to dodge and avoid sharing. Ethnographically, this process does not present itself as an individual prob-lem of distribution but rather as one of mutually recognizing implicit or explicit demands and the responses that they require. Those who are possessing goods may (or may not) have a preconceived plan as to what they are going to do with the resources – and so do those who expect goods to arrive in the camp and who may have preconceived ideas as to what should happen. But sharing in fact commences much earlier with the mutual practical recognition as distinct social beings with whom we share our lives. As a consequence of being present and being recognized as such, the subsequent practices feed into one another to the extent that things may flow without the need to make explicit choices at all. In many small-scale events of routine sharing no choices have to be made except for the basic choice of continuing a social relationship. Sometimes some of the constituent practices also clash and lead to tensions. It is therefore a matter of tracing ethnographically how potential "donors" and "recipients" establish in interaction the shared basis from which a certain "depth" and "breadth" is reached (or not reached). In other words, we need to ground our theory and understanding of sharing in the ethnography of recogniz-ing the presence of others, as this chapter will explain in more detail.

Sharing as a complex institution

If sharing is not a biological programme but a cultural institution it should not come as a surprise that there is considerable variation in how humans organize sharing in their everyday lives – and variability in the ways in which they concep-tualize and rationalize what is going on. This is ever more so since sharing is one of the cultural universals to be found among humans which, again, does not imply that it is directly "hard-wired" into our brains or behavioural repertoire but rather that some form of sharing has been part of every observed society and culture around the world.[1] Correspondingly, sharing is likely to be coloured by the whole spectrum of human languages, kinship systems, economic systems, political and religious systems and so forth. Despite this variability, however, there are emerg-ing patterns which we find in the ethnography and which we can rely on if we want to build up a more general practice theory of sharing "from the bottom up".

One of the recurrent patterns that has been observed is that sharing occurs not in one instance but rather in several waves, temporally speaking, and at a number of levels, systematically speaking. Sharing is spread out in ways that other transfers are not (see Chapter 7). There is, of course, a sequential dimension to all human transac-tions and indeed actions. However, it is easy to conceive for a market exchange in which all buying and selling takes place at once, at a certain time and place. This would be the case for instance in rural West Africa, or historical rural Europe for that matter, where each village has a set market day and an agreed upon place for these transactions. Today, current online and financial sales transactions not only take place in a split second, but they are less temporal in the sense that there are no longer times or places for trading since it takes place all the time whenever buyers and sellers are on the internet. Times are collapsed into time. Specific times are collapsed into time as a unified measure which in itself becomes a trade item. Similarly for redistributions and gift exchanges, it is easy to conceive of a single ceremonial moment in which the transaction is carried out, for instance the harvest ceremonies in Melanesia or other distributive feasts. This is not coincidental because the public visibility and display of who gives what to whom is key in redistributions such as the harvest ceremonies, just as the conterminous and concomitant offers and demands are key for creating a market. Sharing, by contrast, not only lacks a distributive centre, as often has rightly been pointed out, it also lacks the need for such a temporal and spatial centre. As we shall see, the decentralization and disconnectedness are properties that facilitate sharing and are part of its own logic.

The prototypical scenario of sharing which illustrates its "distributedness" is that of foragers who share the food they hunt and gather. Similar sequences have been described for hunter-gatherers of the Central African rainforest and for those living in the savannas of East Africa and southern Africa. Typically, sharing takes place firstly *in situ* where the food is collected (the animal is killed, or the plant food or honey is found) secondly in the home camp where the food is processed (meat cooked, nuts cracked etc.) and thirdly between fire places of families and individuals, after the food has been cooked or stored, either by sending plates to the neighbours or by inviting them to sit at the hearth. The parallels between Marshall's account of !Kung sharing (Marshall 1961) and of Bahuchet's account of Aka sharing (Bahuchet 1990, see Box 6) is striking and many similar ethnographic accounts could be added here. At the same time, many of the details vary, not only between regions and cases but also between these stages or levels where sharing takes place. For instance, Bahuchet notes that sharing at the killing site of an animal follows fairly clear prescriptions according to who contributed to the hunting gear and the hunting effort, but that there is considerable room for giving preferences to certain relatives at the second wave of sharing while there is indiscriminate sharing to everyone present at the third stage. Thus, the sequence of sharing can be connected with different levels of more or less widespread and more or less prescribed sharing. The "breadth" and "depth" of sharing as a social practice are inherently, by "institutional design", responsive to the changing circumstances.

BOX 6 WAVES OF SHARING COOKED AND UNCOOKED FOOD IN THE CENTRAL AFRICAN FOREST

The complexity of sharing becomes visible in case studies that allow us to trace in detail how items are shared, down to the level of particular parts of hunted meat and individual plates of dished food. One of the first ethnographic case studies with the appropriate level of detail was compiled by S. Bahuchet (1990) among the Aka, foragers living in the rainforest of the Central African Republic. Like the other so-called "Pygmy" groups, the Aka are neither isolated nor do they live on hunting and gathering alone. They engage in exchange with villages of neighbouring ethnic groups that cultivate crops, i.e. starchy food that makes up half of the weight in the Aka diet. However, both in terminology and in style these exchanges are differentiated clearly from the sharing that takes place among Aka. The Aka procure their food in collaborative hunting and joint gathering expeditions and Bahuchet collected data from four camps with an average of 26 occupants.

Sharing takes place at three levels: the task group of those contributing to a hunt; the family group of those connected through kin ties; and the consumer group of those living in proximity in a camp (including visitors). The modalities differ at these three levels but all three levels are linked in a sequence which allows for considerable room for manoeuver in the process while ensuring that, on the whole, no-one is left out. At all three levels there is, in principle, a possibility of using some of the food not for sharing but either for direct consumption or for exchange with the neighbouring villagers. At the level of the task group, typically for hunted meat rather than for gathered food, there are recognized rules as to who has legitimate claims. Those who participated in a hunt, in particular those who provided the hunting gear (spears and nets) are given certain portions of the animal. The bigger the animal the fewer parts are reserved for the hunting party. A small duiker antelope of 50kg may be divided into 12, 7 or 3 parts which are all earmarked, whereas a gorilla or an elephant may be divided into many more parts with only a few being reserved for those who killed the animal or who own the hunting tools that were used. The second wave of sharing takes place when the gathered food is brought back to camp and it is geared towards particular family relations, in particular to spouses, classificatory spouses, parents and grandparents. At this level the food is still uncooked and the receiving kin take the food to their cooking hearth in front of each hut (typically a camp has 5–8 huts) but may also decide to store some of the food or to exchange it. Once the food is cooked it is dished out on plates that are taken to the other huts in the camp which includes distant kin but also visitors who happen to be in the camp. Some meals may be consumed with the co-residents of one's hut only but the larger number of meals are shared with most other huts. With 5–8 huts in each camp, a pattern emerges whereby for every dish that a hearth group shares out to the other huts it will receive several times more dishes from others during the same period. The exact ratio of dishes given and dishes received varies considerably with hunting season (availability) and hearth group composition. Individual contributions to resource procurement are very uneven and only every second hunt is successful so that on average only one hunter brings back meat every day. The three levels of sharing, however, ensure that at least small amounts of meat (as in cooked stew) reach everyone in the camp, including children and old people. Without any central authority or strict rules regulating the system there is at each level some room for flexibility as to what is shared (see Figure 1.2).

Many of the diverging reports that we have on sharing are, I propose, a consequence of this situation. Especially when informants were asked, out of context, as to how game animals or other objects were shared, the respondents would phrase their answer with regard to one of these settings, probably the one that they were mostly involved in or that they considered to be most important to mention, or simply the one that was freshest in their minds. Hence, in the ethnographic literature on sharing we often find diagrams of animals and how the various parts of that animal were allocated in sharing (see, for example, Altman and Peterson 1988: 79). And indeed these things matter in particular at a killing site, where the first wave of sharing takes place, but it does not give the whole picture of what is shared by whom and in what way. A much better picture emerged with improvements in ethnographic method which moved from merely questioning people about hypothetical cases (of how they would or should share) to the actual process of sharing in everyday life. Documenting the process *in situ* provides the appropriate time depth that sharing involves and it appropriately moves it away from the abstract egocentric decision-making problem of allocation. Elsewhere (Widlok 2013), I have noted how recording meta-statements about the proper way of sharing gave way to documenting the realities of sharing in which situational factors such as the number of people present and their skills of pushing for a share impact what was happening on the ground. For our understanding as to why people share, and how sharing works despite the lack of a centralized authority that would organize it, it is important to consider these waves, levels and situational constellations taken together. For instance, although people argue a lot about sharing, the fact that there is less open conflict about meat allocations than one might expect can be related to the fact that later waves of sharing will make sure that basically everyone will receive something through one of the sharing channels even if they did not receive a piece in the first instance. Conversely, the question as to why people give in to demands even by distant kin or non-kin can be related to the fact that at some (other) stages in the sharing process there are possibilities to have more influence on who gets what and to express preferences.

On the whole the diversity of sharing processes is such that it would be futile to describe a unified sequence that would hold across all cases. Even within a single case, the sequence can vary, as we can see in the Aka case from Central Africa where the flow of food is different for game meat and gathered food, and yet slightly different again for honey (see Bahuchet 1990, see also Box 6). It is more promising to identify recurring constitutive practices which resurface in many ethnographic reports. I have suggested three main constituents that will be discussed at some length below in terms of the key notions of relatedness, conversation and presence (see Widlok 2013). In some instances these coincide with the waves and levels of sharing, but not in every respect. For instance, in the Aka example sharing in the consumer group is clearly all about presence, in the family group it is all about kin relations, and – arguably – in the task group sharing can be linked to conversations about ownership about "one's due" and so forth. More generally, however, the constitutive practices discussed in this chapter need to be in place for sharing to flourish and to take on the importance that it has in hunter-gatherer societies and elsewhere – but there are many possibilities as to where and when exactly this occurs in the process. The identification of three constituents is not a complete list, but it appears to be fairly representative of what many ethnographers have found among hunter-gatherers and other small-scale societies. Other practices may come in when we include examples from peasant or other larger societies (see Chapter 6). My argument is that in ethnographic literature the three sets of practices do have some predictive value in the sense that we see a rise in sharing when these practices are in place and we see the fall in sharing (and equality) when these practices disappear or are transformed considerably. After introducing the relevant modes of relatedness, the modes of conversation and the modes of bodily presence I shall therefore inverse the picture by depicting how the disappearance or transformation of those three features ultimately results in a decrease of sharing and in emerging inequality.

Sharing and kinship

There is an intricate relation between sharing and kinship. Sharing among close kin seems to be a cultural universal and the argument has been made that sharing in effect creates kinship in societies in which to be kin is not premised on descent or genealogies (see Nuttall 2000). Residence and nurture, or more concretely the sharing of shelter and food, can create relatedness and social bonding just as much as blood ties may do. In this context, sharing receives central importance as part of the attempt to redefine kinship on the basis of performative, constitutive acts of sharing, suggesting that the notion of kinship based on genetic or otherwise narrow biologically conceived links is a Eurocentric bias (see Holland 2012). If to share is a way of becoming kin, then conversely, sharing can also be said to be made possible and facilitated by kinship as an idiom.

There are a number of turning points in the process of "discovery" of sharing in the social sciences. In some instances these turning points seem to be provoked primarily by changes to do with opportunities and strategies of the researchers rather than with the actual sharing practices of the people under study. Consider, for instance, the reports of early explorers about frequent and wide-spread sharing that gave rise to ideas of collective ownership or "primitive communism" (Lee 1988). We now know that many of these accounts were conditioned by research situations in which the local relationships were little understood. Information was captured in a snapshot fashion so that neither the long-term dynamics nor the personal histories between the givers and takers were included in the description. In field research today it is still a challenge to trace the many sharing transfers that take place at any particular instance, for example during pay-day, during drought relief food distribution or when social welfare payments are paid out. Within a short period a lot of items change many hands in multiple and rapid ways and they often do so in opaque manner, so that it would be near to impossible to record these transfers even by a whole team of researchers, let alone by an individual with little local knowledge. When researchers began to systematically interview those who were involved in sharing, they first and foremost elicited normative systems of distribution (or justifications thereof). Typically these got represented ethnographically by drawing a sketch of a game animal in which the various body parts were designated as portions "earmarked" for particular categories of relatives (see above). There are observer effects that such elicitations regularly create. The descriptions that I received in early periods of my own field research were highly idealized and never corresponded to actual sharing patterns *in situ*. This is true more generally and for a number of reasons. One is that situational circumstances influence what happens since not all types of kin may be present or may press their demands with equal force in each case. Quarrels about sharing indicate that there can also be considerable disagreement as to what should go to whom, depending upon whom one asks. Individuals may seek to exempt portions of meat from sharing but may fail to do so in the process (see Figure 3.1 and Chapter 4). Furthermore, as Peterson (1993: 866) has pointed out, it is usually only up to half of the resource that falls under the distribution rules and the remainder, often the larger part, gets distributed in other ways. As a consequence we have a much better record of gift-exchange systems, for instance the !Kung *hxaro* system (see Wiessner 1982) than we have of their local sharing system. Gift-exchange systems like *hxaro* with clearly designated gifts that are handed over between designated individual partners over an extended period of time are easier to trace for both participants and observers. They comply with the requirements, for instance of network analysis (see Schweizer 1996, 1997; Wiessner 1998) and meet many of the Western expectations of rule-bound strategic behaviour. The most recent turning point in the research history therefore is the realization that the ethnographer's search for rules that can account for transfer and allocation practices is actually to some extent detrimentally opposed to the interests of those involved in the sharing process. While researchers want to account for what goes to whom, those who share often explicitly do not. Peterson (1993) has listed a number of good reasons why they do not follow an accounting approach:

> An alternative strategy to this bookkeeping approach is simply to respond to demands as they are made. This has at least four advantages: difficult decisions are avoided; the onus is placed on others; discrepancies in the evaluation of relationships are not laid bare; and an excellent excuse is provided for not meeting some obligations within the context of behaving generously. Further, it fully recognizes the inherent difficulty in delayed reciprocity: time alters the value of objects and the perception of relationships, compounding the difficulties of calculating the correct return.
>
> *(Peterson 1993: 864)*

Graeber (2011) has provided a complementary historical account in which he argues that the application of book-keeping and accounting based on standardized and convertible currencies to social exchanges only developed under very specific cultural

FIGURE 3.1 ≠Akhoe Hai//om men attempt (and eventually fail) to reserve portions of ostrich meat in northern Namibia. Photo: Th. Widlok

and historical conditions. He reminds us that it is by no means natural to apply the logic of exact debt-reckoning that requires a particular type of money to be applied to all exchanges and to all transactions. The ethnographic literature is full of examples in which people very carefully distinguish different spheres of exchange, that were kept separate and with strictly regulated conversions between them (see Bohannan 1967, Hutchinson 1997).[2] Kinship relations in particular may be said to follow a different logic than the book-keeping that is assumed to underpin means–ends calculations in all domains. Even where there are very specific ideas as to what should go to whom, in cases of bridewealth or bloodwealth compensations for instance, the underlying concept is exactly that these payments will never even out the debts incurred by the gaining of a bride or the loss of a family member as Graeber (2011) has pointed out.

It is therefore important to note that despite the emphasis on kinship and social relations that is found in the ethnography of sharing it is not the case that certain kinship terms inevitably trigger a particular form of transfer (or vice versa). Rather the transfers and the kin terms are relevant for establishing what the status of mutual involvement is for the persons concerned. Sharing does not simply follow the rules of kinship but it is also an everyday means to test one's relationships. In societies with a very high incidence of sharing, kinship is often "classificatory" so that it potentially extends to all humans one encounters and any two individuals are related in a number of ways. In southern Africa San people who have good relationships with their agropastoralist neighbours and share resources with them tend to construct kin relations very widely, even across ethnic divides (Widlok 2000). Since there are always multiple ways of calculating kin relations in such small-scale societies, the participants have considerable room for manoeuver as they either try to draw the other person near or keep a distance by using specific kin terms (see Widlok 1999). Especially among foragers, who tend to put a high premium on individual autonomy, being in a particular kinship relationship is no guarantee for sharing to take place and conversely sharing is not restricted to certain categories of kin. Hence, the occurrence of sharing and the categorization of kin are mutually informative rather than causative. Negotiating a kin-term successfully is an open process but when related persons have found common ground in a kin relation upon which they agree, this provides them with a heuristic for knowing whether sharing is likely to take place or not. It also provides them with a tool for pushing towards sharing.

How exactly sharing is tied in with kinship and other forms of social related-ness differs between cases, the ethnographic example given in Box 6 is therefore not to be generalized across regions and societies. However, what can be general-ized is that sharing constitutes one of the prime means whereby individuals in these societies manage autonomy and relatedness (see Myers 1988). The fact that kinship is typically involved does not mean that there is no escape from sharing. Numerous strategies have been recorded whereby individuals seek to avoid sharing – also among kin. Hiding items is the most common form, but attributing objects to a third party in a certain kin category (like mother-in-law) is another one since it can make objects taboo to potential recipients. It reduces the pressure on a potential provider who may "hide" an object by claiming not to have the authority to give it away (see Peterson 2013). At the same time, the complex kin talk that goes with many instances of sharing reminds us that the benefits and costs of shar-ing are not calculated in an abstract way (as, for instance, models of tolerated theft suggest) but that people go out of their way to channel sharing according to the meaning they give to particular social relationships. Demand sharing often involves the invocation of kin terms ("I am your brother/aunt/father in-law, there-fore you should give me ...") and it is clearly not only driven by basic needs such as hunger, but typically by the more subtle needs of establishing and maintaining one's social relations with all its contingencies and the personal histories that go with it (see Chapter 7 and Box 9 in Chapter 4).

Moreover, not all types of kinship and social relatedness go equally well with sharing. While kin practices not only form a necessary pre-condition for sharing to take place, the demise of these forms, and the rise of others, can correspondingly also affect sharing negatively. My argument (more fully developed in Chapter 6) is that this occurs as soon as corporate groups such as clans and lineages, or legal cor-porations such as NGOs for that matter, begin to overshadow open and classifica-tory kinship networks as I have sketched them above for the San. In this shift, social agents reduce the multiplicity of potential kinship links to a fixed set of membership roles in social groups. Commonly corporate membership status is permanent, or very hard to change, once it has been established. In the past this was spread with the emergence of clans and lineages as organizational forms. In the present it is the creation of so-called community-based organizations in Africa, or the registered incorporated land-holding groups among Australian Aborigines or indigenous people in Papua New Guinea (see Chapter 6). Many of these organizations receive mining or other revenues or welfare payments. For legal and administrative purposes membership has to be clearly defined and cannot easily be changed. At this point sharing tends to break down and to give way to fixed entitlements based on membership in a particular group. Somewhat paradoxically it is exactly the introduction of the seemingly equal status of being (any old) member of a specific corporate group that reduces sharing and as a consequence allows for personal accumulation. It allows for the emergence of unequal status which is no longer levelled out through practices such as sharing. What emerges instead is inequality between members and non-members, between different corporate groups, some more successful than others, but also within corporate groups in which positions for representing the corporate group are being created. Previously, these were positions of clan or lineage elder and currently these are typically positions of being "chairperson" or "board member" with privileged access to money and opportunities.[3] As with all kinship phenomena these transformations have two dimensions: forms of social organization "materially" alter the situation, for instance by drawing groups of people closer together on a larger scale or by systematically excluding others. At the same time the kin talk also "symbolically" and "communicatively" re-draws boundaries. Kinship thereby connects to the wider relation that sharing has with language and the communicative setting in which potential providers and potential recipients find themselves.

The language of sharing

As I have already pointed out (in the previous chapter) a focus on the labels that are used to categorize transactions and modes of allocation can be deceptive and misleading. Calling something "sharing", or refusing to use that term and using a different one instead, is in itself part of the phenomenon under study. Participants in these transfers may disagree as to which term is the most appropriate one and they may have strategic reasons to employ one term rather than the other. Moreover, in parallel to what has been discussed with regard to the notion of "giving" we need to concede that "sharing" and its equivalent terms in other languages has a host of meanings, some of which fall outside of the phenomena under consideration here.

While the sharpening of our terminologies when talking about sharing is an important issue, language also comes into the discussion in a much more direct way, namely in terms of linguistic speech acts that structure sharing in action. What has struck many European observers who have recorded sharing is the fact that it typically works entirely without any exchange of "please" or "thank you", without elaborate politeness or honorifics. A large part of the explanation is that generosity, conceived of as a free gift, is not a necessary precondition for sharing to take place and that the strong opposition drawn between altruistic and egoistic behaviour that dominates many European discussions is not applicable here. As I have pointed out elsewhere (Widlok 2010: 92) giving egoistically by putting one's own goals above that of others and giving altruistically by putting the goals of others above one's own goals are both to be contrasted with sharing practices that are all about the realization of intrinsic *goods* rather than about derived *goals*. Altruism and egoism, as Marten (1993: 14) pointed out, are both ideas of a "filosofie a solo", a philosophy of the isolated self. Sharing practices, by contrast, presuppose a shared life in which everyone is distinctively positioned and related to others form the start, a point to which I shall return below. Another part of the explanation is that declarations of thanks tend to introduce status differences that members of egalitarian societies seek to avoid (see Dentan 2011). The deference and dependency that saying "thank you" implies is conspicuously absent in situations in which individuals treat one another as very close kin or as distinctly equal in status. Graeber (2011: 123) points at the social distribution of expressions of gratitude that have become normative in bourgeois society but not in "the lower classes". In fact, today one does hear the equivalent of "thank you" in the conversations of many (former) hunter-gatherers but with two characteristic modifications. Among ≠Akhoe Hai//om, for instance, the terms used are "*dankie*", "*ehalo*", "*aio*", often exactly in this triple manner which combines an Afrikaans loanword (*dankie*) with a Bantu loanword (*ehalo*) and a (probably) vernacular form (*aio*). These expressions are largely restricted to dealings with outsiders, who are known by the Hai//om to expect these expressions and who see it as signs of deference which many hunter-gatherers are nominally happy to give without actually subscribing to them. This fits the general observation that hunter-gatherers opportunistically use such formulaic self-depreciation and forms of respect with regard to outsiders if that helps elicit goods and resources from them. As one Mbendjele man put it: "When you want to kill elephant you must follow it. [...] You must smear its fresh excrement on yourself. It is the same for us with the Bilo! [their farming neighbours]" (Köhler and Lewis 2002: 296). When these expressions are used among Hai//om themselves, they often fulfil a different pragmatic function. The actual use of these terms is that of demand pragmatics, i.e. they are uttered before one is given something (rather than afterwards) in an attempt to *stimulate* giving. Note that it is also possible in English to say "Thank you for the butter" when reaching out for it and in fact asking for the butter to be handed over. In many hunter-gatherer settings this is not the unusual usage of the term, but the default pragmatics. Similarly, even in languages in which there are no lexical items equivalent to "please" and "thank you", there are of course ways to pragmatically decode utterances as a thankful recognition. Many ethnographers have found that making a positive remark about an object creates an implicature that amounts to a "please give me that thing". Similarly, conversations in which demands and complaints are rife, any action that is *not* accompanied by muttering and complaint can be interpreted as a "thank you, I am pleased". Just as every language has a host of terms to express both direct and indirect demands, there are also direct and indirect ways of expressing gratitude or satisfaction. Insofar as there is a notion of a "rightful share" (Ferguson 2015) involved, the gratitude may not be directed to the generous heart of the provider but rather to his or her recognition of what was being reasonably demanded. It may also be a diffuse gratitude of being able to satisfy one's needs, independently from whom or what enabled this satisfaction.

In this sense, conversation and language is a series of speech acts and plays a key role in most sharing events. This involves direct demands and continual mutterings of complaints but also other forms of speech acts. The main feature that characterizes sharing events is the parallel talking exemplified by Liberman's work on Pintupi in central Australia (1985) and by my own work on ≠Akhoe Hai//om in northern Namibia (Widlok 1999). Parallel talk implicates that diverse and even contrastive statements can be made and juxtaposed without there being a linear "argument" of talk and counter-talk. Many utterances do not get a response, many questions do not get answered (Hoymann 2010), many statements are apparently ignored as if they have not been heard. At the same time, even harsh statements can be made without necessarily provoking a direct harsh response. Of course, the pragmatics of all languages include overlaps and questions that remain unanswered but the overlapping discourse style observed in egalitarian societies is so pronounced that it is often cited as a critique of assumed universals of turn-taking in human conversation.

In parallel with what was outlined above with regard to kin-terms, there is no single formulation or figure of speech that would guarantee sharing. Direct demands often stimulate sharing – but they cannot enforce them, as respondents may try to hide their resources, find excuses or simply lie. There is a host of indirect ways to initiate sharing by simply expressing a need or shortage ("There is no water!" "Imagine there was something to drink", see Widlok 1999: 60). The implicature is on the respondent to offer what the speaker has declared to be missing. However, again, not all implicatures are fulfilled since there are strategies of pretending not to hear, of excusing oneself for not being able to help, and of simply refusing to make the implicature. All of these strategies are typically embedded in parallel talk which diffuses the roles of speaker and respondent who are not tied into strictly dyadic exchanges. With several strands of conversation going on in parallel, every person within hearing is potentially speaker, respondent and overhearer at the same time. This lays the groundwork for sharing transfers in which again everyone, including the ones who have just received, are in turn potential providers and witnesses or mediators of transfers. Everyone can own things personally but has to be prepared to give them up as demands are repeatedly made from a variety of interlocutors. As in decision making leading to the moving of a camp or to conducting a hunt, the decision to share is made cumulatively in the process of an ongoing stream of conversation.

In many settings in which people routinely share and know one another well, explicit and elaborate formulations of demand may not be necessary at all. In many sharing events that I have observed among ≠Akhoe Hai//om small interjections are sufficient to set sharing in motion (see Widlok 2016). People may, for instance, simply use an exclamation of surprise such as "*etse*" (hey you) or "*!Xũtse*" (my God) when seeing food or an object that they desire which is enough to exert some pressure on the owner to give away at least parts of it. Sighting or other interjections that express displeasure or need are also instrumental in conveying to others a sense of need. There is, therefore, a seamless boundary between vocal demands (direct or indirect), paralinguistic signs (whistling between one's teeth, shaking of head in surprise) to completely silent demands or offerings to which I turn now.

Given the wide spectrum of (para)linguistic means to initiate and channel sharing, we may ask, in parallel to our discussion of kinship above, what speech acts or modes of conversation there are which may be detrimental to sharing and may lead to its demise. Broadly speaking, it seems that sharing as a levelling mechanism breaks down when parallel talk is replaced by disciplined rhetoric. Disciplined rhetoric in this context refers not only to the use of honorifics, ritualized praise songs and so forth which as speech acts directly elevate individuals (see Strecker 1988 for a systematic inventory). It also refers to changes to established pragmatic rules that provide some individuals with the right to speak before (and for) others (men before women, older versus younger members of the group etc.). This involves rules and practices according to which some retain the right not to be interrupted, of having the right to grant others the right to speak. It includes the privilege that some have the right to ask questions and to impact on others who have the duty to give answers. Some of these features already exist in predominantly egalitarian societies, for instance the right to be asked before a resource is used but the default is inverted in hierarchical societies. The transformation from parallel to disciplined talk is likely to proceed in a piecemeal fashion as language shifts occur gradually. We may go as far as saying that in every single speech act there is the potential for such transformations, as speakers may try to get away with imposing rules and restrictions as to who talks and when. There are also situations in which certain thresholds are being reached and changes occur on a larger scale. In conjunction with what has been said above about the emergence of membership identity rules that replace multiple kinship-reckoning, there are typical communicative roles that come with such a transformation (to be discussed in Chapter 5). The role of "speaker" in corporate or incorporated groups is such a landslide change since such a speaker (or chief, spokesperson, chairperson) may use his – mostly it is a he – right to name advisors (e.g. a board, a council of elders etc.). The speaker and his advisors reserve the right to speak and to delegate that right. Since these transformations often go hand in hand it is hard to isolate "ultimate" causes in the package as these are changes that are mutually reinforcing. What may start off with a slight change of language pragmatics may gain momentum and amplify other changes. This can then lead to a landslide disappearance of important levelling mechanisms that ensure equality and that in turn leads to the rapid emergence of unequal positions and opportunity.[4]

Sharing and bodily presence

One may argue that modes of kin talk are largely a subcategory of modes of conversation which in turn may be considered a subcategory of bodily presence. In any case, the mode of personal presence is a critical factor, a prompt and a trump in sharing as a social practice. Speaking may take place from a distance, negotiating kin can take place in a cursory fashion and both are still conducive to sharing. But conversation and kin talk are trumped by physical presence and more precisely by what we could call practical presence. The scene that so many ethnographers working in egalitarian societies have witnessed so many times is that persons who seek a share stay close to those from whom they expect a share. ≠Akhoe Hai//om has a separate verb that means exactly that, namely "hanging around waiting for a share" (see Figure 3.2 and Box 7). The sequence is documented in many hours of field video recordings: people sit at a fireplace preparing food, cooking tea or simply having a smoke. Someone walks by, positions him- or herself next to the cooking pot or fire place and waits until those attending to the fire or pot provide him or her with a share. Occasionally, a hand is stretched out but often this is not necessary. In other instances, third parties, preferably children, act as intermediaries. As Peterson (1993) and many others have observed, children in many hunter-gatherer societies are free to move around and stimulate sharing from people whom they visit throughout the camp. Many sharing transactions take place via children (see Figure 1.2), that is to say they may be sent with portions of food to others, especially the elderly or visitors who are seated or housed at a distance. In many cases the distance is small enough for a direct transfer between adults but still the direct handing over is avoided. This leads us to the interpretation that an attempt is made to disconnect the act of giving from that of receiving, keeping the possible imposition or asymmetry created in transfers at a minimum. Occasionally, children are also sent to ask for things elsewhere but usually this is far less effective than showing up yourself in person at the hearth of whomever it is that one expects a share from. Bodily presence is a very strong prompt for sharing. "Disembodied" messages sent by intermediaries to ask for food or other things often get ignored because they are not backed up by the presence of the person who makes the demand.

It is important to note that physical and temporal co-presence are not enough, it is practical presence that needs to be established. Practical presence is presence that is recognized by both parties in the encounter. Practical presence can be denied when physical presence exists and, as we shall see below, there can be attempts to create some practical presence despite physical distance. Different ways of constructing practical presence are visible in apparently banal situations such as greetings. In many egalitarian societies a visitor may approach a camp quietly, squat down at the margins and wait for local residents to take note and to initiate greetings. This recognizes the others as being present. Oftentimes there is a long time lapse between physical arrival and practical recognition, which can be irritating for ethnographers who have just arrived. Ethnographers are likely to

FIGURE 3.2 The silent ≠*gona* demand (left) that initiates a sharing response (right).
Graphics: G. Hoymann based on the ≠Akhoe Hai//om video corpus

---

BOX 7 HANGING AROUND FOR A SHARE IN THE KALAHARI

≠Akhoe Hai//om is one of the Khoisan languages of southern Africa, spoken by people who are called "San" or "Bushpeople" in the region (see Widlok 1999). With other Khoisan languages, spoken by many different groups of hunter-gatherers and pastoralists, it not only shares click sounds (written with the symbols /, ≠, //, !) but also some distinctive aspects of language pragmatics. In comparative perspective it is remarkable that speakers of ≠Akhoe Hai//om tend to refrain from putting pressure on their interlocutors by posing yes/no questions, and if they do pose questions many of them do not get any direct response but get integrated into the flow of conversation in which there are often concurrent parallel strands. ≠Akhoe Hai//om also has a separate verb "≠gona" to designate a behaviour whereby individuals "hang around and wait for a share". They may approach a hearth where people cook or another place where others have congregated to consume food, drink or have a smoke. Their bodily presence is interpreted by those cooking or consuming as a silent demand. Usually standing close to someone who has sharable food is sufficient for that person to hand a portion to the one who practices ≠gona. Occasionally, the demanding presence is underlined by small utterances (e.g. by just saying "tobacco") or by stretching out a hand, but in many cases the bodily presence is sufficient to stimulate and initiate sharing (see Figure 3.2 and the ≠Akhoe Hai//om corpus at www.mpi.nl/dobes/akhoe).

---

come from a cultural background in which presence (just like giving) is initiated by the approaching party.[5] Agropastoralists in southern Africa (like visitors in Europe) are expected to announce their coming with loud greetings, anything else would be considered "sneaking in", but the pattern is inverse in societies with a high incidence of sharing. Among San in Namibia I have observed many times that visitors were kept waiting for a considerable amount of time. In Australia I have accompanied visitors who were not supposed to enter a camp but instead waited at a distance to be welcomed (and to move on if they were not).

These practices of establishing and recognizing presence make sharing phenomenologically quite distinct from various forms of barter and gift exchange in which the handing over of the items is often highlighted and elaborated ceremoniously. Here, by contrast, the transfer takes place without "giving" in the sense of directly handing over and only after the other's presence has been recognized. Once co-presence and interaction proceeds, it becomes very hard to evade sharing. By not being on the scene yourself your chances of receiving a share decrease dramatically. Being bodily present and staying on the scene trumps those who are faced with a demand but are reluctant to give. Being physically and practically present in itself establishes a potential claim and providing a share is a further acknowledgement of the presence of the other as a person. Elsewhere I have suggested that this presence already constitutes a "silent demand" (see Widlok 2009a, 2013). Following this line of thought I suggest that we should not consider demand sharing as a different or special type of sharing since in a certain sense there is no sharing without a demand. However, some clarification is in order here in the light of Altman's (2011) observation that after initially being ignored "demand sharing", in particular in Australian Aboriginal studies, has in the last two decades been wrongly assumed to stand for all kin-based transfers in Aboriginal relations, with politically detrimental consequences (to be discussed in Chapter 5). Altman reminds us that there is a lot of "unsolicited giving" in Aboriginal Australia as much as elsewhere (2011: 190). He rightly points out that there are a number of ways of allocation and distribution in Aboriginal economical relations but I think we need to draw somewhat different conclusions from the evidence. Many transactions in Aboriginal Australia, even pre-colonially, are more akin to trade and gift giving, for instance the transfer of songs and items associated with the so-called "travelling business" in Aboriginal ritual life (see Widlok 1992). Similarly, many Aboriginal demand practices, including much of what is glossed "humbugging" (aggressive demanding), are just that, demand practices and not sharing practices and there is a local repertoire of deflecting these demands. Hence, it is primarily the notion of "sharing" that is overstretched and overused when people increasingly talk about "demand sharing" in Australia. All ethnographic accounts agree that successful sharing events involve a seamless spectrum ranging from overt, vocal demands to a host of indirect, polite forms of requesting (Altman 2011: 190). The rationale for highlighting demand in a comparative view of sharing here is different: if sharing is "enabling access to what is valued for its own sake", i.e. in terms of the intrinsic properties of what is shared (see Widlok 2004: 63) then a very basic notion of demand is built into "access to what is valued". Valued properties are sought-after properties and it is part of human sociality to understand the presence of others as a "silent demand" for realizing what is valued (Løgstrup 1997). The silent demand need not be uttered, and it need not be the demand of a specific interlocutor since it is a demand for provisioning and for taking care which is a direct consequence of moral relationships (see Gell 1999: 87). Sharing water, for instance, realizes the intrinsic value that drinking has for humans through enabling one another to access water. Acts of taking meat from a hunting site to kinfolk living elsewhere (the "unsolicited giving" in Altman's examples) is following the recognition of others as being present (here as my kin), and their presence as being one of continuous silent demands for sustenance. Insofar as these demands are pre-reflexive they can be said to be incurred simply by a situation of co-presence. In the context of human sociality, mere bodily presence always constitutes a demand for being acknowledged as a partner, as a personal being with legitimate needs. And talking and thinking of others in terms of kin (for instance) is one way of realizing this presence even when the others are not physically present right then and there. Importantly, the demand can be rejected just as recognition of presence can be rejected.[6] Once it is conventionalized it may be hard not to recognize the presence of others but the fact that there is an element of freedom is constitutive to it being a practical presence and demand.

If we restrict the term "demand sharing", as many anthropologists do, to explicit demands such as "Give me ..." we need to keep in mind that this is only one (vocalized) manifestation of a practice that only works because of an underlying phenomenological presence that continually implies "silent demands" (Løgstrup 1997). The demand is that of turning towards, and not turning away from, someone who has addressed me through her actions, words or mere presence. This continual silent demand is most felt when there is a refusal, a breakdown of recognizing one another and one another's needs in realizing the intrinsic goods of what is valued (see Widlok 2009: 26). The explicitness of the demand may differ but the underlying pattern is the same. Humans are sufficiently able to put themselves into the situation of others to be able to know what the intrinsic goods of shared objects are for fellow humans.[7] Moreover, any encounter between humans is also one in which there are asymmetries. In practice, humans who encounter one another differ in many ways, which is implicated in the fact that they need one another in multiple ways, being of different sexes, ages, occupations etc. The encounter therefore is sufficient to create demands without any utterances. This is the ultimate reason why humans share so much more widely than animals do who lack this ability. It is therefore useful to introduce and highlight the notion of "sharing *of* demand" and to distinguish it from "sharing *on* demand". While demand sharing may vary situationally, *sharing demand* with one another is at the heart of sharing in all its manifestations. Sharing may occur as a result of demand sharing, but it only occurs when demands are shared.

Demands are not automatically shared, partly because they often conflict. The mythology of many forager groups is full of examples that depict the dilemmas between contradictory demands, above all between the expressive wishes and needs of others and the autonomy with regard to one's own actions and decisions. As van der Sluys (2000: 432) has observed for the Jahai, these myths "invariably contain the message to show care for others by not expressing one's desires too forcibly". Or, as Myers (1988: 52) has put it, there is a dialectic between personal autonomy and social relatedness which is also played out with regard to the transfer of objects. The more general observation beyond these culture-specific cases is that bodily presence and sharing demands, as discussed above, need to be recognized by others before they become practical presence and shared demands. Concretely, the presence of those with demands has to be recognized by those who are, for example, sitting at a hearth preparing or having food. Although presence is a pre-discursive phenomenon, there are ways to actively deny others the recognition of their presence, or at least to deny others to wield this presence. As just mentioned, visitors to a hearth may only be greeted and addressed a fairly long time after they have sat down quietly somewhere, or in extreme cases they may not be spoken to at all (see Widlok 1999: 145). Thus, physical presence is not only due to those who move to a place but also to those who already are present. Co-presence is an intercorporeal act in the true sense of the word in that it depends on the bodily movements of everyone on the scene. It matters when and how (and for how long) someone decides to get closer and it matters how (and for how long) those "at the receiving end" decide to acknowledge the presence of the other person.

In the case of "presence", the transformations that can lead to its demise and to the rise of more unequal modes can be traced across a number of settings. An important feature relates to changes made to the architecture and to the layout of settlements. A typical hunter-gatherer settlement in southern Africa (and among egalitarian foragers elsewhere) allows an open view across the camp, open access to fireplaces in front of individual huts, and the right to erect and move huts nearer or further away in an unrestricted fashion. This changes with transformations that have been observed by ethnographers at many resettlement or farm settings: people begin to erect more permanent buildings that are not easily moved; they use building materials that are impenetrable to sight (or sound); they build little court-yards around their hearth places; install doors and gateways and a number of other measures that not only change the spatial but also the social permeability of a place (see Widlok 2009b). Such small changes often suffice to undermine physical presence which has such an important role for prompting sharing. People eat with-out witnesses and they make it harder for visitors to "hang around and wait for a share". Stricter residence rules take their toll and reduce the flexibility for seeking the assistance of those who have gained certain resources and to make demands on them. The changes to spatial layouts are bound up with other changes such as the emergence of corporate groups and with the establishment of certain positions connected to these corporations. The hut of the household head in the kind of set-tlement preferred by the hierarchically organized neighbours of the San in south-ern Africa sticks out in spatial permeability maps as the hut that has the least "distributed" space, i.e. the hut that is reached by passing through many more spaces than any other hut in the homestead (see Widlok 2009b).

The transformations that I have sketched here for the domestic space of the house or the settlement may also be upscaled since they may cover the man-made landscape at large, sacred spaces, places and regions that are restricted in access and so forth. However, it is not just the attributes of the built environment that matter, but also how much autonomy people have to move around in that environ-ment. Being able to come closer is just one side of the coin. Being able to move away is the other side of it. At a very fundamental level, violence and domination can be defined as imposed presence (Marten 1993: 17). When egalitarian and shar-ing systems break down, it is donors who impose their presence onto potential recipients and not vice versa. The money lenders and liquor producers who "give" on credit and thereby create dependencies are a case in point (see Widlok 1999). Other examples are the neighbouring raiders who control exchange relations by their presence (see Willerslev 2015) and finally the state and NGO agents who impose their presence and reduce the exit options for those to whom they give what was not demanded. Many acts of "unsolicited giving" are therefore not sharing in this technical sense. Gift giving and other forms of transfers may also enable access to what is valued not for its own sake but for the sake of some "derived goals" (Widlok 2004: 64), for instance the sense of obligation or indebtedness, that are imposed onto the situation. All of these groups control the terms of transfer by controlling presences, imposing their own presence and disallowing others to be absent, to take their leave, often literally by preventing them from moving on.

Opportunities instead of obligations

The preceding sections have provided an ethnographic sense of what constitutes sharing in the practical lives of people whose economic and social needs are primarily satisfied by sharing. It is now also possible to flesh out further what has already been suggested as a technical definition of sharing that distinguishes it from gift exchange and other transfers: *sharing is enabling access to what is valued through a bundle of soical practices of responding to demands.* Let us consider some aspects of this ethnographic definition of sharing in more detail: "demands" here, as just explained, include vocal direct demands as much as silent demands of physical presence. While "demand sharing" has been used in the literature to refer to special cases of sharing that are directly initiated by those who want to receive something (Peterson 1993, Kishigami 2004) I suggest that there is no sharing without a demand in the sense outlined above. It may still be useful to distinguish direct demand (vocalized or by gesture or by moving physically close) from indirect demand. But the more relevant dividing line, I propose, is elsewhere. The dividing line is between, on the one hand, gift giving that is initiated by the giver and that constitutes a prompt for a counter-gift from the recipient, and on the other hand sharing that is prompted by the situation (if not the action) of the recipient. The human ability to put oneself into the place of another person is such that I cannot help but be aware that others need to eat regularly, for instance. The awareness is a direct product of sharing one's life with others. As we all know this does not preclude the human ability to willfully ignore this awareness and to act against the needs of others, by letting them starve or suffer in other ways, but that does not take away the fact that the awareness is there, implicated in our lives as humans who share their lives and who recognize what other humans value – without the need to formulate it explicitly. Therefore, as we have seen, much about the "social work" of sharing revolves around the ways in which I as a potential recipient can make my presence felt to you and how I can invoke our shared lives in order to elicit the share that is due to me as a fellow human being. This is a specificity of sharing which is, for instance, not entailed in instances of gift giving. It is not entailed in the development aid of state and non-state agents (see Chapter 6) and it is not entailed in putting up "give boxes", boxes or shelves in public spaces where people leave things for others to take (discussed in Chapter 7). In all of the cases just mentioned the interaction is initiated by the giver without responding to any need at the receiver's end. An isolated action, e.g. dropping something at a gift box that no-one ever looks at or picks up, would not in itself count as a form of sharing. There is no feedback, however vague or unspecific, by someone else, an interactant, and it is not generated through shared lives but rather through unilateral and solitary decisions to give things away – for whatever reason.

The implications of conceptualizing sharing in this way are considerable: the "problem" of sharing is now no longer that of those who have something and who need to make decisions about how to split things up. Rather it is an issue between those who do not have but who need to decide how and how far they can make demands on others and those who need to respond to such demands. Only once the demands are made is the issue one of how to adequately respond to these demands. Then it is something that those who have need to worry about. If we accept that silent demands are there as soon as we encounter other humans in need, it is something that those who own something will not be able to stop worrying about. For all parties involved there is an element of choice and freedom here insofar as assessments of whether any particular demand is "appropriate", or not, may differ. As we have seen above, many responses are "pre-fabricated" typically in the idiom of kinship (or friendship for that matter) which contains cultural templates for determining who can legitimately ask what from whom and what the legitimate answers to these demands are. Once I have agreed to be in a particular relationship with someone, it is hard to avoid the implicatures that this entails in terms of sharing. However, since there is always the possibility that the person demanding has misjudged the situation and made an inappropriate demand, my response is principally open. Moreover, by hiding or lying I can respond without complying with the demand for sharing but run the risk of changing my relationship, or possibly destroying it. Why does this not lead to a situation in which demands are constantly rejected out of egoistical reasons? To begin with, in many cultural systems the situations are set up in a way that I do not need to actively give anything but simply allow others to take what they consider theirs. In other words there is an in-built default towards the demand being fulfilled unless one takes action by *preventing* others from gaining access to what is valued. As I shall discuss at length in the last chapter, the work of culture more generally may be seen as training towards letting (things) go. If culture is all about conveying things and skills to others, in particular to those who grow up while I grow old, then learning to let go of things that others appropriately demand is a permanent process. Just as those from whom I have received skills and knowledge (and positions and objects and my life) had to let go of their possessions in the course of their lives, so will I have to learn to let go since it is inevitable that I will lose all those things eventually. Being able to let go is therefore not only morally valued in many societies but culture often involves constant practical training towards it.

We are now in a position to rephrase and replace Mauss' tripartite sequence of the obligation to give, to receive and to return (Mauss 2002) in the following way: *sharing creates and maintains social bonds through the opportunity to request, the opportunity to respond and the opportunity to renounce.* The first departure from Mauss' scheme is the replacement of "obligation" with "opportunity". This is partly a philosophical and partly an ethnographic point. Ethnographically, the evidence from hunter-gatherer societies suggests that they succeed in creating social order without obligations that are imposed from an external position of authority or a force that Mauss saw in the law but also in the *hau* of objects. Apparently, modern humans, including the small groups of egalitarian foragers, all can lead a satisfactory social life without an externally defined and upheld law or authority – simply through sharing their lives. As mentioned before, this does not mean that the opportunity is always taken but it is there through the force of a shared life alone, with no need of an external force. Phrased slightly differently and more philosophically, where there are ligatures (Dahrendorf 1969) that ensure social life, no enforced obligations are needed that are derived from an absolute or transcendental source outside the social practice that humans share with one another (see Marten 1993).

Replacing "the obligation to give" with "the opportunity to request" has two implications. Firstly, it places the potential recipient rather than the forced giver at the focus of attention (see above). There is a need to request because things are neither out there ready for everyone to use as the image of primitive communism might suggest. Nor are they readily offered; they have to be requested. Secondly, it highlights the realistic point of departure that interaction is driven by individuals who realize that fellow human beings can provide what they need – and who therefore request it from them. This is much more realistic than individuals realizing from the start that *they* can provide what *others* need. There is clearly an element of means–end rationalization involved but also of empathy in that I do need to emphatically understand and experience how I can reach my goals through the help of others (and vice versa). But I do not need generosity that is forced on me by an external morality. I would even go as far as to say that what Mauss called the "social lie of the gift" is replaced by the "individual truth of sharing", namely the realization that connecting to others is beneficial to me since it allows me to make requests of them and it is beneficial to me and others to share our lives. While gift theory is forced to suggest that people may think they are free to give while they are actually not (i.e. by tricking themselves into the necessary mutual obligations), sharing theory simply recognizes that people are free to request what they actually need (i.e. no need to trick either themselves or others) and to be free to deliberate over the requests that others make. There may still be lies or illusions involved but they concern the uncertainties of understanding what one truly needs rather than the fact that making a request of others is one of the key features of what it means to be a social being.

Replacing "the obligation to receive" with "the opportunity to respond" underlines that instead of a "social *contract*", all that is needed is "social *contact*". Being able to respond implies that one is oriented towards others (e.g. I notice my neighbour who has a hat that I would like or who demands a hat from me). It also implies that the others are expecting my response (e.g. expecting to make an appropriate demand or my insistence that I need my only hat for myself against the sunshine, if that is the case). Moreover, that contact is constantly updated and thereby affects future responses (e.g. when I get another hat or when there is no sunshine anymore, I no longer have a reason for making a demand or for rejecting my neighbour's claim if he still demands it). In other words, where Maussian gift theory introduces a legalistic element into social life, no doubt generalizing from a specific historical situation in which contracts were required and designed by legal institutions, sharing theory relies on the ongoing social interaction that is universally evident. Instead of installing a contract, once and for all, contact constantly conditions which responses are acceptable and which ones are not. To be sure, keeping contact also has social costs, costs of keeping in touch and of negotiating, for instance, but none of the costs of coercion that a social contract typically carries.

Finally, replacing "the obligation to return a gift" with "the opportunity to renounce or to let go" alludes to two different ways of coping with asymmetry (see above). The obligation to return seeks to get rid of unevenness while the opportunity to let go accepts that things may be gained or lost and that unevenness is an inherent property of humans engaging with one another, each with their distinct properties (age, gender, health etc.) and the capabilities and limitations resulting from these. Where gift theory has to assume a "magic glue" that keeps a part of the person in the object that is exchanged, sharing theory asserts the universal experience that human life is finite and that humans may be capable of gaining things but are incapable of clinging on to them forever as life proceeds. "To let go" is an appropriate way in which agents typically phrase the fact that things were gained and things were lost. I adopt the term "renouncing" from Turner (1999) although it contains a connotation of active striving for relinquishing things which need not always be present. It also need not be the case that the renouncer is happy about having lost something to someone else. Typically, he or she would resist and bemoan the fact but ultimately has to comply with it. Turner maintained that Australian hunter-gatherers cultivate the letting go in a religious stance of renunciation, but it is important to note that this is different from the strategic "sacrificing" that is found in religious or worldly utopian thought. In the latter case it is part of a *do-ut-des* (I give so that you give) strategy, giving up so that one achieves eternal life or a better life for future generations or for humanity in the abstract. The renouncing involved in sharing is not directed towards a utopian resolution. However, it is also not necessarily directed towards a fatalistic end of the world. Rather, the expectation is that within a lifetime everyone who has forgone something also receives opportunities to request again which can start a new sequence, but not endlessly. In many hunter-gatherer societies, for one, old people may give up power and goods as they grow older but they do not give up on their opportunities to make ever more requests on others.

In terms of kinship, language and presence, as I have sketched above, we have identified modalities that are the foundations of sharing which in turn functions as a levelling mechanism for ensuring equality. As these modalities decline, for whatever reason, this puts sharing at risk and it opens an avenue for inequality. Some of the side-effects that gift-giving systems have, as Mauss has rightly pointed out, are that they provide an entry point for antagonistic and competitive systems of gaining status, an entry point for emerging inequality (Hayden 1994). Gift-giving systems may be said to create solidarity by creating a substantive communion so that the receiver embraces something of the giver who presented something of him in the gift. This idea has been developed in theories of partible dividual personhood (in Melanesia, see Strathern 1988) and permeable dividual personhood (in India, see Busby 1997) and into more general theories of distinct ontologies (see Descola 2011). By contrast, we are not forced to construct different ontologies for understanding how sharing systems differ. In sharing systems the autonomy of the individual is highlighted through practical means, the collective is not put before the individual and there is no necessary assumption of a shared substance between giver and taker. Here persons are not participating in the substances of given things and givers but they may feel they can extend themselves beyond their own confines by temporarily (rather than substantively) recognizing each other and themselves in their game animals or in superhuman beings (Widlok 2001a).

As a foundation for social theory at large, the theory of sharing presented here need not assume ontological discontinuities but rather relies on understanding continuities and discontinuities in social practice. If sharing is so full of opportunities one wonders why it got replaced by other modes of transfer in many social settings. Part of the answer is that a practice approach also allows us to conceive of unequal social relations as the unintended consequences of ongoing practices in changing settings. Discontinuing sharing and enabling inequalities can be the unintended consequences of changes that took place elsewhere, at the level of the wider setting and at different scales. Changes may occur with regard to modes of constructing settlements, of maintaining certain language pragmatics or modes of kin reckoning, for a number of unrelated reasons. But the concerted outcome can be the destruction of the basis that sharing practices do need to function effectively. In contemporary settings many of the changes are induced from the outside, oftentimes state interventions and possibly with good intentions relating to improved conditions of health, material wealth, etc. They indirectly create lasting inequalities that may in turn provoke a host of new social problems. A second point worth mentioning is that these transformations may not only be non-intentional, they can also proceed without being master-minded by a group of exploitative individuals. After all, altruistic or other moral principles are not necessarily part of the sharing modality that I have sketched above, all require complementary actions by several parties involved, those who speak and answer, build huts and visit hearths, accept or deny kin links and so forth. Accepting a certain set of kin relations, responding to speech acts and recognizing physical presence are interactive processes with many active parties may have cumulative effects for which we may find it difficult to identify a single cause or agent that can be held responsible.

I suggest that the demise or decline of sharing is not that of an emerging void that then gets filled with another set of completely different cultural activities or values. Rather, I suggest that it is a consequence of the shared common ground crumbling away or being transformed. The ethnography of (former) hunter-gatherers shows how sharing breaks down when the shared common ground disappears, in terms of modes of relatedness, of distinct modes of language pragmatics and of corporeal presence. When social agents reduce the multiplicity of potential kinship links to a fixed set of membership roles in social groups, when they abandon certain ways of conversation (such as talking parallel to one another) in favour of disciplined rhetoric, and when they start living in secluded homes and hearth places that make co-presence less likely and more cumbersome to achieve in practice, then the institutionalized practice of sharing loses the foundations on which it is built. If this general pattern is valid we can easily imagine historical and evolutionary scenarios whereby the diminishing of sharing is neither a purposeful abandonment nor one that becomes inevitable and irreversible as other forms of transfer became more dominant. Rather, we can easily imagine scenarios where the abandonment of sharing was an unintended consequence of changes at the level of some other social practices (of kin relations, of linguistic pragmatics and of corporeal movements) that underlie sharing and that make it possible.

Making and unmaking demands

The prerequisites of sharing that have been described above may be less familiar to economic theory (in science and the Western everyday) but they are no less complex, involving recognized modes of physical presence, of articulating demands and of responding to them in ways that are considered appropriate, and managing relations between providers and receivers that minimize the interference with personal autonomy. None of these requirements are "simply there", they have to be culturally "invented" and have to be kept in place through social processes of "enskilment" not only among children but also among adults. However, it is also important to note that human repertoires can encompass several modes of transfer so that someone may share with some social partners, keep gift-exchange relations with others and commercially trade with yet a third group of people. We may consider these modes like languages that make up the linguistic repertoire of what we describe as the typical multilinguality of humans. Just as people can speak more than one language, they can engage in more than one mode of allocation. We have tended to prioritize language as a system over the practice of speaking (Agar 1994). Similarly, there is a danger of overdrawing the boundaries between different modes of transfer. Nevertheless, the architecture of each of these systems is such that in their complexity (Schüttpelz 2006: 16) they cannot be combined in an arbitrary way. As with languages, these modes of transfer constitute recognizably different systems that are not cumulative and that do not respond to the same requests. It is misleading to assume a sequence starting with "primitive sharing", on which more elaborate gift giving builds and out of which commercial transactions would evolve. Where we find people juggling with various modes of transfer it is not as if sharing was needed so that people could trade. In fact, many people trade so that they have something to share. The fact that commercial transactions appeared later in human history than sharing or gift-exchange systems does not imply that we are dealing with a unilinear evolutionary sequence or directional change that is irreversible.[8]

There are continuities as well as specificities in the role that demand plays in different modes of transfer. Sharing gives priority to demands, and in a sense there is no sharing without there being (silent) demands since the responsiveness to the perceived needs of others is a defining and constituent feature of sharing. A great deal of the invention and convention of "cultural work" that goes into sharing is to tune such demands and the possible responses to these demands. Although we are used to thinking of other modes of transfer like gift giving and commercial trade in terms of offers being made, to which those to whom the offer is being made have to find ways to respond to, there are, of course, also elements of demands in these other modes. If there is an obligation to return a gift, then the gift-giver can be said to make a demand, a very specific demand on those receiving. In sharing the cultural skill that is at its heart is to make a demand that will be considered appropriate and that will elicit sharing from others. The cultural skill of gift giving can be seen as a different modulation of that process, if under changed circumstances. Just as not all demands for a share succeed, there are also attempts for gift giving (and for receiving counter-gifts) that fail. In both cases there are multiple reasons for failure. In the case of sharing it might be that the potential provider actually has nothing to share, or that he or she has very good reasons not to share or that the demand was put forward in a way that provides good reasons to fend it off. Similarly, a gift exchange can fail because those to whom one has entrusted a gift may simply not be in the position to return a gift, either because they lost the appropriate item or they lost their ability to reciprocate. Or they may have found other partners or other reasons that allow them not to fulfill their obligation to return the gift. Commercial transactions can also be read as demands under specific circumstances. We see this most clearly in cases where they fail: i.e. where they incur a debt that is not repaid after all. Hunter-gatherers, too, occasionally attempt to sell things, sometimes also to relatives and friends. Typically the commercial transactions fail to the degree that immediacy in repayment is not possible, i.e. the relatives may promise to pay for the liquor that they have just received, but they never do. As Graeber (2011) has shown, failed repayment has been part of the story of commercial debt ever since it began 5,000 years ago. As time goes by, arguments may arise as to what was agreed upon as payment and whether that payment is still appropriate after the lapse of time and other contingent factors that may have emerged in the meantime. The many commercial transactions that are based on debts which do not get paid could be read as unsuccessful attempts for a commercial demand by the creditor.

There are also specific conditions under which a demand becomes successful, be it a sharing, a gifting or a commercial demand. The difference lies, above all, in the social resources that can be summoned to make the demand "hit" or "register" as spelled out above. Some social features enable just one mode of transfer but not others. Arguably, equivalence is a case in point which is central to gift exchange but neither to sharing nor to commercial transactions since history has many examples of commercial transactions that are apparently lacking equivalence (think of various real estate and other "bubbles"). Other social features are more or less required for all modes, including some minimal mutual recognition of the needs or interests of one's interlocutor or interactant.

Making the right kind of acceptable demands under changing circumstances is not the only continuity between modes of transfers. The same, I would argue, applies to accepting to give up demands in the sense of allowing yourself to let go of things. Making acceptable demands and accepting to unmake demands are both constant features of human interaction and communication. If making demands is a human universal that grows out of the inability of humans to live lives of individual autarky (or, conversely, our ability to live cooperative lives) then accepting to let go is a universal that grows out of the inability of humans to live constant and eternal lives – a point to which I will return at the end of this book. Giving things up temporarily or permanently is a constant in human experience which is conditioned by knowing one's finiteness and by the expectation of giving up one's life eventually. As humans undergo their lifecycle they constantly give up things, their status as babies with constant attention by caregivers, their status as adolescents with particular pressures and freedoms and eventually their active lives as they age, becoming old and frail. Sharing cultivates this preparedness to give up things on an everyday basis with regard to objects of personal property but also with regard to being in a privileged asymmetrical position towards others. Being a successful hunter not only means owning meat (that one has to give up to others) but also of having had the privilege of hunting luck that lasts only that long.

Gift giving and commercial transactions also include giving up demands, but in their specific ways. The whole point about gift-exchange systems such as *kula* is that one does not keep the items of value forever but that one receives them knowing that one will have to give them up again at some point in the future, in the interests of keeping the exchange going and, of course, in the interest of receiving other items. The difference is that in gift giving the principle of *do-ut-des*, giving to elicit counter gifts, is prevalent which is absent in sharing as explained above. Commercial transactions may be unequal but they involve, by definition, one thing being given for another and unlike with gift exchange the demand can be made and can be counted on. As was pointed out above with regard to the making of demands, there is diversity and cultural discontinuity emerging in the unmaking of demands, in the general human ability of letting go. Again it is some enabling and disabling factors that generate particular ways of cultivating this ability. Gift-exchange systems make it easier for agents to let go of their gift objects if there is an elaborate system of memories, maybe praise songs, that go with ownership and that ensure continuities beyond specific times. *Kula* participants find it easier to let go of armshells and to keep the exchange going since their names (or that of their villages) are connected to the particular objects from then on. Again, membership in corporate groups is a key factor that facilitates the personal act of giving up something and of letting go – because things that individuals give up may continue to be part of the clan or lineage. Inheritance (of objects or offices) becomes a conventionalized way of asking people to let go of things, to step down from office. Individuals comply with these conventions as members of a particular lineage, clan or house, which are considered to be the ultimate owners of the property. By contrast, the emergence of clans or similar corporate groups makes it harder to share indiscriminately since it generates a conflict, or even a dilemma, between accumulating wealth along the lines of membership to a corporate group and distributing wealth according to the needs of those who are present. Commercial transactions with immediate returns facilitate giving up by the immediate gratification of receiving something else. Commercial transactions with delayed returns are facilitated by the invention of interest, i.e. receiving more than what was given. Time here is collapsed into rent and interest and is in a way neutralized. At the same time, considerable ideological construction is needed to reconcile the accumulation of wealth during a lifetime with the experiences of human life being finite. Religious ideas are created that compensate for losses received (redemption) by providing ways of accounting between things given (alms and personal sacrifices) and things received (in heaven). Atheist ideologies such as communism work in a similar way by compensating present sacrifice (during economic misery and revolution) with the life of future generations or the society of the future.

The two constant human dynamics are those of making demands on one another and that of unmaking one's own demands. These are constantly at work in all human societies and in all modes of distribution and transfer that make up part of these societies. However, they show considerable differences and they are interwoven with other features such as individual autonomy and the emergence of corporate groups. They interact in particular ways with these other features so that we end up with discontinuities in the sense that some societies maintain sharing as a focal mode whereas others are primed on gift exchange and yet others see no alternative but to commercialize as many transactions as possible.

What is more, the modes of transfer not only interact with other features of social life such as spatial arrangements, degree of corporate organization and so forth, but also with one another. As we have seen above, the everyday of many hunter-gatherers is dominated by sharing with strong obligations to provide for anyone present independently of personal affection or of the strategic formation of specific friendships with individuals. But in most of these societies there are possibilities to create and foster specific friendships or particularly close exchange relations by entertaining gift exchanges (such as *hxaro* among the !Kung) that are distinct and complementary to the largely indiscriminate everyday sharing. Similarly, sharing may be limited to particular things such as food whereas ritual objects or dances can be commercially traded as among the Baka and many central African forest foragers (see Tsuru 2001, Lewis 2005). In the same vein, high degrees of commercialized exchange may be said to rely on a backdrop of gift giving or sharing relations both for its emergence during early industrialization and repeatedly at times of crises or ineffective commercial systems. Commercial exchange and gift exchange have also been shown to interact in complex ways within the practical life of one and the same cultural group. The point is that despite the marked differences that are highlighted here, these modes of transfer can be complementary parts of a repertoire. This does not mean that they are interchangeable.

It also does not mean that trying to combine different modes of transfer would not, at times, create conflicts.

Conclusion

This chapter provided an outline of the enabling and disabling social factors that have shaped the path of sharing in societies in which it has become the dominant mode of transfer and allocation. I have highlighted how the aspects of relatedness, of language and presence that are enshrined in social practice itself are sufficient for generating sharing and how, conversely, the discontinuation of such modalities can lead to the breakdown and the decline of sharing as a complex social practice. It is an ethnographically grounded outline of a theory of sharing. In order to show how it differs from gift-exchange theory I have formulated it along the lines of a similar tripartite scheme. In many ways it is the opposite of what Mauss and his followers suggested for gift exchange. Ethnography provides cases of social groups in which sharing is the dominant mode of transfer and suffices to provide adequate social cohesion (see Widlok 1999). The social commitments involved need not be defined as abstract principles but they can be generated through following certain practices that I have outlined. To highlight the differences between sharing and gift exchange with its obligations to give, to receive and to return, we can explicate a corresponding sharing scheme consisting of the opportunity to request, to respond and to renounce. This scheme is informally institutionalized and does neither require explicit cultural systems of rules of generosity nor centralized authorities that enforce them from the outside.

What needs emphasizing is that the diversity of informal practices in sharing systems is greater than the range of gift-exchange systems. Given that it is actual practices and not abstract principles which are driving the system, it is not surprising that the resulting social systems are also more diverse than in the commodity-based and gift-based societies to which we have become very accustomed in anthropology. Moreover, in practice we do find all of these modes interacting in individual repertoires. An ethnographically grounded sharing theory is therefore not only (and not primarily) a critique of existing theories of gift exchange and of liberal theories of market exchange but it also provides a new perspective on social relations as contracts and roles more generally. What gift theory shares with libertarian theories of commodity exchange is a certain disregard vis-à-vis the actual contents of actions and the substances that are being transferred. Modern economizing looks at production and trade independently of what it is that is being produced and traded. To put it somewhat provocatively: economic growth and exchange is considered to be good independently of whether it is arms or luxury items that are involved or health and food items. Similarly, Mauss' gift theory highlights the social formation of exchange independently of who gives what to whom. For Mauss, food is the prototypical gift in comparative perspective (Mauss 2002: 10) but in his analysis feeding the guest is ultimately secondary to the creation of solidarity between host and guests.[9] This reduces the food that is transferred to a means for a specific goal and does not see it as a good in itself. The ethnography presented in this chapter, by contrast, suggests that it does very much matter for sharing as a system. What is shared by whom and with which degree of appropriateness is key, and the lack of appropriateness can bring the transfer to a halt. It is therefore necessary to look more carefully at what the subject matter is that is being transferred – the subject of the next chapter.

Notes

1 In most lists of cultural universals (compiled by Antweiler 2007: 359–375) "sharing" is not listed but is instead subsumed under "gift-giving", probably for the reasons explained in Chapter 2.

2 In Chapter 4 we shall see how the nature of the things that are shared (their affordances like countability and partibility) are relevant. It is no coincidence that many sharing experiments focus on items that are not only easily administered by the experimenter but that also lend themselves to book-keeping.

3 There is no automatism here. If other levelling devices are firmly in place, the leaders who may have privileged access to resources may be forced to give them up as they are subject to demand sharing. Moving towards leadership and corporate groups is but one change in a complex whole.

4 Such a transformation can be found even within one language, for instance when moving from Khoekhoe-speaking foragers to Khoekhoe-speaking pastoralists in southern Africa (see Widlok 1998).

5 One could argue that the pattern spills over into modern means of communication technology (see Chapter 7). While hunter-gatherers tend to send "missed calls", indicating their availability for conversation, but often do not receive a reply, it is a breach of social convention in "the West" not to react fairly quickly to the various forms of unrequested text messages (emails etc.) that are sent out to attract the attention of others.

6 An extreme case of non-recognition, I would argue, is to be found in infanticide when the newborn – without a name and without status as a person – is not granted a presence in one's life (see Widlok 2009). Conversely, imposing one's presence on others may be seen as the most basic trait in violence. Recognized presence is no birth right but has to be achieved in social practice and conversely there are various forms of imposed presence (see Marten 1993: 17–18). What Altman (2011: 191) and others describe as being "interfered with, having one's peace and autonomy invaded" (in other words "humbugging") is one form of imposed presence.

7 Phenomenologists, who have long considered the notion of presence to be key for understanding human relations feel, that recent neurological evidence about mirror neurons connects phenomenological and physiological approaches (see Fuchs 2008: 195).

8 Arguments have been put forward that commercial transactions have preceded gift giving in some contexts and arguments could be constructed both ways for a possible sequence between sharing and gift giving (see Valeri 1994, Gell 1999, Rio 2007). Finally, there is evidence of all three modes of transfer discussed here to break down and to disappear, at least for a while.

9 In fact this seems to be only partly born out by the evidence presented by Mauss insofar as the local terminology in the *potlatch* is all about "feeding" and "getting satiated" (Mauss 2002: 10, see also Därmann 2005: 98).

4

THE THINGS WE SHARE

Introduction

The previous chapter has looked at sharing in terms of the constituent practices that enable sharing across settings. We have seen how "details" matter, in terms of how co-presence is achieved and how responses tie in with demands, whether they are implicit or explicit. Against this background we can also expect that the "objects" of sharing also have an impact, an issue to which we turn in this chapter. The first point to note in this context is that sharing "objects" need not be objects in the narrow sense of things at all. As the Inuit example (see Box 2 in Chapter 1) already indicated, paying a visit may also be considered sharing. Damas' study showed similarities in both cases, with only some slight differences. Similarly, sharing in many contexts around the world not only applies to granting others access to material objects such as food, clothes and tools but also to services, in particular labour and knowledge. It is noteworthy, though, that many of the community services work on a reciprocal basis that is more akin to a gift economy than to sharing in that they create specific personal obligations. Favours need to be returned and can be called upon from specific partners. Typical examples are work parties in South East Asia (see Figure 4.1), African "beer parties" (Figure 4.2) but also the so-called "blat" system of favours in Russia (Ledenena 1998) and the notion of *zhanguang* reciprocal gifts in China (Yan 1996). In many societies individuals draw on the work support of others, especially when facing larger tasks such as building a hut, house or tomb, and when preparing fields or when conducting a ritual. Correspondingly, these collective enterprises have been discussed extensively in anthropological literature, sometimes misleadingly as sharing or more appropriately in terms of exchange labour. What may look initially like the sharing of food (e.g. in a beer party) is a long-term exchange of services, work for work, or under more hierarchical conditions "food for work".

There are also instances in which sharing extends beyond objects into the domain of services. Notions of demand sharing may be usefully extended to cover not only material things but also the "demand cooperation" when trying to entice and mobilize enough participants that a trance healing dance and other rituals require (see Widlok 1999). In forager camps there is a host of services ranging from tending one another's fire, to keeping insects away or caring for others when they are ill and to giving advice (Hill 2002: 123). In a similar vein the sharing of knowledge has been discussed in anthropological work on apprenticeship and training (see Lave 2011). In this context, the notion of "communities of practice" has become a productive concept which will be explored in some detail in this chapter. The main objective when investigating these cases is to trace the effects of the substance of what is being shared onto the sharing relationship.

Affording to share

The difference in sharing between the meat of large game and gathered food items has been touched upon above (see Chapter 2). The distinction followed ecological considerations relating to the fact that large game animals provide more food than one or a few individuals can readily consume. Gathered food items are more pre-dictable and more readily available to anyone. Even children from a fairly young age and unsuccessful hunters of an advanced age can gather food through their own efforts but cannot gain large game on their own. Many languages spoken by hunter-gatherers distinguish lexically between eating and eating meat ($\neq\tilde{u}$ and o, for instance in $\neq$Akhoe Hai//om). Meat is often not only relatively difficult to obtain, it is also a high-prestige food and often stricter rules of sharing apply to meat than to other types of food. For the sharing practices of African rainforest foragers it matters whether hunting gear was provided for the hunt or whether plants were individually collected (see Box 6 Chapter 3). For Southeast Asian foragers it matters whether labour was provided in the joint acquisition of fish or yams or whether fruit were gathered individually (Lye personal communication). Objects are integral parts of practices and the notion of "communities of practice" that I will develop below tries to take account of that.

Although the argument that big game is shared primarily because the meat cannot be stored has been repeatedly refuted (see Woodburn 1998) it seems still to matter what the object is that is being shared. It appears to be a combination of intrinsic properties and of the evaluation that humans attach to the object in ques-tion. If we expand along this line of thought we get to what Gibson has termed the "affordances" of objects (Gibson 1979, see also Ingold 2000). Affordances include basic properties such as "being portable" and "being divisible" but also more derived qualities such as "being excludable" or "being amenable to be owned indi-vidually" that incorporate relational qualities that links an object to its potential users. To say that an object affords "ownership" or is "ownable" means that it invites particular uses and makes other uses less likely or even impossible. It is part of the affordances of domesticated animals, of fish runs or of fixed paddocks that they can

FIGURE 4.1 Exchange labour: Rice transplanters in Cambodia. Photo: Lye Tuck-Po

become property more easily than herds of wild animals or migrating flock of birds. However, it is important to note that affordances are not just material qualities but are also subject to the practical context in which they are found or approached. For instance, in a context in which food like bread cannot be talked about in conjunction with possessive pronouns ("*my bread", see Edel and Edel 1968: 71) it may lose its

FIGURE 4.2 Exchange labour: Agriculturalists in East Africa having a "beer party". Copyright: Peristiany (1939), reprinted with permission of Taylor and Francis

affordance of being "ownable". Similarly, previously "unownable" things such as air can be institutionally equipped with the affordance of being ownable as we see with the introduction of "pollution certificates" that are traded on "emission markets". We may therefore also investigate what the distribution of the affordance "sharable" is with regard to the universe of objects and services that enable human life.

Economic and psychological experiments that target sharing usually take care to include food items (usually sweets) and non-food items (usually beads) as their "stimuli". The quantities are usually small so that individuals can grasp and handle them easily. Recent research on experimental "ultimatum games" has shown that "stakes do matter", that is to say the size of what is offered has more impact on the results than was previously thought (Anderson *et al*. 2011). So far we have not seen strong effects on sharing across the food / non-food divide but note that in the interest of comparability stimuli are kept constant across cultural settings and give little room to the interpretations and backgrounds of the subjects. One distinction that is relatively regularly considered in this context is the difference between money and non-monetized items. Many economic experiments rely on money which they ask the subjects to divide or share. This is because money has affordances that experimenters value – it is easy to administer and it is easy to count and measure which is what probabilistic experiments and statistical analyses are all about. Unfortunately, this can easily introduce cultural biases. The problem is not only with money per se but with any monetized and monetizable items that are included. After all, the integration into market economies appears to be one of the major cultural factors that create significant differences in the way in which respondents behave in sharing and trust experiments (Henrich *et al*. 2005). Correspondingly, one could expect considerable criticism against these experiments raised by anthropologists especially about the assumption that objects (and subjects) remain unchanged as one moves from the context of experiments to those of everyday life and vice versa.[1] It does not go without saying that objects in a laboratory setting have the same meaning as they have outside of it, nor that the subjects act in a similar way within and beyond experiments. Some observations concerning experiments involving sharing suggest that especially subjects with little experience of experimental settings behave quite differently as soon as they step outside the confines of this artificial environment (see Henrich *et al*. 2005). All the modalities that the previous chapter has highlighted (kin relations, conversational pragmatics, presence) are usually minimized and excluded from experiments, while in everyday life they are the ones that determine the setting and whether people share or not. Arguably, sharing is therefore even less amenable to experimental research than more strictly codified forms of transactions.

Outside the methodological discussion on stimuli in experiments there have repeatedly been observations that suggest that some items are particularly hard to share so that they provoke a lot of conflict in sharing contexts. In contemporary settings this applies to cars, other vehicles and similar items that require considerable accumulation before they can be purchased. Many remote communities in circumpolar regions, Africa and Australia who otherwise practise a lot of sharing, increasingly rely on vehicles (often expensive 4x4 vehicles, snowmobiles or motor boats) to maintain links with their land and to facilitate access to new resources including state welfare. One of the best known examples is that of "burning the truck" (Myers 1988), that is the case of indigenous Australians who are facing the "ambivalence about 'proprietorship'" (Myers 1988: 64) of the community vehicles that they are given by the welfare state. Although these are controlled by individual persons, whole communities depend on access to the vehicle and to the places that can be reached with it. When these car-holding individuals die and their property is supposed to be destroyed or given away, destroying the truck may seem the only way out. The importance of access to vehicles in places like Australia is also underlined by Stotz (1993) who has argued that for some remote communities sharing a car in these communities is more decisive for defining social units than living together in a house. In this context, she argues, it makes more sense to talk about "carholds" than about "households". Central Australian Aboriginal people may not live in houses, nor stay together as stable households that form the basic economic units in farming communities. What matters to them is their seat or share in a car that regularly takes them to town where they shop, visit relatives and collect social welfare payments. More generally, this is a good starting point for analysing sharing in terms of "communities of practice".

Lave and Wenger (1991) have used the concept of "community of practice" as an innovative way of understanding skill and situated learning, for instance with regard to West African tailors (Lave 2011) but also with regard to the knowledge that "simple" workers such as photocopy maintenance staff possess and convey to one another. In these contexts the learning takes place beyond maintenance manuals or the formal teaching that a company provides or the technology itself demands (Lave and Wenger 1991: 109). To speak of sharing in terms of a community of practice highlights that sharing, too, is a skill that is built up through situated learning in practice. It is neither contained in codified moral rules nor is it an afterthought of what the objects (game meat, cars etc.) require. What people need to know about sharing they pick up from the people they share with and the situations which prompt sharing. Conversely, the range of people who engage in sharing is not fixed but it is primarily constituted through the practice itself. A social practice is not just an individual problem-solving strategy but it involves from the outset the relation with others as well as objects and services that are at stake.

As was argued above (see Chapter 2), human sharing is not easily aligned with particular pre-existing groups but it deserves the label "widespread" because it can work in very diverse social settings. Humans may share only with close relatives, but they may also share with (relative) strangers. Moreover, they may be sharing with some of their close relatives, but not with others, and with some relative strangers, but not with others. The neat correlation between sharing and particular categories of people, suggested by Sahlins (1988), has not stood the empirical test. As has been observed (Guenther 2010), hunter-gatherers sell (or try to sell) some resources to close relatives, only to share some other food with the same individuals soon after. The Penan of Borneo may sell bushmeat to relatives on one day but share it on another day (Lye personal communication). Examples multiply when we consider industrial or post-industrial society in which on some occasions money changes hands between siblings or between parents and their children who conduct household chores like mowing the lawn but who, at the same time, share food, a house and many other things. While it is difficult to predict sharing by simply looking at the shared objects and their affordances, there are still good reasons to look more closely at how the things we share are integrated as constitutive parts into a community of practice. After all, the most basic affordance of any shared object is that it creates something like a community, however loosely constituted. In the remainder of this chapter I explore this perspective with regard to different types of shared items, and the particular communities of practice that they bring about. The first one is the rather precarious community surrounding large bulky items (such as vehicles and big game) that are being shared. The second is the community of commensality created by sharing food, and the third one is the residential unit created by sharing sleeping places. Finally, I shall return to the most inconspicuous objects that get shared, the ones that are not even considered finished objects but *Halbzeug* ("half-stuff", semi-finished products).

Sharing big items and big packages

While 4x4 vehicles are prized items for remote communities in savannah and desert environments, the most valuable items that people may own in coastal or riverine places are boats and outboard motors. Baka pygmies in Gabon depend on owners of outboard engines for their long-distance travel and many aim to become an engine-owner themselves (Weig 2013). Similarly, for Batek foragers in Malaysia, boats with strong outboard engines or motorbikes in logged environments provide an important alternative method of moving through the forest (Lye personal communication). With regard to coastal and island communities there is an extensive literature about the modalities of sharing a place in a whaling boat in Nordic communities (see Bodenhorn 2005). Being part of a whaling crew is a major factor in gaining access to shares of the meat or fish that is produced with the help of these boats. Moreover, in many circumpolar regions snowmobiles are of similar importance as 4x4 vehicles are in the remote areas of the south (Pelto 1973). While dog-sledges usually bring people together in the sense that the individual dogs may be borrowed or given in return for whatever gain is made by using these sledges, snowmobiles are a main driver of economic and social differentiation in these communities. In other parts of the world, for instance in Africa, people have up to now had less access to the large amounts of cash needed to purchase motor vehicles. In many San communities individuals strive to buy a second-hand vehicle (or, previously, a bicycle or donkey-cart) but find it difficult to accumulate enough capital for the purchase because their income is constantly under pressure by demanding relatives, neighbours and friends who depend on them if they have no paid job themselves. Several strategies have emerged to cope with these difficulties. In southern Africa, many San people ask their employers (European settlers or African agropastoralists) to control some of their assets in a way that allows them to withstand demand sharing pressures. Farm employers may keep some of the wages in a private bank account so that it cannot be cashed in at payday and the neighbouring agropastoralists may look after San-owned live-stock which may be used as a kind of saving account, an off-limits asset that can be cashed in when large expenses become necessary (Widlok 2000). In Australia, many Aborigines try to circumvent the problem by having non-Aboriginal people being in charge of stores, accountancy and related financial matters. Alternatively, they register vehicles not in their own name but in the names of elderly residents, which gives them the room to reject demands since they can claim not to have immediate control over this large resource that is in constant demand.

Therefore, when looking further afield than big game animals, it seems that "big items" are actually more difficult to share than smaller items. This is partly because they are non-divisible but also due to the fact that they need a "holder" to look after them if there is to be shared usage. One affordance of large game is its "bulkiness" but there are also affordances of social organization that are implicated. A giraffe or an elephant does produce a lot of meat at once. However, when we include into the equation the way in which this large amount of food is shared, it is striking how quickly the large game is reduced to smaller entities that reduce the amount that is open to request and it also provides a way of dealing with the fact that bulky items provide a challenge to sharing. Correspondingly, there are a number of ways in which big game is reduced to size and is made manageable.

Game animals, for most people, are not just any old "object" to share. There are a number of culturally specific precautions of approaching and treating wild animals. To consider them primarily in terms of a bulky amount of calories, as models of optimal foraging sometimes do, is the odd view out. More typically, hunters consider themselves in a relationship with the animal so that the animal itself becomes an active part of the "community of practice" of hunting since its behaviour is continually teaching the hunters a lesson. It may trigger constraint or it may invite and require particular action. We could go as far as to say that the sharing of the meat not only involves fellow humans because the community of practice includes the animals themselves, the conditions under which they are hunted and, in many cases, also the guardian spirits that hunters respect, appease or try to trick. Even "rationalist" observers realize that the fact that hunters treat the animal as an intentional partner in the process of hunting has clearly observable effects on the process of hunting and of sharing. Hunting taboos, for instance, may restrict what can be hunted – and shared – at a certain point in time. Personal food taboos may make successful hunters give away the whole animal because "it does not agree with them" and eating it would make them sick. I have often seen and heard this with regard to lizards and other small animals that men and women among the San are hunting in southern Africa. Conversely, there is a widespread pattern that game animals are seen to actively "offer" themselves to the hunters (see Duerr 2010), which invites the interpretation that successful hunters are not the original source of food but that they, too, have received their share from "the giving environment" (Bird-David 1990) which they in turn share with others. In other instances there are restraints on talking about the hunt and the animals, often phrased in terms of respect towards the animals but also in order to raise hunting success by not sharing one's intentions with the game or the spirits connected to them (as in the case of southeast Asian foragers, Lye personal communication). Hunters who are tracking a large animal will not talk much about it, and they tend to understate the size of the animal, dampen the expectations and preferably only talk among themselves about their expectations (Szalay 2002, see also Sugawara 2001, 2005a). Another specific feature is the so-called "insulting the meat" among southern African foragers (Lee 1993). This is a levelling mechanism that kicks in after a successful kill or any other particularly lavish provision of meat. The recipients talk negatively about the meat, insisting on its bad quality and how little there is – and these complaints are the more intense the better and the more substantial the meat in fact is. This effectively reduces the danger of the successful hunter elevating himself, it cuts down to size the meat as much as those who provided it. It makes it difficult for the hunter to use his hunting luck for aggrandizing himself and to create dependencies. While these are all culturally specific and diverse attitudes, they do lead to functionally similar effects in that they divert attention from the position of the hunter as a potential centre for distributing large amounts of meat and they facilitate the waves of sharing that follow. Despite the cultural diversity there is a pattern here which in turn contrasts with other patterns that we find in more hierarchical societies in which gift giving and ownership are important status markers. Cattle among pastoralists in Africa and shell ornaments in Melanesia are subject to elaborate praise and are shown off and exhibited. In this regard they are similar to markers of status and proof for upward mobility among the bourgeoisie of the industrial age who show off their cars, boats and houses (see Bourdieu 1979). The practices surrounding the treatment of big game animals may invite and facilitate the sharing of their meat as outlined above. Conversely, praised and literally "earmarked" individual cattle – or, elsewhere, the connection between particular consumer items and individual status for that matter – discourage sharing and make it more difficult.

Apart from the attitudes towards the objects involved, the actual process of dividing the kill has also a number of social implications. Since the kill is usually made away from home, the meat is being transported, creating a number of potential sharing sites with particular conditions. At each site the meat is divided ever further, initially to what a single person can carry, minus what has already been consumed on the spot. Those who carry the kill take it to a number of fire places, *not* to a central place, where they are expected by others who cut down the meat further, minus what they consume as they do it. The smaller chunks then find their ways to other huts and fire places, minus those bits that the owners may try to sell to outsiders. Those places are visited in turn by people who have not had their share but who now succeed in taking some of it along. Alternatively, it may be handed to children who have the task of taking it to the elderly or others who are not on the scene (see Figure 1.1, p. 7). In other words, considering the large amount available, the speed by which the game is divided and dispersed is considerable. As will be discussed in Chapter 5, this is closely paralleled by what happens when large amounts of money, e.g. the pension money in 100 (Namibian) Dollar notes arrives. There are rapid ways by which the amount disperses into many hands, going back and forth and further. While outside observers tend to see this as a sign of gluttony or limited foresight, it can also be considered a very reasonable strategy to overcome the "bulkiness" of the resource that needs to be shared, and that makes sharing difficult unless it is practically resolved.

If we think about "big items" such as fields, buildings or large machines that may be collectively used, we realize that typically there is some redistributive position necessary that goes beyond a loose network of sharing partners. Take the simple case of a "settler association", a housing or farming cooperative as are found in many parts of Europe. Typically these are associations of horticultural-ists, small-scale farmers or owners of small houses who have created some sort of "*Genossenschaft*" that becomes the legal owner of major assets such as large gar-dening tools, tractors, club houses, water pumps etc. The larger or more valuable the items, the larger and, typically, the more hierarchical these associations are. The larger ones employ functionaries to look after their assets and require external auditing. And the more recent these associations are, the more diversified are their pursuits, not necessarily limited to rural farmers, but extending to urban housing cooperatives, trading or banking circles and so forth. Many of the LETS (Local Exchange Trading Systems) that exchange services based on their own currencies of vouchers also fall into this category. Although small objects may be transferred in these schemes, the infrastructure of locally recognized alternative currency has similar affordances to many "bulky" items elsewhere. In all these cases there is a membership structure, some form of incorporation (see Chapter 5) and hierarchy that oversees the pooled resource. This is much more than what a loose sharing network can typically provide. At least in the case of many hunter-gatherers, creating such associations, membership and delegation structures is a social requirement that people may not be happy to fulfil because it tends to compromise other valued properties such as individual autonomy, mobility or flexibility. Some objects are simply "unwieldy" as they require formalization of social organization, member-ship and ownership.

Big items therefore not only have material affordances to do with their divisi-bility but potentially also social affordances to do with administration, control and domination. Rapid consumption of large quantities need not be a case of "glut-tony" but it is also a common strategy of dealing with the social problem inherent in storage. Complementary strategies are the attempts to "store away" (see Figure 2.3, p. 47) and to keep things out of sight. But what about small items? Received wisdom has it that small, gathered items are not worth sharing. This argument is often put forward by gatherers themselves but it deserves further attention. To begin with, gathering berries or other food items is, in practice, not separated from eating. While gathering, people almost constantly eat (if it is small berries) or at least frequently eat up much of what they find while having a short rest (if these are tubers for instance). Since it is often the larger part of the resident group that goes out on a gathering journey it is not surprising that often the majority of the items gathered are consumed before arriving at the camp where only a few individuals remain who have not had anything, as yet. We may consider this a case of "share as you go" since it is not the individual berries that are being shared but the bushes and the landscape from which they are taken. In principle, the quantity of gathered and jointly consumed items can actually be considerable. Although most vegetative food is quickly perishable and is best collected fresh rather than in bulk, other gathered food such as honey or swarming termites can generate a large amount within a short period. There are exceptions such as the Mangetti (Mongongo) nuts in southern Africa, a nut which can be kept with no effort for months without it rotting. In a number of cases I was able to measure the gathering returns of a one-day gathering trip which could amount to sufficient calories that could make someone last for several weeks! However, such large quantities were typically only gathered when people had specific plans for exchanging the food against agricultural products or when trying to sell them. Otherwise, the preference was *not* for bringing back large quantities but instead to go out on another gathering trip the next day or two days later. Again, I suggest that this is a result of the social issues that surface when practicing sharing involving large quantities. There will be endless demands and there will be the need to manage and protect the collected asset. The final piece of evidence comes from those events when people who regularly share find themselves in the lucky if rare position of being given large amounts of food at once. Today this is the case when drought relief food arrives in settlements – or when the departing field researcher decides to throw a farewell party (Kempen 2016). Often these cases lead to problems and tensions in the camp that can be most effectively avoided by reducing the amassing of unwieldy amounts to begin with. The joint attention that big items require can create extended communities of practice but it can also put considerable pressure on these communities and lead to fission rather than fusion.

Sharing commensality

Food is not only important in sharing transactions but of course also in other modes of transfer, including gift exchange and market transactions. Handing over edible resources that in turn become incorporated in one's own body are marked events, not only in South Asian contexts (Busby 1997) but near universally, since communal meals have a marked importance everywhere (see Bloch 1992). It is important to note, therefore that some gift-exchange systems (largely) exclude food items, the San *hxaro* exchange is a case in point, and focus on tools or "jewellery" instead. This does not mean, however, that all food transfers are automatically sharing events. Like many other fieldworkers in Africa I often received gifts of food, cooked and uncooked, from farmers. When doing field research in rural parts of southern Africa that are occupied by farmers and herders, we were given garden vegetables, fruit, various meals but also live chicken and occasionally a whole goat. Most of the time these were extended as gifts by the local agropastoralists and not the hunter-gatherers, typically as a welcome sign that was meant to initiate good collaboration and future exchange. It is noteworthy that in none of these cases the foodstuffs were consumed together with us. Visitors to Owambo home-steads in Namibia, for instance, will regularly receive food and drink which they are always expected to eat separately from their host. The same is true for the live animals that are given as presents: local residents assisted in slaughtering and cooking these animals but they would not sit down with us to eat.[2] The same applied to food that the farmers gave as payment in kind to San employees. Eating meals separately was the norm also within many of the larger homesteads which have separate hearths and seating places (*olupale*) for guests, men and women, unmarried boys and other youth.

Are these transactions cases of sharing or of other modes of transfer? In many cases, I would argue, these were gifts because they were initiated by the giver. Moreover, especially in the case of living animals, it was clearly a case of creating a personal link of mutual obligation. They allowed us to take the animal with us and to do with it as we pleased, i.e. consume it, give it on to someone else or even sell it, but the importance was that it had been given to us by them. With rare exceptions we were not travellers in need who depended on such gifts for survival, as could be seen by looking at our packed vehicle. Often the gift was actually directed to the political or church leaders on whose recommendation we had been introduced. In some cases it was seen as a tribute paid to us as visitors of high status, especially if we did some work in the fields, which in this part of Africa is seen as a sign of blessing when it is conducted by visitors to whom high status is attributed. Thus, these were not instances of allowing us access to resources in which we had an intrinsic interest, driven by the intrinsic need and joy of eating and drinking, but there were specific strategic goals attached to these transfers which highlights their status as gifts. Moreover, although cooked food or edible things were transferred, our agriculturalist hosts did not share their table with us; commensality was not created.

There are other instances of transfers involving food that are less clearly gifts and more readily recognizable as sharing events. Examples are the slaughtering of animals and provision of food at family lifecycle events, especially at funerals. Again, in large parts of southern Africa (but also, for instance, in Aboriginal Australia) it is funerals that bring people together in large numbers. Funerals are often extremely costly affairs, not only due to the expenses related to the burial itself but also because they usually comprise an invitation to free drinks and meals for everyone attending. In many parts of the world the radio services in vernacular languages have a regular section, widely listened to, of announcements having to do with funeral arrangements and people travel large distances to be able to par-ticipate. There are many functions in which communal meals may serve as a form of gift giving where the food that is given out works as a social glue that binds people together and creates mutual obligations in Mauss' sense. In these cases the meal may be said to be part of ritualized events that create a bounded community (see Bloch 1992). In Germany expectations of mutuality are implicit as participants of the meal after a funeral will reciprocate with gifts of flowers and wreaths. In Japan the circle of participants expected for a funeral is clearly demarcated and everyone makes a monetary contribution that is carefully and explicitly noted and is later returned in the form of consumer vouchers. In other cases, as Klocke-Daffa (2001) has pointed out for Africa, there is an emphasis on the funeral being open to everyone, even to those who are only remotely connected in a kinship or neighbourhood network. For many poorer individuals the free meals associated with these events are of prime importance. When goats or oxen are being slaughtered this provides many people with one of the rare opportunities to consume a good portion of meat, typically jointly with their neighbours and distant relatives with whom they do not share meals on a daily basis. In other words, the feeding of participants realizes the intrinsic goods of bringing people together and of feeding them what they often lack. A universal occasion such as a funeral can therefore bring together quite different communities of practice. A joint funeral meal can be instrumentalized for exclusive membership or, to the contrary, it can serve to blur differences of status and wealth depending on how exactly it is arranged in practice.

Food is therefore not only an important item for sharing because it lends itself to being transported, apportioned and distributed but also because it opens up the possibility of immediately realizing the good of sharing community in commensality and of feeding oneself, often with things that one may otherwise find hard to get. Non-perishable non-food items, by contrast, have other affordances. They are typically not consumed jointly but they can be put to work for long-term purposes, for instance as tokens of mutual bonds and obligation. Not surprisingly therefore it is small, carefully manufactured items, e.g. ornaments with beads, tools and weapons that feature prominently in exchange systems across a host of relations ranging from hunter-gatherers to state visits (see Ssorin-Chaikov 2006). My main argument is that it is not the item per se that determines how it is transferred but the community of practice of which it is part. In this context, a community of sharing practice not only involves certain objects but it usually also goes hand in hand with practical co-presence, for instance sharing a visit or sharing the table for a communal meal. Apart from sharing as commensality, it is the sharing of a place to stay and to sleep that stands out in this context and to which I shall now turn.

Sharing a place

For many people today the establishment of private houses and homes appears to be a prerequisite for sharing since sharing is seen as being limited to the family that inhabits a house. Sharing outside these confines is often seen as either not feasible and impracticable, or as outright dangerous and morally inappropriate. In anthropology, too, the market and the house are often considered to be opposites with sharing being positioned on the house side of the equation together with gift giving (see Gudeman 2001). There seems to be some conceptual confusion insofar as sharing and pooling resources get fused when it is useful to keep them apart. Within houses the two often coincide since the limits of what is pooled or stored in and by a house or a household often corresponds to the limits of sharing. However, this need not be the case: the pool can be wider, as in the case of share-holders in a company, who pool their capital but who do not actually share it (see Chapter 5). Conversely, the circle of sharing can expand beyond the circle of those who pool their resources; at least the two need not coincide. There is sufficient ethnography to indicate that assuming congruence between the extension of a house-based community and a network of sharing is a rather biased view from societies that take houses and walls for granted. If it is true that the erection of the first wall is the greatest invention and revolution in human history (Wilson 1988, see Christensen 2010: 84), coinciding with the divide between egalitarian hunter-gatherers and hierarchical societies, then sharing needs to be placed on the side that is opposite to the house. At least, it is important to broaden the spectrum beyond houses and the communities that they create. Unfortunately, living quarters without house-type walls, i.e. the camps, tents, caves and so forth have for too long been neglected by anthropologists as practical spaces. It is only fairly recently that they have been included with the more elaborate forms of architecture. Across these settings the creation of spatial permeability has repercussions for maintaining social permeability and vice versa – prominently through sharing living space (see Widlok 1999, Musharbash 2008).[3]

BOX 8 SHARING A PLACE TO SLEEP IN AUSTRALIA'S CENTRAL DESERT

Not only things are being shared but there are other ways in which life is being shared. In the Central Desert of Australia, the Walpiri and other groups either spend much of their day and night out on the verandah or, weather permitting, they sleep around houses rather than in the houses. The *yunta* (windbreak shelters) are often constructed in a similar manner as in the old days, when the row of sleepers was protected by a windbreak at the head-end of those sleeping between two fire places. Today, sleeping places still have named spatial orientations according to cardinal directions (heads towards the east) and according to the places at the margins (towards the fire) or in between. Hence, far from lying down at random in these camps the composition of who slept where was flexible and continues to be. Yasmine Musharbash, who recorded sleeping in Walpiri camps over more than three years, reports that there were less than 20 nights in which there was no change in how the sleeping space was shared (Musharbash 2008: 82). Individuals took their beddings to sleep near the person(s) with whom they had spent much of the day. The individual swags and sleeping bags are cleared away every morning which "wiped the slate clean of the affairs of the previous twenty-four hours" (Musharbash 2008: 88).

Sharing space here closely parallels sharing of objects in the sense that there is room for drawing the people around us closer or for increasing the distance, but without creating lasting obligations of indebtedness or account-keeping. There is room for strategic movement as Musharbash (2008: 88) illustrates in one of her case studies which traces two women, Greta and Mabel, who shift their swags to different *yuntas* over the course of a week (see Figure 4.8). There were three dimensions to these shifts in sharing sleeping space. Firstly, Greta was looking after her sister Mabel, who had been ill, by staying close to her every night, sharing her presence. Secondly, her moves underlined that she sought the presence of all the other members of the camp in an equal fashion. And thirdly by taking Mabel with her to these other members at night she successfully ensured that during the day, when she herself was away, these other members who had slept close to Mabel would also look after her during the course of the day. In other words, sharing a sleeping place opens up possibilities which are not there when people settle in houses with designated living and sleeping spaces. This case study also illustrates how spatial arrangements have an impact on how we share our lives and conversely how sharing space gives shape to our living spaces.

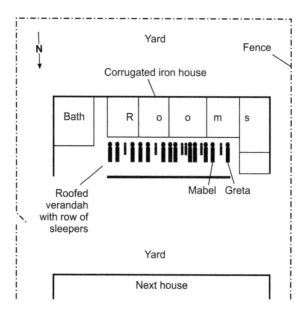

FIGURE 4.3 Sleeping arrangements in a Central Australian settlement. Graphics: M. Feinen, adapted from Musharbash (2008)

The Central Australian case study (see Box 8 and Figure 4.3) illustrates how much the possibilities for sharing a place widen as we move out of the house. It also illustrates why it makes sense to broaden the view on "the things we share" to a community of sharing practice involving not only the transfer of objects. More clearly than in other cases, the object of sharing in question, joint sleeping space and joint company, is intimately tied in with the social and spatial settings in which sharing takes place. Ever since assimilationist policies began in Australia in the second half of the last century Aboriginal people have been equipped with Western-style housing by the Australian state. However, more often than not these government houses were simply mapped onto suburban "White" housing. Houses and other "community facilities" such as playgrounds were standardized to the extent that the layouts and equipment used in the relatively cool and relatively urbanized southeast of the continent were imported one to one to the tropical and remote north where most Aboriginal settlements are. In the 1980s in places like Wyndham, in the northwest of Australia, the state took care to provide identical housing to its Aboriginal and non-Aboriginal residents, allocating neighouring houses in alternating order to one family of Aborigines and to one of non-Aboriginal decent each. The results deepened the rift between the two groups as Aboriginal residents "restructured" the houses according to their pre-colonial patterns, often getting rid of door blades, windows and blinds that were obstructing movement and the permeability of houses. Instead they spent much of their everyday life in the open. Residents of European origin were appalled by what they considered to be a destructive and inappropriate use of the houses by their Aboriginal neighbours, reinforcing claims that the state was spending too much money on Aboriginal citizens. More recently, some architects and Aboriginal communities have attempted to adapt housing to the practical needs of the occupants (Ross 1987, Morel and Ross 1993, Read 2000). In many Aboriginal settlements there continues to be a high incidence of mobility even on a daily basis. The Walpiri example from Yuendemu (Box 8 and Figure 4.3) shows how the sharing of sleeping spaces is very much in line with the sharing of objects. Sleeping arrangements express the interactions throughout any particular day. They do not create lasting obligations. Instead, sharing a sleeping place intrinsically realizes a desirable good, namely that of staying close to those with whom one has undertaken activities during the day. There is also an element of demand sharing as moving one's bedding to those who form a joint sleeping space for the night also enhances the prospects of looking after one another during the day that follows the shared night. In line with what was said above, these demands are clearly silent demands, since actions here speak louder than words. The action of moving one's swag works by implicature. In other words, there is always the possibility of dodging or ignoring the demand which in turn means that there is potentially always the necessity to back up this demand with other actions. The example of sleeping arrangements also shows that unlike in a typical gift-exchange setting, the roles of the participants in the "community of sharing practice" are not dyadic but rather diffused. Although there are individual motivations and strategies at work, it is largely impossible to define a giver or taker among the women, in this instance, who jointly share their time and space. Unlike in gift giving the relations created through sharing a sleeping place are not of a long-term binding obligation. Every morning "wipes the slate clean" of the interactions of the previous day (Musharbash 2008: 82). Note that the sleeping arrangements discussed here are not about sexual relations. These often take place outside the camp and sharing sexual partners is a topic that has been discussed as a separate case with its own cultural intricacies (see Sugawara 2005b). What matters here is the mutual recognition of spatial closeness. In many cultural settings moving in with one another is sufficient to create married status. In the case of elopement or clandestine relations, staying together can even enforce this status against seniors who may want to arrange marriages. Spatial closeness with one another and spatial distance to authority can thereby demand the recognition of a relationship.

BOX 9 SHARING A STUDENT HOME IN JAPAN AND GERMANY

In many industrialized societies the prime locus of sharing is the family home, or native house. Among university students, sharing transcends these confines. The reasons are a combination of weak economic status due to little personal income and a liminal period of experimenting with relationships that are neither family nor business but more akin to *communitas* among equals who share similar problems (e.g. exams) and privileges (e.g. flexible schedules). Here are the living arrangements of students living in shared student housing in two countries, Japan and Germany; the ethnographic present is the 1990s.

The student home in Kyoto is a rather shabby looking building with a disarray of second-hand household items, bicycles or parts of them, and furniture in narrow corridors and on balconies. The Münster student home looks somewhat more orderly from the outside but here too some students have deposited items in the communal space, for instance old TV sets for repair. Both buildings share an important feature: they are run by students who resist interference into their affairs by the university administration or senior academic staff.

In the Japanese case, students freely take from the food, the cutlery and utensils that they find in their shared kitchen but they also enter one another's room and take or "borrow" things from fellow students, even without asking but usually with notifying them later on. One resident reported that fellow students regularly came into his room to look for things even when he was still asleep. In one instance someone took his bike and returned it a day later without telling him.

In the German case some of the utensils are for everyone's use but the rooms are usually kept locked and personal food is kept separately in the fridge. Flat-sharing groups, so-called "*Wohngemeinschaften*" differ with regard to their agreements concerning joint or separate food. Food is often shared if there are up to four students sharing a flat but it is uncommon if there are 10 or more students sharing a kitchen. One resident reports having occasionally had serious conflicts about small things like yogurts that were taken from the fridge by someone who had not b(r)ought them. Independently of the individual arrangements with regard to property rights of food in the communal fridge the residents often eat together, they take turns in cleaning, with more or less success, and they agree that some of their rent is used to purchase a few collective property items.

Despite a general sense of self-determination, both living arrangements are not completely independent of structuration from the outside. The German student home has given itself a constitution and it has selected one member to receive a little salary and more room in exchange for some housekeeping tasks such as organizing the selection of those who have applied for moving into the home. The house regulations prescribe service time that every resident has to spend for the community in the way of serving and selling drinks at the bar downstairs at least twice during each term. Sharing drinks at the bar is more frequent than sharing food in the kitchen. In the Japanese case, allowing fellow students to freely take food occasionally leads to shortages in terms of supplies which the professors and supervisors of the students feel obliged to cater for as a fall-back option. When students and professors go out together there is a tacit agreement in both cases that the former do not have to pay or pay considerably less. In both countries there are living arrangements that either tie students together more closely than in the student homes described, e.g. the German "*Burschenschaften*" with lifelong membership in an alumni network, but also arrangements that are more fleeting, e.g. in commercially owned and rented student flats. In the Japanese and the German cases, sharing is hedged by an underlying infrastructure and the sharing practices are not carried on beyond the student days.

The second ethnographic case in this context (see Box 9) looks at sharing in settings that are situated in densely built environments of countries that have been urbanized for centuries. Examples from student housing in the West (Germany) and the East (Japan) illustrate that irrespective of distinct cultural values there are some features that have an imprint on the students as a community of practice These features are due to the fact that students are at a particular life-stage and in a joint dependency relation with regard to professors and the university administration that provide them with space to work and live. Relations among fellow flat-sharing students are informed on the one hand by the fact that they temporarily provide a substitute for the home families that the students have left and the families or firms that they will join afterwards. On the other hand, practical closeness is created through their shared student status that is characterized by dependency and specific needs. Students in these countries are notoriously short of money and at the bottom end of the university hierarchy. Given the infrastructure surrounding the sharing that takes place in German and Japanese students' homes, both the sharing of goods and the sharing of space is channelled in many ways very differently from the examples that we encounter in hunter-gatherer societies. However, despite the large structural differences – houses built and owned by outside agencies, sharing being limited to an age-set over a limited number of years – we are still dealing with a face-to-face context. In these contexts much of the variability can be understood in terms of situational factors to do with the community of practice that informally provides participants with the guidance they need. Whether something can be taken from the communal rooms, cupboards and fridges and from the possessions that are considered to be personal property depends on the practical arrangements of space. There are patterns emerging that characterize the students who share a flat or hostel as a community of practice in which those already resident can be said to train the newcomers. Still, there is room for manoeuver in these situations. Demands may be rejected as impositions or they may be accepted as a sign of friendship and being close to one another. This has wider repercussions for the social fabric of student life. The corporate agencies, above all the university or student welfare organizations, are enabling actors in the background but they are kept at a distance. Students in both instances insist on self-determination and self-regulating their space. Rather surprisingly this relative freedom is largely respected by these outside agencies, or at least was up until fairly recently. The involvement of professors (in the Japanese case) and of salaried housekeepers (in the German case) was only accepted upon invitation of the students and had to be directly negotiated with them. As I shall argue in more detail in the next chapter, things change drastically and rapidly as soon as sharing no longer takes place between persons but is instead delegated to institutions with incorporated persons who act as delegates and representatives. The changes that this new type of player introduces to the community of practice are particularly visible in the case of "modernization" measures that indigenous minorities see themselves confronted with. They are forced to register as legal bodies and to organize themselves according to the standards of representational democracy, financial accountancy, individual responsibility and disinterested functionality that NGOs and government agencies demand of them. Arguably, the difference between hunter-gatherer and student communities is exceeded by the difference between sharing practices among natural persons (anywhere and at any time) and sharing practices involving delegates or corporate representatives. Corporate settings now not only characterize countries such as Japan and Germany but also influence countries like Namibia and Botswana, an issue to which I shall turn in the following chapter.

Sharing *Halbzeug* in a community of practice

Up to this point we have discussed the influence of properties of the things we share with regard to bulky items, to the food versus non-food and the perishable versus non-perishable distinctions and with regard to the practices of sharing a meal and sharing space. I noted in passing that ornamented non-perishable items are prime candidates for gift exchange, things like the shell necklaces of the *kula* or the copperplates of the *potlatch*. There is also a category of objects that lend themselves to sharing and in a sense constitute sharing in a very basic way and these are called *Halbzeug* in German or "semi-finished products" in English. In industrial contexts the use of semi-finished products, for instance in metallurgy, is a highly efficient way that allows the production of a host of very specific items for a precise fit into machines or constructions from a limited range of wrought products. Typical "semi-finished products" in other societies (see Figure 4.4) are, however, more varied and more common than the English term suggests. They are neither always products nor exactly semi-finished but rather partially altered stuff, *Halbzeug*. They include almost any type of object that humans have altered in some way and which are left near the house or camp for potential future uses. The category in its widest sense should also include what animals or natural processes have "produced", for instance broken trees left behind by elephants or useful stones left behind by erosion. Especially the settlements of former hunter-gatherers are often considered untidy "rubbish heaps" by outside observers. And indeed, there is often little effort made to discard objects permanently since their future uses are not excluded. In camps with few industrially produced items this is not quite so noticeable since most items are made of natural products that quickly rot and since most settlements are not permanent. With sedentarization and the influx of mass-produced items made of plastic or other materials that take a long time to rot, the environment quickly looks like a rubbish dump. However, in both of these contexts objects are typically not "dumped" in the sense of "finished and done with" but rather "left for future use by oneself or others". "Semi-finished" is not quite fitting here since it implies a clear goal of a finished product with precise "semi" stages in between. Metal tips, cut feathers, resin, poison or wooden shafts that are components of a completed-poisoned arrow are first and foremost just that, metal tips, cut feathers, resin, poison and wooden shafts, i.e. objects that have been worked on but which can be used in a number of ways. They are not precisely half-way products that will become arrows because they can end up in quite different things and for different purposes at various stages of the process (see Figure 4.4). Moreover, the arrow itself may look "finished" but it may also at a later stage be used for other purposes, such as stirring or cutting things, and with goals in mind that can range as widely as playing or gambling – or threatening to kill someone or oneself. Often items need refreshing or sharpening to retrieve them from disuse back into usage. Sometimes they may be "finished" in the sense of no longer being any good for hunting but then start on another trajectory as an item that can be sold to tourists, given away to children to play with or simply used for poking or fuelling a fire. Many objects are multipurpose tools in any case. A bow may be a hunting bow during the day but a musical bow at night. A metal container can serve as a container, a chair or as an extra resonating body for the musical bow, changed within moments through practice.

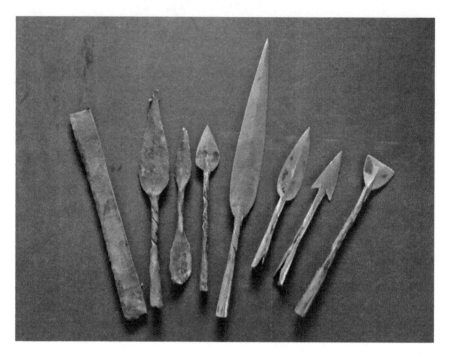

FIGURE 4.4   Semi-finished products (or *Halbzeug*) of a local blacksmith in southern
Africa. Photo: Th. Widlok

The notion of "product" also needs to be widened since in some instances the
objects involved are not produced, in the narrow sense, but rather made useful
through continuous practice. A pair of stones, differently shaped, for cracking nuts
(see Figure 4.5) is a case in point. A round stone has received its form through a
combination of "natural" processes, when taken from a riverbed for instance, and
"productive" processes such as handling it for a long time, thereby smoothing its
surface. Both stones would constitute semi-finished products – and they are particularly prone to being shared. The particular stones shown in Figure 4.5 are used
in Namibia in an area of sandy soils where such stones are in fact relatively rare but
also in high demand since they are perfect for cracking the nuts of the local
Mangetti tree, a rich staple food. Occasionally, such a pair of stones is found along
footpaths along rows of Mangetti trees (see Widlok 2006, 2009b). Since they are
heavy to carry they are left for anyone to use who travels along the path and who
needs them for preparing a snack of nuts from the local trees. When these stones
are left for others to take, this is appropriately considered an act of sharing. And
this extends to many objects which are left in the vicinity of the camps and settlements; they are there for people to take and use. We could even go as far as saying
that it is not only the stones along the footpaths which are shared but the footpaths
themselves. After all, they are semi-finished and semi-produced by everyone who
uses them. Every time I use the footpath, I help to keep it clearly visible and I help

FIGURE 4.5 Stones for cracking *Mangetti* nuts on a footpath in northern Namibia.
Photo: Th. Widlok

to keep it clear of branches or weeds that may threaten to overgrow it.[4] There is
another parallel here between the stones and the paths: both typically improve and
become more valuable as they are shared and used by others. The stone which I
allow others to use for cracking becomes smoother through their handling of it
which helps to shape it according to need. The path I allow others to walk on
thereby (typically) maintains or improves its affordance of allowing me to recognize and use it in the future. The community of practice in this case extends beyond
those who at any one point in time share an object and it includes those who have
shared and used it before. A "community" of practice in this context does not
denote a tightly-knit collective since members of this community may never meet
and need not know one another at all. This is underlined by examples from the
digital age that match the use of stones and paths whether email or fax-machines or
other forms of media technology: "the more people who share these things, the
richer the possibilities become" as "benefits grow exponentially as more people
share" (Belk 2010: 727). Other examples for the same phenomenon can be found
with regard to many instances of infrastructure (think of sewage networks in urban
centres). Those who share these infrastructures neither need to know one another
personally, nor have particular sentiments of generosity towards one another.

There is an ideology of newness and scarcity surrounding most objects that are
being used in market exchange. Their value increases when they are new, when

they have not been used before and when they are innovative. However, despite this discourse currently being the dominant one, it may actually be exceptional when seen in the larger spectrum of human practices. There are not only exceptions in commercial exchange. An antique piece or a family treasure may be old but grow through age (see Appadurai 1986, Kopytoff 1998). In many gift-exchange contexts the pre-ownership also enhances an object and its value, the most famous anthropological examples are the Melanesian *kula* valuables, crown jewels that gain value through their histories of having been pre-owned before and transferred across generations. When items are shared, this can enhance their value in two very different ways. Firstly, it enhances availability, that is to say when objects are available to sharing requests there are many more chances that I can receive such an object for use when I need it than if I had to wait until my preferred gift-exchange partner is in possession of such an item or until I have the equivalent means to purchase an item commercially. Moreover, things that I have given up for the moment can also be subject to being reclaimed at a later stage when I need them again. Secondly, it also enhances my personal freedom and autonomy in the sense that I can free myself from the burden that owning an object usually also has. The burden may be quite literal in the sense that I would have to carry heavy stones, or carry the costs of maintaining a path, or a house or whatever, myself. But owning and storing also incurs other costs, costs of defending items against others, and opportunity costs since my attention and time is tied to them and cannot freely move to other, maybe situationally more appropriate items. And finally, sharing also frees me of obligations to counter-gifts and of dependencies of repayment vis-à-vis particular others, allowing me to be more flexible in choosing with whom I want to transact and interact in the future. It is possible to see yet another advantage to sharing (to be discussed in more detail in Chapter 7) and that is the training effect that letting go of things can have for cultivating an appropriate habitus of equanimity. Philosophically speaking this training through practice achieves a realization that human existence has its particular quality through being limited and being finite and through being aware of this finiteness (see Marten 1987). The ultimate human community of practice, one could say, is that in which humans who are as mortal beings aware of their finiteness and who limit one another. Sharing their lives with one another allows them to be aware of themselves as a person that is not everyone and always.

Researchers have tended to focus on the sharing of large game meat, elephants in Africa or whales hunted in the Arctic, partly because the local people emphasize the importance of this meat and partly because of a bias in sharing studies to focus on the calories and material benefits involved. In the light of the ethnography presented here it appears that the everyday sharing of quantitatively small and unspectacular items may be just as important or even more relevant for leading their lives with one another. Whether things are shared most of the time or in the majority of cases is less important than the fact that they contribute to social life because they can continually be made subject to sharing demands. The relative calm and lack of agitation that ethnographers have observed when large amounts of meat are shared can be explained by the fact that people grow used to sharing, to letting go of things through the practice itself – and without the need of moral indoctrination towards generosity or altruism. The self-image of humans who are embedded in sharing relations is not one of *homo faber* who creates his or her world out of nothing and without anyone else. Rather it is an image of what I have called *homo sumens* (Widlok 2015) who takes into use what is available through the company of others and that can be claimed from them. And the category of "others" is here not limited to one's own family but potentially to anyone around, including animals and the wider environment. Even those who may have left stones somewhere but whom one may not encounter personally are included. Even more widely, agents who need not be human but who could also be animals may be involved. As I have shown, the material quality of "the things we share" often does matter if only in the sense that anything material typically not only has affordances that enable me to do something with it but it also limits me, it can constitute a burden in one way or another because I have to attend to it.

Conclusion

Having gone through a number of things that are being shared, it is time to come back to the notion of "community of practice" already mentioned repeatedly in this chapter. The extensive sharing observed among hunter-gatherers initially provided a major puzzle for research since there was no redistributive centre, no chief or any other central institution that coordinated the transfers. The puzzle was aggravated when ethnographers underlined that there was also no need for a codified system of generosity for sharing to take place but rather, to the contrary, that people were usually reluctant to take the initiative to give unless they were being asked. Ideas connected to the notion of a community of practice can help to solve the puzzle. Anthropologists who had worked on education and training noted that a considerable part of the knowledge and skill that individuals acquire in apprenticeship is not conveyed through formal teaching but rather through allowing newcomers to participate in a process of "situated learning" or "legitimate peripheral participation" (Lave and Wenger 1991). I have argued elsewhere (Widlok 2004) that sharing can be seen as a moral skill rather than a technical capacity. The underlying logic is similar, namely a process whereby it is the practice itself that creates the group of those who know what is appropriate to do in a particular situation. They achieve their knowledge and skill through participating, initially mimicking the expert old timers, often pre-discursively. They learn by improvising and by eventually taking over the role of those who have become expert over time. The necessary framework is provided not by explicitly conveying contents and instruction but rather by entering a particular constellation, by dealing with certain objects and by mixing with peers who are involved in the same practice.

As we have seen, all of this happens when we share things, or more generally, when we share our lives. In the case of sharing, the community of practice involves those who demand and those who have to respond, but also those involved as intermediaries or onlookers. Ultimately it also involves the objects transferred as well as the setting, the infrastructure that includes accessible hearths, a classificatory kinship system and so forth. As we shall see in the following chapters, the notion of "community of practice" is also a useful starting point for comparing practices as distant as car-sharing and sharing software codes. In many cases the term "sharing" is being used and there may be similarities with regard to the actions of dividing or handing over. However, to the extent that the practical constellation is likely to differ, it can also generate very different implications for the social order and for the relationship of the persons involved.

Notes

1 In fact, there is surprisingly little direct debate between mainstream anthropology and the "tens of thousands" (Anderson et al. 2011: 3427) who conduct these game experiments in economics and psychology since these are separate scholarly discourse worlds (for a debate see Henrich *et al.* 2010 and comments).
2 The noteworthy exceptions were some households of church pastors who made it a statement of distinction that everyone was seated around one table consuming the meal together after a joint prayer.
3 Other examples of interrelations between spatial arrangements and sharing possessions have been investigated in consumer research (see Belk 2010: 724), for an early example see Stack's (1974) monograph on African Americans in the US.
4 There is no need to venture far for other examples that are very similar: consider the English system of public footpaths across private property, a right of access that members of "rambler associations" (www.ramblers.org.uk) are keen to maintain by regularly using the footpaths and keeping them "free" and accessible for the public (see also the "land for free" initiative by B. Sieverts and others (www.neueraeume.de/?cat=14).

5

IT IS A SHAREHOLDER'S WORLD

Introduction

Who can hold a share? What may appear to be a simple question is in fact often difficult to answer. Earlier sources with a comparative perspective were quick to suggest two options, namely individual and collective holding of shares. During the last two centuries many accounts about the ways in which humans "elsewhere" were sharing their resources were discussed on the basis of a European ideology that contrasted "Western individualism" and the "collectivism" or "primitive communism" of the "Rest" (see Chapter 1). The default assumption was that self-contained and self-interested individuals are exchanging objects with other, similarly bounded individual subjects for their mutual benefit. All sharing phenomena encountered that departed from this expectation seemed to indicate "collective property" or "common goods". As we shall see in this chapter, this has also got to do with the self-image of the shareholding society that was emerging in the modern capitalist world. What this chapter tries to do is to overcome the simplistic and misleading individualist versus collectivist dichotomy. In an attempt to arrive at a broader understanding of what it can mean to hold a share, I focus on contemporary indigenous groups. These relative newcomers to the world of capitalist shareholders are today faced with a novel situation. Their lives are increasingly governed by commercial markets, nation states and international corporations. Their experience, I suggest, provides a diagnostic view of sharing under the emerging conditions of corporate shareholding. These conditions are a reality for all of us but they tend to be more difficult to see for those who have been thoroughly immersed in them for a long time. Towards the end of the chapter I shall return to those who consider themselves longstanding "natives" of the capitalist world but who are faced with an increasing inequality between the few who dominate corporations by owning the larger part of the world's wealth and "the remaining 99 percent".

To hold a share – and to hold on to it

For behavioural ecologists who seek to develop formal models (see Chapter 2), the question as to who owns what is being shared is a fundamental one. If those who provide shares do not hold property rights in what is being transferred – or in their parlance if "the producers have [no] control over distribution" (Gurven 2004: 548) – then we are dealing with "a collective action problem". Non-producers who "consume portions without paying any production costs" (Gurven 2004: 547) are at the centre of this problem and research should focus on how free-riders were to be excluded or sanctioned. If, however, the individuals do own what they distribute, then the question shifts and research attempts to establish behavioural rules according to which the individual is assessing and carrying out the allocation of material items. The point that the previous two chapters have elaborated on is that, as anthropologists, we do not actually need to "imagine" such situations, and we do not need to limit ourselves to these two scenarios because we do have a strong ethnographic record that covers a whole spectrum of practical sharing situations. Here are two instances from my own field notes when doing research with southern African San:

> An elderly man has received three onions from a junior relative. When the onions change hands, another man from the neighbourhood is also present, he grabs one and starts walking off to his fire place. The elderly man complains and demands for the onion to be returned but the response by the second man is simply that he needs it to prepare a sauce to go with his food. He walks off and the matter ends.

> A senior woman is cooking at her hearth, having a conversation with some of her children and grandchildren. Food and a smoking pipe are next to her. A young man from the neighbourhood drops in, stands next to her and marginally participates in the conversation. He remains standing next to her for a while until she passes him the tobacco. He takes some tobacco out of the pouch, helps himself to a piece of paper from one of the food packages to make a cigarette and then returns the pouch to her. Once the cigarette is prepared, he lights it at the cooking fire and walks off.

These everyday sharing situations neither match the individualist nor the collectivist framing of the problem. Rather, most ethnographers agree that what needs investigating and modelling is a spectrum of such complex situations in which there are people engaging in practices that involve a range of individual strategies as well as various social relationships. Both are inextricably linked in the social practices that enable and foster sharing, e.g. practices of making demands, of establishing kin, of communication, of managing interpersonal space (see Chapter 3). There are also practices that enable persons to keep and consume things, e.g. practices of establishing legitimate ownership, of rejecting inappropriate demands, of hiding or otherwise excluding things from sharing. People may agree, in principle, that everyone should care for their close family and that appropriate sharing is a positive value. However, as we have seen, this does not preclude debates among participants as to who needs to be considered as close family and what is appropriate in any given situation. In other words, there is the two-fold danger of overemphasizing either the individualist character of sharing – following the image of the hunter who is left with a problem of allocation – or the collectivist character of sharing in the form of social conventions that regulate social access to common goods. It would be misleading to contrast sharing in small-scale societies as one of collectivism (regulating access to collective goods) with sharing in modern large-scale societies as being one of individualism (strategic choices of allocation). In both cases there is room for individual agency but in both cases these choices are structured by social relationships. The diversity found on the ground is that of a shifting repertoire of practices which all have their specific limitations and possibilities. Moreover, what changes as we move from face-to-face contexts to contemporary settings embedded in the modern commercialized economy is that a new corporatist dimension is being added, or, if you will, the corporate person enters as a new agent in the negotiation of what is shared and who holds shares.

Corporate holding and incorporated holding

In recent decades the long-dominant self-image of Western liberal political and legal systems as "individualist" has been repeatedly re-assessed and criticized. After all there is a growing importance of national and international incorporated bodies, organizations, lobbies, agencies and globally operating companies. Political scientists have argued that the self-proclaimed individualism of many liberal polities and economies is in fact undermined by strong corporatist tendencies which can constitute threats to the rights and opportunities of individuals as well as to the democratic principles of these societies (see Saul 1997). In a similar vein but at a much earlier point in time, Coleman (1982) had pointed out that the emergence of corporate persons was indeed the hallmark of modern society. Pre-modern corporate agents did exist in Europe and elsewhere; consider for instance guilds or brotherhoods (see Weber 1985[1922]). However, what Coleman refers to is the emergent flexibility of individuals who are relatively free to join (and leave) associations and corporations. This modern development has boosted the exponentially growing number of modern corporate bodies and their power over transfers between individuals. A major incentive in this process was the aim of holding and protecting property. Individuals formed trusts to protect their assets from being appropriated by tax-collecting states and to ensure that property could be held and preserved transgenerationally (Coleman 1982: 11).[1] Holding property, and holding positions of power, also played a role in creating corporate actors such as "the Crown" as a *corporation sole*, as a legal person that could be detached from the "natural person" of the actual king or queen, resulting in persons who effectively had two bodies, a physical body and a corporate body, personifying both these bodies (Kantorowicz 1957, see Coleman 1982: 8). Since then, the legal forms that were initially developed for the Crown, the nobility or the church have become accessible to any member of society. This process of incorporation has been accelerated in the early twentieth century with the "invention" of the corporation of limited liability in Euro-American economic systems (see Drucker 1972). This historical process of defining new rights and new legal bodies that hold and manage shares and rights to property continued to expand into other fields. Not only commercial companies but all kinds of associations have become incorporated, among them institutions of higher education and knowledge production but also the non-governmental organizations (NGOs) that govern much of the life of many indigenous minorities today.

The two case studies from indigenous groups presented in this chapter both testify how "infectious" this incorporation process is. The emergence of corporate players tends to spawn new corporate agents around them. In the Namibian case (see Box 10), a small but incorporated non-governmental organization (NGO) was founded by Claire Ritchie and John Marshall (anthropologists and filmmakers). This was at least partly their response to pressure from corporate agents such as tourism and conservation agencies, the army and other quasi government organizations who were keen to appropriate the land of the San. Since the NGO was foreign-based, it needed a local counterpart, a CBO (community-based organization) which got renamed and reorganized with changing legal and political requirements. It then joined WIMSA, a new networking NGO that would recruit similar San CBOs and which would only accept other corporate bodies as members. This NGO in turn became a member in a body called the Namibian NGO Forum (NANGOF) and which actively trained other San groups to form development trusts and other corporate bodies. Corporations therefore create more corporate bodies, directly through spreading the organizational formats into every corner of the world and indirectly by simply increasing the benefits for those individuals who join corporations and decreasing the benefits for those who are as yet not incorporated. Individual San felt the need to create such corporate bodies in order to politically gain more power and to economically be in the position to accept and administer external funding.

BOX 10 BUILDING A SAN ORGANIZATION

Probably the oldest surviving San organisation in Namibia, the "Ju/wa Development Foundation" was founded in the 1980s, before Namibian independence, by Claire Ritchie and by John Marshall whose family had conducted a number of expeditions into the area. Its biography can serve as an illustration for the ways in which corporate bodies evolve and spawn one another. In the course of German and South African occupation of southwestern Africa the Ju/wa (also spelled Zhu/'hoan) San had been disappropriated of their land. Unlike with all other San groups in the country, some of their land was earmarked as "Bushmanland" during the apartheid period. This allowed the Ju/wa Development Foundation to rename their community-based organization from an ethnic label ("Ju/wa" is their autonym) to a regional one (NyaeNyae) which was acceptable as the country became independent but which maintained an ethnically homogeneous membership. Moreover, the organization's name initially included "Farmers' Cooperative" and later became a "Conservancy", reflecting a general shift in development policy from support to agropastoralists and from socialist ideas towards a conservationist agenda. The original, internationally funded "Ju/wa Development Foundation" very soon generated a local community-based organization (then called the "Ju/wa Farmers Cooperative") that would act as a counterpart to the Development Foundation and that in turn would become a member to larger non-governmental bodies. From the start there were important and influential individuals involved in the setting up and the running of these organizations – but the organizational requirements "on paper" had to be such that the positions and parts of the organization would provide a separate architecture – independent of the actual persons that were filling these positions. The contrast between the ideal of disinterested positions or functions and the realities of individuals with very specific interests and capabilities emerges when talking to the members that bring different cultural expectations and understandings to the corporative setup. When I asked expatriate development workers to sketch and describe this organization they provided an organigram that showed relationships between corporate entities at various levels, ranging from international to national and local "stakeholders". The local San employee, however, did not hesitate to put personal names and the names of ethnic groups into the diagram, as these were the ones who were in fact interacting on a daily basis. Personal and ethnic relationships were often crucial for the success or demise of the corporations. Conflicts had a lot to do with personal animosities and allegiances. The conflicts remain largely invisible if the personal and ethnic designators are deleted, as they were in organigrams, in annual reports and other official documents. Like many organizations elsewhere, this organization not only equips its members with "two bodies" (natural and legal personhood), it also leads a double life – one in which actual persons with their distinct profiles interact, quarrel and cooperate, and another one in which functions, rights and duties are distributed to "stakeholder" slots in an organigram that are devoid of these personal properties and that had to be filled with interchangeable staff, in principle.

In many countries of southern Africa, the most valuable asset of indigenous people, their land, was taken by force in the course of colonization. Conflicts ensued about "the land that they [the European settlers and their descendants] won't share" (title of the *New African* magazine in June 2000). The only means for indigenous groups to re-gain access to land is through re-distribution by the post-colonial governments, in particular through court cases aimed at Crown land. In the Australian case (see Box 11) the prototypical European corporation, the Crown, generated a host of new corporate bodies in this process.[2] Above all, these were "prescribed corporate bodies" that Aboriginal people had to form were they to negotiate Native

Title of land with Australian government agencies and courts, all of them corporate bodies that had been created by the Crown. In a fascinating cartoon-like story, Aboriginal artist Jimmy Pike and his English wife Pat Lowe tell the story of how the Walmajarri of Western Australia learned that "the Queen" owned their land and that they could now ask for it back from her (see Lowe 1997). In the story the Queen is denied her dual body, as it were, because the Walmajarri ask Elizabeth of Windsor to come to the desert and prove her ownership claims by identifying waterholes in the desert. She arrives in Australia with her dogs, the story continues, cut to size to the natural person that she is out of office. She enjoys her time but – not having shared Aboriginal life in the desert – is unable to find any waterholes so she concedes that the land must therefore belong to the Walmajarri. "And so the Walmajarri Republic was born", the story ends (Lowe 1997: 29).

The story reflects two diverging views on the relation between indigenous Australians and their claims to hold their share of the land. One is the uneasiness of granting any right to land to corporate bodies like "the Crown" which is dispensed from the need to actually know the land as a natural person living on the land would. The other view is that the Crown may indeed hold land and that it requires "the Walmajarri mob" to form a corporate body, a republic in the story and a "Registered Native Title Body Corporate" (RNTBC) in the current administrative system, in order to be a legitimate holder of their share in the land. This creates one of the great paradoxes and dilemmas of indigenous communities today. Having relied extensively on flexible sharing practices based on sharing life with one another across everyday situations, they can now only retain or regain land and resources if they create bodies that define fixed membership to exclude others from access. Moreover, their claims to land are usually only successful in the legal system when they can provide proof that they have also a track record of exclusivist practices before colonization.[3]

In southern Africa, as elsewhere, various San groups have also sought legal advice to prevent further disappropriation of their land. But even when claimants had legal success they are still confronted with serious problems when seeking to transform this legal success into practical benefits. In the case of the Central Kalahari Game Reserve (CKGR), residents' rights were restored to individuals who had been named in the claim but not for the many others who had also lived in the reserve but had not been part of the corporate claim against the state of Botswana (Zips-Mairitsch 2013). The government also made it clear that they would not support any collective infrastructure at the former dwelling places in the reserve but instead would continue to support the resettlements outside the CKGR. In Namibia, the Hai//om traditional authority, appointed by the national government, received farmland purchased south of the Etosha National Park for resettlement but many Hai//om individuals felt that they were not properly represented by the appointed traditional chief and sought to establish other chiefly positions and alternative incorporated groups for which they sought state recognition and support. In these situations the lawyers advised these groups to either provide water-tight criteria as to who would be an eligible beneficiary of a group claim or to collect a near-to-complete list of all members now living dispossessed and dispersed but who would potentially be beneficiaries in sharing the revenues of any legal agreement with the government. Given high rates of mobility, of intermarriage and co-residence, any stringent membership criteria is near to impossible. Similar problems occur not only where there are large assets (like national parks and the income connected to them) but also resources at a smaller scale. At many settlements indigenous San populations are being made a minority by a large influx of members of other ethnic groups. Making legal claims on assets on the basis of ethnic membership is problematic, in particular in post-apartheid southern Africa, while at the level of practice ethnic membership is often highly relevant as the various groups are very unequally represented in political and economic power positions. Non-San dominate decision-making bodies because of their education degrees or their connections and they dominate resettlement farms because they may be the only ones who are financially in the position to fund the diesel-driven water pumps and to run other infrastructure. Again, San find themselves in the paradoxical situation that in order to protect their economy of sharing they have to find strategies to exclude others from usurping the local economy. And although they put a high premium on individual autonomy they are forced to create ever-larger incorporated collectives in an attempt to secure their rights, including the basic rights of access to water and land.

The Mabo decision of the High Court of Australia that granted indigenous Australians rights to their land under "Native Title" has become a model which is invoked in many debates about land-sharing agreements involving indigenous people worldwide. In the Mabo case the court ruled that "the Meriam people", a group of Torres Strait Islanders to whom the family of Eddi Mabo belongs, "are entitled as against the whole world to possession, occupation, use and enjoyment of the lands of the Murray Islands" (quoted in Mantziaris and Martin 2000: 77). However, the court gave no hint as to how the land was to be held communally by a group of local people who identified themselves with that land. It is "one of the most striking features … of the NTA [The Native Title Act]" that it does not allow individuals or groups to hold and manage their native title directly (Mantziaris and Martin 2000: 98). Under the NTA, individuals and groups have to create corporations, artificial legal personalities, and more specifically either trust or agent corporations, in order to hold and manage their land title. The corporate restrictions do not follow logically from the premise that native title is intended to benefit the community as a whole. The Australian Government believed that there was a need for a corporate body, given that the High Court assumed that native title rights were "held by a group" which changes over time. This raises a whole set of issues concerning "group rights" and the way in which these can be reconciled within a liberal constitution. As case studies indicate (see Box 11), the internal dynamics of these groups, including the flexibility of membership and the role of influential individuals within them, seems to have been seriously underestimated. This is in parallel with the situation in sub-Saharan Africa in which "traditional rights" in land are typically granted only to groups with "traditional chiefs". It reflects the European bias of assuming that land was traditionally shared in a collective and not between individual persons with a considerable degree of autonomy. Among the specific restrictions imposed on native title holders in Australia or recipients of land reform in southern Africa is that the land received and redistributed is inalienable, i.e. that shares in corporations designed to hold indigenous land cannot be sold or let (Mantziaris and Martin 2000: 50). This follows the historical experience that people with very limited means and a weak political and economic position are frequently lured into agreements that made them sell their land for short-term benefits. Exempted from this restriction to sell the land is only the one corporate body that provides the legal basis and the regulations under which land claimants have to incorporate themselves, namely the British Crown (in Australia) or the nation state (in southern Africa). Mantziaris and Martin (2000: 50) have pointed out that this is a major limitation for the beneficiaries concerned, since "the most important asset that the native title group members might possess" (i.e. land) cannot be used freely in their economic development under the current legislation. As a consequence indigenous groups are forced to become incorporated in order to pursue their claim for a rightful share since they otherwise face a loss of land. In an economy in which market principles are increasingly replacing all other forms of transfer, sharing land can only be practised within the corporate pockets left by a shareholder economy. I shall argue towards the end of this chapter that this situation is not only characteristic for indigenous people. The case of indigenous people sheds light on a much more general problem. The increasing market orientation is hard to reconcile with other modes of transfer that people adhere to in their everyday relationships.

BOX 11 FIGHTING OVER SHARES WITH AN ABORIGINAL CORPORATION

One of the many Aboriginal corporations that was created for the purpose of claiming and holding Native Title near Broome in Western Australia is the "Kunin (Native Title) Aboriginal Corporation RNTBC". With less than 30 members it is one of the smallest registered corporations. The corporation is the result of a long and convoluted process that began with one of the earliest Aboriginal claims in Western Australia (the so-called Rubibi case 2001) aimed at regaining a share of the land that they had lost. Colonization had been intense in this region for more than a century with the influx of European ranchers but also Japanese pearl divers and Malay fishermen and a recent rapid growth of Broome as a tourist destination. There had been a number of influential Aboriginal spokespersons in the area, the late Paddy Roe (Muecke, Benterrak and Roe 1984) and Patrick Dodson (Keeffe 2003), currently one of the Kunin directors. As part of the legal procedures of establishing this Aboriginal corporation two well-known anthropologists were involved, Patrick Sullivan as consultant for the claimants and Erich Kolig as expert for the government of Western Australia. They both reviewed the anthropological archive in this region and conducted research themselves. Key questions concerned as to whether and how much cultural continuity there has been to substantiate the native title claim and which social groupings were to be legitimate title holders. The first issue concerned the question as to how ritual knowledge was maintained and shared – given the considerable colonial disruption – among the local Aborigines. Some individuals, including Dodson, claimed to be fully initiated and legitimated but at the same time were dismissive about the claims of younger men. The second issue concerned the question as to whether clans or "hordes" or tribes existed in this region, how they were embedded into one another and to what extent their membership was flexible or fixed and the degree to which they excluded others from their land. The anthropological evidence that had accumulated over the period of one hundred years was equivocal and so were conflicting conclusions drawn by the two anthropological experts during the court hearings. Moreover, there were tensions between various corporate bodies involved, including the Kimberley Land Council (KLC) as the prominent political lobby group in the region with some overlapping membership in the original Rubibi claimant group and the current Kunin Aboriginal Corporation. Much of the inner conflicts remain hidden as the KLC has a policy of secrecy and refuses researchers insight into the relevant documents of the court claim, which is not untypical in Australia (see Burke (2011) for a detailed account). The Rubibi/Kunin claim shows the conflict-torn process whereby individual claimants, with their individual interests and positions based on their specific shares of knowledge and ritual obligation, have to found an organization and find enough common ground with experts and courts to claim their share of the land. In the course of the process, associations adopt many rules of Western legal practice (http://register.oric.gov.au/document.aspx?concernID=104364). However, in the Kunin constitution the members point out that "We are required to comply with the kardiya [European] law in setting up this PBC to hold our native title. But the restrictions of the kardiya law do not reflect our understanding of our community under Yawuru law and custom." They go on to specify that according to Yawuru law leaders are not elected but that they are the ones who determine membership.

Becoming a shareholder

Entering an economy of shareholders is often lamented as going hand in hand with a loss of sharing. San people in southern Africa like many people in a similar transition constantly complain about the current lack of sharing as a side-effect of market integration. These complaints underline their own demand sharing in particular situations. But they are also reflections of the changes described in this chapter which have been disabling sharing practices. Similarly, in the perception of many indigenous Australians their economy has undergone dramatic change from a situation of "caring and sharing" to one of dependency on "welfare money" (Macdonald 2000: 87). When they lament the loss of an "economy of sharing" they do not simply refer to the distribution of material items but also to changes in the social relations that are indexed by transfers (Macdonald 2000: 90). Sharing as a practice, as Macdonald points out, recognizes humans as "desiring creatures". Any obligation that results from this recognition "pre-dates the asking" and "does not arise as a result of it" (2000: 91). In other words, the default assumption in their sharing economy is that fellow humans always have desires that allow them to make legitimate demands on others. From the agents' point of view the problem is not one of deciding what to give to whom but rather what to demand of whom. The onus is on the potential receiver to make his or her claim acceptable and the rules for appropriateness are not about acceptable giving but acceptable demanding. Correspondingly, Gaynor Macdonald has suggested that the Aboriginal choice of the English term "sharing" relies on it being the closest equivalent to "responding to each other" as individuals continually make demands on one another (2000: 94). As pointed out in Chapters 3 and 4, this does not require or imply generosity on the side of the giver. Quite to the contrary, indiscriminate giving is considered to be stupid and there are very few occasions of spontaneous giving since this may in fact destroy the relationship. Gertrude Stotz (2015) has recently underlined that "sharing" in Aboriginal Australia is really "asking". Undemanded giving may create dependency for the recipient and power for the giver. It can create obligations and interfere with the personal autonomy of the receiver. It is also considered a loss of autonomy of the provider if he or she meets demands of "bludgers", i.e. demands that are out of proportion (Macdonald 2000: 96). There is, hence, both a danger of "over-giving" and "over-asking" (2000: 97). Establishing what the right proportions are is an ongoing social process. In this process the transferred objects provide the medium that helps to establish a relationship and to test and update one another on whether the relationship is as close and reliable as the partners expect it to be.

In the economies dominated by sharing, the important question of the appropriateness of demands and of fulfilling demands was hitherto primarily a matter of kinship relations. In Australia, the system continued beyond hunting and gathering as Aborigines moved into a ranching economy in the twentieth century. For most ethnographers this illustrates the relevance of sharing for maintaining sociality and cultural values beyond the mere distributive function of allocating material benefits among foragers (see Macdonald 2000, Peterson 2013). Giving up hunting and gathering in favour of labour in the pastoralist economy seems not to have led to an immediate breakdown of sharing relations. What has instead seriously challenged the system is the introduction of welfare payments and the new corporate structures created by the Australian welfare state. The nation state not only provides a host of regular individual payments (unemployment benefit, housing benefit, child benefit, pensions etc.) but it is channelling these services through organizations, i.e. resource agencies, land councils and other corporations. As a consequence the multiple modes of acquiring resources that were accessible in the past times of hunting and gathering and of pastoralist labour are now reduced. Government agencies have become the sole source of income. Pivotal positions that individuals attain in associations create the potential for monopolizing resources (see Box 11). Whereas the uncertainties of hunting, or gambling, or seasonal labour for that matter, used to topple strategic accumulation, the more recent steady incomes from government funding seem to fundamentally alter social relationships. Accordingly, the creation and management of incorporated associations is a major field of contestation and conflict. There were around 3,000 Aboriginal corporations in place at the beginning of this century (see 2015 yearbook under www.oric.gov.au). The Registrar of Indigenous Corporations (previously Registrar of Aboriginal Corporations), the federal government agency that keeps a record of all Aboriginal corporations and oversees the way in which they are run, currently lists 2,688 indigenous corporations (see www.oric.gov.au). The employees of the Registrar (of which 40 percent currently identify as indigenous) report many complaints about fissions and fights and frequent problems concerning the election of chairpersons. From the perspective of Euro-Australian bureaucracy numerous cases of misappropriation of funding, a lack of accountability and accusations of nepotism and official complaints, mostly regarding misconduct of directors and managers, were filed against Aboriginal corporations (834 complaints altogether in 2014/15). The Registrar's office in Canberra, by contrast, explicitly underwrites transparency by publishing detailed information on all registered corporations online, including annual reports, membership lists, statutes, court cases against misappropriation of funds etc. Often this information is more detailed than that of commercial corporations, although the sole property held by many corporations is their land title. Some so-called resource agencies are externally audited, for instance Marra Worra Worra (Moizo 1991) which actually own assets and support their members financially in terms of transport, or for social events like funerals and cultural festivals. In several cases corporations have become dominated by single families so that more distant family members who feel disenfranchised split up and create their own incorporated association. The result is that the average number of members in a corporation is no more than a few dozen individuals, often of a single family. While this "plethora of Aboriginal organizations" established since the 1970s was to channel state support more effectively it has created a "dual economy" with two types of transfer geared towards the different types of persons Aborigines now have to deal with: sharing with kin, and a market-type competition with regard to government funding (Macdonald 2000: 106).

The resulting conflict is particularly felt by those who have begun to engage in an accumulating mode of economic activity. Their attempts are regularly frustrated because of the kin pressure to share. Alternatively, people become more isolated accumulators as they reject demands and the social relatedness with others (Peterson 2013: 173). Moreover, the two goals of keeping relations going and of accumulating funds for individual purchases are often in conflict with one another. The rules of corporate bodies are compromised by kin obligations and the sharing between individuals is compromised by the new sources of income that have replaced and restructured access to resources. At the same time, Peterson has recently argued that there is a two-fold reason why demand sharing continues to be high among Aborigines today. One is the social dimension of sharing already alluded to above.

Being asked for a share, and thereby being able to provide for others, is still the main way of establishing social relations and of receiving recognition as a sociable and acceptable person. Therefore, these practices are likely to continue despite changes to the ecological or economic conditions that may have previously stimulated or even generated such practices. The second reason as to why sharing continues to be high in Aboriginal Australia is that the asymmetric relationship that the receiving young men had with regard to the senior men (above all through gradually receiving potent secret-sacred knowledge) is now transposed onto the state. The major difference, Peterson points out, is that instead of gradually moving up in the "nurturant hierarchy" the dependency vis-à-vis the state is chronic, non-dialectical (non-revertible) and disempowering (2013: 174).

Native Title legislation has in a way aggravated the situation since the interpersonal sharing between persons of adjacent generations (and places) has been replaced by the relation between members and non-members, and between "traditional owners" and the rest of the Aboriginal community. Installing a community-based organization or another corporate entity tends to be a lengthy and at times painful process (see Box 11, see also Biesele and Hitchcock 2013). One of the general problems is how to define the relation between the group of people entitled to land and the corporation that would apply for and manage the claim in practice. In Australia the "Prescribed Body Corporate" (PBC) became indispensable for registering with the National Native Title. The minutes of the parliamentary debate on the Native Title Bill show how parliamentary procedures, including the dynamics between incorporated party interests, led to this situation (see Widlok 2001b). Initially, the question of individuals being titleholders and succession to their title after the death of an individual was to be left to subsidiary regulation but eventually, amendments systematically substituted "body corporate" for "holder" in the Native Title bill. A major issue in the debate was whether or not the new legislation would conflict with the Racial Discrimination Act which puts restrictions on property being managed for Aboriginal people by outsiders (possibly against their interest and will) as was commonly the case in early Australian history. Whereas the opposition compared the proposed corporate land management to that of corporate companies, the government underlined that the corporation would be formed by the sum of all members of a native title group. The opposition in turn feared that powerful collective bodies would arise that would override individual interests.[4]

The parliamentary debate (totalling more than 50 hours, the longest debate in the history of the Australian parliament) was not able to resolve the matters concerning the definition of "native title parties" and "bodies corporate", and the relation between them. Instead the problem was delegated to lawyers and bureaucrats who now in effect occupy positions of redistribution. This has created a third mode of transfer between the market exchanges and the sharing economy, or the domain of Euro-Australians and the Aboriginal domain respectively. In an attempt to solve the question of how corporate representation is to be organized, the bureaucracy and lawyers took centre stage. Mantziaris and Martin (2000) outlined some of the implications and design possibilities for Australia's Aboriginal groups in the given legal and bureaucratic framework. There are striking similarities between Aboriginal Australia and San Namibia with regard to questions of localism, autonomy, and representation in these corporate bodies. In both contexts localism, as the tendency to favour local values and interests rather than more encompassing ones, is a marked feature which is, however, paired with a strong interest in regional links. There is also a shared emphasis on autonomy and reluctance to cede control over local affairs. In both cases it is increasingly the legal frameworks (and lawyers) who specify the makeup of these groups and indirectly the modalities of the way in which welfare money is (re)distributed. Again, the underlying issues go beyond indigenous groups. Being faced with the corporatist situation that gives tax benefits and other privileges to corporations, individuals in Western welfare countries have sought to establish families as corporations which, for instance, would have turned expenses for the education or care of family members into tax-reduced investments (an idea already proposed by action anthropologist Sol Tax in the 1970s).[5] These attempts have largely failed but the debate continues as to how similar families and corporations are. Coleman calls the extended family "the oldest corporate form" (1982: 9). Tuscola (2005: 325) sees no firm boundary between corporations and the modern American nuclear family (following Becker 1991); he considers the Chinese "clan corporation" as a prototypical case for economic and political governance. Belk (2010: 720) disagrees because he attests "caring and sharing" to families but not to corporations. There is agreement that the corporate dimension of families has facilitated the emergence of modern corporations but that there remain tensions between what people want families and corporations to be. It is important to note that corporations have kept their privileged position while in fact becoming more like natural persons in that they often live shorter lives than the individuals who set them up for specific purposes. In the process of large-scale outsourcing and the establishment of individual labourers as self-employed, branded entrepreneurs ("Me incorporated") there is no longer a clear-cut difference between "large corporate companies" on the one hand and "individuals" on the other hand.

Being a claimant

Anthropologists working with and for indigenous people tend to read these processes of incorporation in terms of state dominance and as an imposition of social forms from a specific European tradition of bureaucracy and social organization. While this is certainly the case, it is also possible to read the process described above in a broader way. After all, the introduction of state rule, of bureaucracy and of corporatism not only transforms Australian and other indigenous societies but social relations everywhere (see Bourdieu 2012). The main difference is probably that the process was more protracted in the history of Europe than elsewhere but the challenges that it poses for social practices such as sharing are very similar.

The corporatism that we see rapidly spreading in the domain of indigenous people is not only a continuation of the general tension between state and individual. It is not simply a matter of the authority of the state that is compromising the liberties of the individual citizens. Rather, we are dealing with a specific restructuring of relations between state and citizens in a way that privileges associations and other corporate bodies that can take full advantage of state benefits and (inter)national politics. Only if citizens become members of incorporated sections of the state or when forming associations that fit the requirements of the state can they hope to defend their interests, to receive their share of the national revenue, to have a say in national politics and to achieve an advantageous position in market exchanges as they are framed by the state. A net effect of this corporatist tendency is that the influence of individuals is diminishing. With very few exceptions it is only the major shareholders that can exert power on the business corporations in which they hold a share (see Box 12). They are themselves in turn incorporated, i.e. companies, governments, banks or association of share-holders. Thereby, incorporation has become a prerequisite not only for receiving a share of the common good but also for making a demand and laying a claim on the common good.[6]

Recall what was outlined in Chapter 3 with regard to the many demands and claims that are made in the face-to-face settings of indigenous foragers. The practices that sustain sharing in these settings included parallel talk and a flexibility of roles in which anyone who has successfully claimed a share may soon become subject to claims from others. It is easy to see how such practices work against the indigenous minorities in a corporatist setting. In these settings unfaltering unity is required while internal flexibility and debate may weaken the impact of the corporate claim.

The logic of political representation requires that parallel talk and situative leadership is replaced by leaders and representatives who would speak for the community at large in matters concerning its interests in disputes over land and its resources (see Box 10 and Box 11). The most successful San group in Namibia that has (so far) clung onto its land are the Ju'/hoansi of the Nyae Nyae area who were quick to form a corporate entity that met the changing requirements of the state over time. The corporation changed its name, from an ethnic to a regional designation, from a socialist label ("cooperative") to a commercial and now to a conservationist format (see Biesele and Hitchcock 2013). This indicates the ability of representatives and their consultants to abide by the corporatist rules that were set up by the government and by overseas donors. Moreover, this group not only incorporated at the right moment, and in acceptable ways, but it was also linked with allied similar corporative entities, other NGOs and CBOs (see Box 10). Compare this to another, neighbouring, San group in Namibia, the Hai//om. They have a similar history of having lost their land to the colonial and national state as well as to neighbouring groups but were much less successful in securing their share of the national territory and of the revenue that this land provides, for instance in terms of tourism levies, game licences or mining royalties. The recent history of the Hai//om is one of competing leadership claims and internal rifts – a problem that many so-called traditional authorities are dealing with in Namibia, and in southern Africa more broadly. In an attempt to claim back their land, (some) Hai//om have now sought legal support. The legal advisors see chances for the Hai//om to reclaim that part of their land which was Crown land, in close parallel to the native title land claimed by Australian Aboriginal communities. However, there were only two ways of filing such a claim in their share of the land – both of which do not comply well with the way in which demands and claims were and are made in their everyday sharing economy. The first option was for the creation of a corporate body that would specify membership in an exclusive manner so that if the land claim was to succeed the group of beneficiaries could be established unequivocally in terms of descent, language or any other group property. This option was hard to follow up, not only because colonial history had diffused any of the uniting features that more isolated groups may have been able to claim but also because it went against the openness of the system whereby claims to a share would be negotiated contextually rather than determined categorically. The second way of complying with legal requirements was to name all the claimants (and potential beneficiaries) individually. This was the strategy that had been adopted by a previous land claim in Botswana. In the much publicized claim for the Central Kalahari Game Reserve, the first major land claim that San had been able to file in southern Africa, the result here was sobering (see Zips-Mairitsch 2013). The land claim was reached on paper rather than in practice and it was subsequently limited to those members of the /Gui and //Gana San happened to be on the list of original claimants. Again membership created a strict boundary between beneficiaries and non-beneficiaries that the previous system was able to avoid since it allowed for degrees of success along the lines of (kin) relatedness that were negotiated and not determined once and for all.

The question that these case studies raise is as to what exactly changes with the arrival of corporative entities with fixed membership? Elsewhere (Widlok in press a) I have argued that even under the transformed conditions or corporatism there are ways of creating "hunting and gathering situations", including what one could call "sharing situations". Repeated social practice produces "open loops" through which sharing relations can be reproduced even under transformed conditions. Moreover, it is not the case that the redistributive force of corporations is detrimental to everyone. For some individuals positioned at the core of corporate groups, for instance the new chairpersons and leaders, it creates amplified access to resources. They may abuse that privileged access but in principle they may also help to raise the average access to resources for people in the group. The question is how much the emergence of corporations necessarily changes "the rules of the game", the ways in which legitimate claims can be made and responded to.

Sharing in the time of shareholding

How exactly does sharing change in a world of shareholders? The initial assumption may be that it is, above all, scale, the size of groups and of shares, but this may be deceptive. The case studies of this chapter show that we are not simply dealing with a problem of quantity or size. Aboriginal corporations tend to have no more members than pre-colonial groups (see Box 11). Multinational commercial corporations are typically big. ThyssenKrupp (see Box 12) is divided into about 566 million shares of which more than half are owned by institutional shareholders and ten percent by "private" holders (see www.thyssenkrupp.com). A share here may look negligibly small in comparison to the shares that individuals can

BOX 12 BEING A SHAREHOLDER OF THYSSENKRUPP

Company shares, despite the name, are not acquired through sharing but by being bought and sold on the market. The shareholder status in business corporations is said to be in principle universally open to everyone. As a stock market-listed company, ThyssenKrupp, has more than 75 percent "free float" shares, freely purchasable (see www.thyssenKrupp.com). It is noteworthy, though, that to become a shareholder requires some group-recognition, usually that of other institutions such as banks and the state. It requires a recognized identity document, permanent residency and a bank account (with its own prerequisites) as minimum requirements, apart from having the financial means of acquiring the shares.

The annual shareholder convention, at first sight, has similarities to the meetings held, for instance, by Aboriginal corporations. Free public transport, free soft drinks and a free meal are provided for every named share owner who has a right to participate in the annual general meeting. Like in Australia the meal provided to members of the AGM was meat, presented in a way (namely as curry sausage) that underlined the self-image of ThyssenKrupp as a hands-on, down-to-earth steel manufacturing company in which shareholders would eat the same food as the ordinary workers employed in the company. There is also a right to speak and to vote for everyone but there are two very distinct types of speakers at these meetings. At the ThyssenKrupp convention in which I participated in Bochum (Germany) some individual shareholders took their right to air their grievances about the course of the company, which the chief executives endured in an almost ritualized setting. But then there were speakers of shareholder associations of various sizes. The "Association of Ethical Shareholders" (www.kritischeaktionaere.com) regularly raises points for the agenda, refuses to discharge the board, and can influence the course of a meeting. Here, the chief executives have to tread carefully in their responses and they underline the trust and shared interests between management and shareholders. Although they are largely immune to individual grievances, individual representatives of large associations and institutional shareholders can make them topple since they represent many shareholders (and votes).

In the run-up to a meeting the right to vote (and to discharge the management) can be delegated to banks or associations which thereby accumulate the dispersed power of the shareholders and in extreme cases can withhold discharge of the board. In fact, most shareholders never appear in person at these meetings but they delegate the task to a bank advisor who, typically, delegates it on to managers of financial asset funds. The physical presence of some at the shareholders' meeting is not to be confused with the *practical* presence that is generated through these delegation processes. Under normal circumstances the company managers do not have to fear the physical presence of shareholders but they are rightly concerned about those who master considerable practical presence through the weight of shares and votes that they represent. At the meeting, shareholders were in conflict with one another: in the end 75 percent accepted a dividend of 15 cents per share (up from 11 cents), their purchase gain for the year, and during the meeting the value of shares fell from 14.80 to 14.30 Euro per share (down from 23 Euro a year ago), a considerable loss on the market if the shares were sold.

Although much of the discourse exhibited at shareholder meetings refers to notions of trust, shareholders and management are not tied to one another in affection but because they need one another. Managers may move on to other companies, shareholders may sell their shares any time.

usually claim from a killed game animal except that the kill would also be considerably bigger if the company was in fact cut up, so that the average share size as a relation between holders and asset may be similar.[7]

Anonymity may be considered another distinctive feature. While shareholder meetings are *in praxi* often run between a few powerful parties (see Box 12), in fact, a company like ThyssenKrupp does not even know exactly who owns how many shares (see https://www.thyssenkrupp.com/en/investor/aktionaersstruktur.html). Nevertheless, the shareholders' meeting is characterized by conflicts that are personal in terms of the board managers who need to be discharged and the representatives of large banks and shareholder associations who have a major say (and vote). Similarly, one could argue that even in the small so-called face-to-face societies, that feature prominently in this book, there is some anonymity in the sense of a theory of practice. Sharing demands, as we have seen, are made not so much on the basis of indebtedness towards specific persons (as in some gift-exchange systems) but towards people in a certain kin category or simply against anyone who is around and who is in a position to give. Both, provider and recipient are interchangeable to the extent that I can go from any hearth to any other hearth demanding food until I get some, and I can face legitimate demands by any person present. Conversely, much of the discourse exhibited at shareholder meetings refers to notions of trust, of being able to identify with the decisions made by the management and with "what the company stands for". Shareholders of a company need not be affectionate, either towards the company's management or towards one another. Typically they could not care less about their relationship with other shareholders since they are completely absorbed by the aim of making a personal profit. Thus, although foragers and financial advisors seem to be worlds apart neither of the two are limited in their exchanges to intimate partners. After all, as we have seen above, sharing does not require an ideology of generosity or affection. Things are shared also with people whom I have not selected on affection but who happen to be my neighbours or relatives.

Hence, distinctions based on scale or anonymity can be deceptive. Continuities notwithstanding it is the different ways in which personhood is constituted in these transfers that demand our attention. It is noteworthy that the financial markets of today – in most cases – are no longer made up of particular individual shareholders at all, who could have particular sentiments towards a particular company. As Appadurai (2016) has recently pointed out, the individual shareowner not only disappears in the sheer size and anonymity of the large group of shareholders but rather in the increasing trading of derivatives. As owners of funds of shares (investment funds or financing bonds) that are in turn subject to trade and speculation, the agents on financial markets become fractal persons, made up of fragmented relations. What is traded in these instances is not the money or obligation of an individual person dealing with an individual financial institution ("me and my bank" or "me and the company whose shares I own"). Delegation has moved on since most people do not own shares but purchase "obligations" towards some financial asset fund. These funds have a constantly shifting mix of shares and often shares in other funds that in turn have shares in "real" companies somewhere down the line. This reduces and diffuses the relationship between those who hold shares and those who give out shares in the capitalist economy. The result, Appadurai argues, is that what is traded are averages across shareholders (and credit holders). The average value that my investment (or credit) has, is subject to transactions between financial institutions that speculate on the likelihood of people being able to repay their loans or to demand their money back at a particular point in time. Shareholder meetings are anachronistic in the sense that shareholding is nowadays largely detached from individual companies and individual "holders". It has become an arithmetic function of what banking tools judge to be "average" risks of the "average holders" who take out a mortgage or some other credit. The main challenge of the latest manifestations of the shareholder world is that it promises its largest profits (for those who are surfing the system) when we disregard the individual person as agents. Where sharing in other contexts is effectively supporting the autonomy of individual persons, the shareholder system leaves little room either for autonomy or for the notion of the person as we know it.

Appadurai recognizes some non-Western concepts of personhood, in particular those of the "dividual" (see Busby 1997), in these new developments. In a similar vein, we may ask whether the new forms of the shareholding economy are indeed radically new in kind or modifications of earlier constellations. After all, diffusing the origin and the destiny of shares is also one of the features of sharing that I have identified above in many foraging societies. My point is that it is misleading to define sharing solely with regard to the intimacy of small bands. Sharing in these small bands does have features of anonymity and dispersal which have some resemblances to features in the transfers of large-scale and hyper-complex transactions. The differences are not constituted simply by quantity or by a lack of intimacy. Rather, the crucial point, I maintain, is that the new shareholder economy makes it more difficult for those who could potentially claim a share to make appropriate demands and it makes it more difficult for us as natural persons to position ourselves to the demands that we face from this complex shareholding system. The ways in which interest rates, retirement benefits, bailout thresholds are fixed not only affect the actual distribution of gains and wealth, it also affects our status as persons who practice sharing and who are potential claimants of shares.

In complex shareholder societies most payments and transfers are transactions hidden away in bank accounts. In Africa, most of the transactions surrounding the pay out of grants and wages are still readily visible because bank accounts have not yet become the norm. In countries such as Namibia and South Africa that do have a system of state pensions and some welfare (for orphans and the handi-capped for instance) the distribution of this welfare money is a major event in many communities. In terms of cash flow it often exceeds what is transacted at paydays at the end of the month since many farmers and corporations have laid off more and more workers over the past decades. State pensions are thus often the only reliable cash income, not only for individual pensioners but also for the com-munity at large (see Widlok in press b). The typical scene at a pension collection point in Namibia is that of excitement for the whole settlement. Locals listen care-fully to the radio to hear when the pension monies will be delivered by mobile units to the distribution points in the remote countryside. When the vehicles arrive, a portable generator is brought on the back of one vehicle while an armed guard and a computer keyboard and a screen emerge from a second vehicle (see Figure 5.1). The locals line up and have their pension cards ready (see Figure 5.2). These are inserted into the machine that automatically produces the pension for the month (currently 1000 N$). There is also a fingerprint recognition device and it works, at least as far as the distribution of the money is concerned. No counting and handling of money is necessary, no manipulation seems possible. As soon as one container of cash is empty, a new sealed box is docked onto the computer and continues to spit out ten red banknotes for each pensioner.

There continue to be problems though. At each of the remote distribution points there are people who are in principle eligible for a pension but who are not yet "in the system" and who only receive an "error slip" (see Figure 5.2). This is because their identity documents were compiled by some civil servant in the past, who may have been ignorant about their birth date, their proper name and, in some cases, even their nationality.[8] For those who have sufficient means to convert their entitlements into claims that can be read by the state bureaucracy the system does have advantages because fingerprint recognition, sealed containers and automated access reduce the possibilities of fraud. The danger of abuse is not entirely elimi-nated but it is alleviated, requiring much more sophistication. What has not changed (as yet) is that recipients are physically beleaguered as soon as they receive money. Debt collectors position themselves right next to the payout points to syphon off the debt repayments. Many bystanders flock to the scene hoping to press for a share. In urban areas the picture begins to change since many payments are no longer made in cash but get put into bank accounts. The attention here has shifted to the cashiers of post offices and banks and to the roadside stops along the routes that pensioners and others take home.[9] In other words, however complex the workings of national and international finance might be, there is still sharing on demand being practiced when the income is ready to be spent.

From the perspective of these groups, gaining a social grant is at present very much looked upon as some big game successfully hunted. From a San perspective,

FIGURE 5.1   Mobile state pension payout in northern Namibia (2014). Photo: Th. Widlok

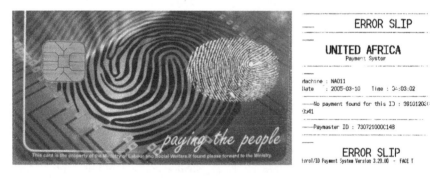

FIGURE 5.2   Documents of automated social welfare payments in Namibia: A service card with biometric identification and an error slip received by a non-eligible elderly Hai//om San person. Photos: Th. Widlok

getting a pension – given the administrative problems – has always been a matter of luck, very much like killing an elephant. It is true that the uncertainties and dependencies are today even greater given the erratic and unpredictable behaviour of colonial and state bureaucrats. It is therefore not surprising that the habitual hunter-gatherer practice of sharing their kill gets reproduced in the new setting (see Widlok 1999). Pension money, like most other resources, is pooled and those who have received a sum of money living among kin without a comparable amount of money are subject to demand sharing. San sometimes explicitly draw parallels between the natural environment and the state. Since the nation state has taken away San land or made it inaccessible, it is expected to provide freely to people in the way that the environment provided for them in the past. Hunting involves a conversational and interactional exchange with the prey animals, but people lament that the state agencies that release state pensions and other benefits are out of reach for conversational exchanges whereby claimants can get recognized as the persons in need that they are. The administrative devices for creating account-able persons not only make it more difficult to be recognized personally by the state, they are also gradually generating a new conceptualization of personhood within these communities. As one elderly man put it when trying to avoid sharing practices: "Now it is independence, now everyone cooks for himself" (see Widlok 1999: 263).

Conclusion

This chapter has summarized what happens to sharing in a world of shareholders, i.e. of incorporated agents whose well-defined circle of members have fixed entitle-ments to a share of whatever it is that the corporation owns, holds or claims. I have focused on the experience of indigenous people in Australia and Africa but I suggest that we are dealing with fundamental changes affecting the relation between indi-vidual persons and corporate persons everywhere. We are so much used to a world in which corporations dominate (above all companies, the welfare state, religious organizations and similar agencies) that our economic categories and our ideas on sharing are shaped by this experience. Looking at the emerging organizations of indigenous people and at other cases in which corporate agents are in the process of establishing themselves can help in this endeavour because they show the impact of ideas and practices of incorporation and membership on sharing.

What we see is not only a move from personal to non-personal, or certainly less personal, modes of transfer and dependency. In terms of a practice approach we see a move away from practices of eliciting shares, of trying to stimulate them and trying to reject them, to practices surrounding membership status. It is not only that the counterpart of a recipient has changed from a person holding (and potentially sharing) goods to an institution giving out a standardized sum of money. Rather, there is a whole new set of practices involved. The officials bringing the pension money to remote delivery points are delegates of the state and its agencies. They are purposefully left unimpressed by demand sharing practices. In the demand sharing practices described in the previous chapter, kin relations or demands are a matter of degree, they can be met minimally, maximally, half-way or any degree in between. And given the changing situational circumstances every sharing event provides new opportunities. Personal relations that are nurtured can become closer or can fade out over time. The pay out in a shareholder economy (whether business or bureaucratic), by contrast, works like an "on/off" switch and it is very hard to change that switch once it is set. The new practices are all about establishing legitimate membership status (through legal documents, identity cards, reports to the registrar etc.) and about establishing a legitimate status as being in need.[10]

In the following chapter we will look more closely at what is now called the new "sharing economy" including initiatives that claim to reconstruct sharing in large-scale contemporary settings of complexity. In some cases the claims are mere rhetoric and in some cases they focus on presumed features of sharing (such as intimacy and generosity) that are not necessarily part of sharing. However, there are also cases which more concretely seek to connect sharing as a social practice with challenges of (re)distribution and allocation in complex economies. I shall particularly look at initiatives that promote a "Basic Income Grant", a basic citizen's salary as an unconditional right that each citizen has in the "wealth of the nation".

Notes

1 Shared property was, from the start, a major concern in the emergence of corporate bodies. In Europe corporate institutions grew in a historical context in which church property, no longer owned by nobility or by church leaders, had to be held by some entity over time beyond the individual lifespan of a priest or a congregation leader (Coleman 1974: 17). As Kantorowicz has shown, theological ideas about Christ as God-man led medieval jurists to a comparison of the inalienability and perpetuity of ecclesial property with that of the fiscal property collected by supra-individual bodies such as empires and kingdoms (Kantorowicz 1957: 176-7).

2 This does not mean that there were no corporate actors in Aboriginal Australia before, although the debate continues as to what extent the pre-colonial entities of clans or skin-groups in various parts of the continent can be usefully considered corporate groups (see Keen 2000). Glaskin (2007: 215) has argued that the outstation movement has led to the "multiplication of Aboriginal corporations".

3 The proof of exclusionary practices succeeded for the Meriam people of the Torres Straits who did practice some horticulture in the past with a land regime that is typical for agriculturalists (not for foragers) and which could be read by the national courts of Australia which share a similar cultural background (see Brody 2001). Since Torres Strait Islanders and mainland Aboriginal groups are treated as a single group by the Australian state the High Court decision on the Meriam ("Mabo") case became the basis for Native Title legislation throughout Australia.

4 The individual interests under threat were not only those of individual Aborigines but also, and maybe primarily, those of non-indigenous Australians. Towards the end of the parliamentary debate an opposition senator made an explicit parallel with gender politics and apartheid policy: "Aboriginal people [according to the proposed bill] have a right that ordinary Australians do not have – that is, the right to exclude people from their land ... There seems to be some sort of curious underlying acceptance by those who come into the category of collectivists that something that is cultural and discriminates against women is okay ... That automatically establishes the possibility of women – Australian women citizens – being discriminated against, simply because we have a piece of legislation setting up two sets of laws ... This is the beginnings [sic] of apartheid. That is something that I find un-Australian." (Senator Bishop quoted in Widlok 2001b).

5 Many issues of corporate organization now faced by indigenous peoples will eventually have to be faced by anybody who has ties to groupings such as families or local co-residents and who intends to protect the rights of these groupings vis-à-vis privileged groupings of another sort, namely corporations be they incorporated private businesses or other forms of corporations. Household heads in Germany and elsewhere have tried

(in vain) to claim income tax reductions on money spent on bringing up children on the same basis as companies whose investments are exempted from tax. Sol Tax's suggestion that families should get incorporated in order to protect their property and integrity over generations is currently being spread on the internet as one model of how to reform social relations in the future (see http://www.globalideasbank.org/BOV/BV-66.HTML).

6   The Australian government, and to some extent also the governments in southern Africa, are relatively strong states – at least vis-à-vis minority indigenous populations. Other national governments are either out of necessity or choice not themselves the main corporate players but conceive of themselves as a mediator between competing interest groups in the country. Thereby legitimacy and power is shifted from the individual citizen to groups with more or less set membership (Saul 1997: 18). This is increasingly the situation in South Africa where land rights tend to be granted to collectives only, increasingly through state-appointed "traditional authorities" and where individuals can only hope for leaseholds, with the state retaining the ultimate right to own the land and the traditional chiefs retaining the right to re-appropriate it from individuals. Moreover, this deflects any claims that people may have against the state, for instance with regard to land claims and other claims to a share in national resources. In this respect nation states often pursue a double strategy. On the one hand they deflect and reject demands for land in terms of conflicting and competing claims from groups within the country. On the other hand they retain the ultimate right to own all land and effectively reduce shareholders with legitimate claims into stakeholders with competitive claims.

7   I exclude the fact that shareholders typically have an interest in keeping the company alive and benefit from it through dividends but there have also been cases where shareholders have allowed companies to collapse by selling their shares.

8   Elsewhere (Widlok in press b) I have discussed the problems that arise in particular for members of indigenous minorities. Ferguson (2015) has pointed out that having a system of allocation in place that can cope with social grant redistribution at a large scale is a prerequisite for this type of sharing the national wealth (to be discussed in the next chapter).

9   In Australia, the introduction of pin-numbers for those collecting welfare payments has led to a situation in which this immediate physical presence is no longer necessary: instead, the stealing and abuse of pin-numbers has increased (N. Peterson personal communication).

10 In many African and Asian countries there is an emerging industry of forging documents that goes hand in hand with the introduction of means-tested bureaucratic social grants. The Basic Income Grant, to be discussed in the following chapter, is an attempt to move away from this cumbersome means-testing approach.

6

INTRODUCING THE SHARING ECONOMY

Introduction

Organizing the allocation of goods and services along the lines of shareholder corporations and stakeholder organizations has been a trend that has affected people all over the globe (see previous chapter). The new modes of organization now frame and limit the ways in which sharing takes place in very diverse settings, ranging from the situation of indigenous minorities trying to secure a share of the land to that of wage labourers and credit users looking after their families in complex societies. While this process has been intensifying over the last few decades, we have recently also seen the emergence of what is often called "the sharing economy" that supposedly boosts sharing rather than constraining it (see www.thepeoplewhoshare.com).[1] Domains of the sharing economy that have been most widely publicized and discussed are mobility (car sharing, urban bikes, carpooling and transport networks such as *UBER.com* and accommodation platforms such as *AIRBnB.com*), secondhand and recycled objects (books, jumble, give boxes), leftover food (food sharing schemes like *foodsharing.de*), and work (co-working spaces, Local Exchange Trading Systems like *noppes.nl*). In other words, the "sharing economy" is not a marginal phenomenon but it is spreading across domains in various formats. As a form of co-consumption the "sharing economy" has been hailed as an ingenious general remedy to global inequalities and as the way forward for a sustainable use of resources (see Rifkin 2014). At the same time it has also been criticized as an attempt to integrate aspects of personal life into the capitalist economy, for instance when private homes, cars and neighbourhood services become items of commercialized exchange.[2] In either case, the new players on the market, the new services and products seem to attract the label "sharing" or feel attracted to it. As innovations they tend to undermine existing ways of transferring goods and services before they become an established part of the commercial market system. In this chapter I look at some of these schemes but I also include a social innovation, the Basic Income Grant schemes, which are not usually covered under the notion of the sharing economy but which, I will argue, retain many more features of sharing practices.

Sharing economy as the answer – what was the question?

The discourse surrounding the "sharing economy" often suggests that this is a radical departure from earlier phases in the capitalist economy since it is said to break with established assertions of exclusive private property and with an emphasis on cooperative rather than competitive market behaviour. However, it is important to note that there are also considerable continuities. To begin with, the "sharing economy", just as previous ideas of capitalist relations, is based on the notion of scarcity. Modernity defines itself as a "culture of scarcity" (Claassen 2004: 11, see also Lewis 2008), of there never being enough goods and information. The assumed "eternal shortage" paradoxically seems to grow, rather than to diminish, as modernity and capitalism unfold and ever more consumer needs are created. The underlying orthodox assumption is that economy is above all economizing (making ends meet) and directed toward utility as being conditioned by limited means employed to satisfy unlimited wants. Co-consumption, which is what most activities in the "sharing economy" boil down to, is presented as a more rational, utilitarian strategy because it allows more people to consume more with less resources. The internet, and related technological innovations that are linked to the new economy, is seen as a "cornucopia of shared information available to all" (Belk 2010: 715), thereby kindling the idea that the scarcity problem could be solved once and for all.

In this context it is useful to remind ourselves of the critique that anthropology has raised against theories of universal scarcity and of utilitarianism. In the discussion surrounding the "original affluent society" (see Gowdy 1998) it has been pointed out that when making ends meet many societies opt for limiting wants rather than hoping for unlimited means. In other words, a limitation can lead to very different strategies of dealing with such a limitation. It can lead people to focus on accumulation (the currently dominant strategy in world economy) or to focus on consumption and distribution (in the discourse surrounding the "sharing economy"). When broadening the comparative perspective it becomes clear that it is a notion of relative abundance rather than scarcity that underlies many economic systems. But as Lewis (2008) has recently pointed out, divergent practices can arise from this worldview. Central African farmer villagers tend to see the abundance of the forest as something that needs to be conquered and controlled while their hunter-gatherer neighbours seek to keep up the abundance by committing everyone to norms of sharing. In some contexts (see Belk 2010: 729) sharing seems to be narrowed down in times of abundance, in Lewis' case of Yaka foragers sharing is intense even when there is plenty of food and "when there would seem to be no need to share" (Lewis 2008: 13). Being able to let go seems to be an important skill independently of whether what is shared is abundant or not, a point to which I shall return. It appears that sharing is driven less by the finiteness of the resource than by the finiteness of human life. The state of resources by itself is there-fore not a good predictor for the observed social practice while the inverse is more likely. Social practices may seem (in hindsight, from a distance) to be strategies to clearly defined problems. Very often, however, the practices are prior and they can be observed not only to create specific new problems but also to respond to condi-tions that are more fundamental than specific problems of resource allocation.

Ever since Malinowski's ethnography of *kula* exchange, the classical utilitarian ideas of "economic man" have been a target for anthropological critiques that take the ethnography of social practices as their starting point. As a description of actual behaviour, classical utilitarian and rational choice models were proven wrong. They are easily proven to not adequately capture the complexities of actual behav-iour and interaction in particular circumstances. Actual humans, almost everywhere and always, have more things on their minds than matching limited means with basic economic wants. They exchange goods for many reasons and sometimes without having a single strategic purpose in mind. People around the world do not only attach different priorities to the various things that are acquired and exchanged. They are also not universally inclined to engage in utilitarian means–end consid-erations in every transfer in their social network. Rather, they are concerned about social relations including power relations, their entanglements with objects and other persons, and the cultural values of what constitutes a good life. Moreover, as discussed above (see also Chapter 2) there are indications that it is often relative affluence rather than relative scarcity which is the engine to emerging hierarchies, innovations and complexities in long-term social change (see Hayden 1994). Correspondingly, humans never and nowhere, act completely "rationally" in the narrow sense of taking decisions based on general information gained that could be gathered from a view from nowhere in particular. They always reflect their particu-lar situation in what is now commonly labelled "bounded rationality", or apparently "irrational" decisions based on emotion, path dependency and local circumstances. Even orthodox economists are often ready to concede to this image of bounded rationality because market choices, for instance, are typically limited by the infor-mation and the time available. The models of utilitarian rational behaviour that were proposed in the emergence of enlightenment thought (and also since then) proved to be just that: idealized models that did not capture actual agency but that proposed a radical idea of what life could be imagined to be like. It is striking that this idealized model still serves as a backdrop for attempts to describe the practical world as a departure from such an idealization.

The ethnography of sharing questions this radically idealized utilitarian model in the sense that it underlines that sharing is the giving away of what you could use yourself, or – as I have phrased it elsewhere – sharing is "allowing others to take what is valued" (Widlok 2013). Sharing in this sense continues to be a challenge to some of the basic assumptions of utilitarian models, namely that individual agents should always strive to optimize returns and that their main concern is how to get rid of free-riders. In this context it is important to consider questions of scar-city in the light of the ethnography of sharing. In order to rescue the model it has been attempted to soften the challenge of sharing by making further assumptions: for instance, it has been assumed that sharing is prototypically a case of a solitary big game hunter who, without the opportunity to store food, has too much meat to eat all by himself so he would allow others to have a share (it is always a "him" in these accounts, and always a single him). In effect, the story continues, this situation makes the surplus meat valueless for the hunter and sharing a no-loss game – which would rescue the rational choice model as a fair description. However, there is ample ethnography showing that this is not a very likely scenario. People share many things, not just big amounts of meat which is not the typical everyday food situation anyway. Hunter-gatherers may often eat meat long after it has passed the best before date. They also store food (see Widlok forthcoming). In the case of the ≠Akhoe Hai//om, referred to in previous chapters, meat is dried, and gathered fruit like the *!no* (Bushmen orange), for instance, is stored in the sandy soil for it to ripen and for it to be protected from uncontrolled consumption by animals and by humans (see Figure 2.3, p.47). However, as soon as the storage is opened, the sharing obligation towards everyone present in a camp kicks in and it is difficult not to share all of it, and impossible to share none of it, unless one manages to eat it in secrecy, which is difficult. All across the forager world there is similar evidence that things get shared that do have a value and that anyone who possesses them could be tempted to hoard and accumulate. It is exactly that latent possibility of accumulation that ethnographers have recognized as the underlying logic of "levelling mechanisms" that are employed to ensure sharing for those receiving and to minimize enforceable obligations and power for those who are providing goods in a sharing event.

The anthropological view is that relationships are never absent from exchange and allocation practices. Embedded rationality, therefore, means a choice of strategies that is deemed appropriate to the specific situation in which action takes place – with the important caveat that these decisions are never made in splendid isolation. In all of these cases the rational agent who makes optimality choices without worrying about the social embeddedness of his behaviour is a rare phenomenon. But it does exist as an idea and that idea has been powerfully affecting economic transactions at least in modern times. As an ideal of the enlightenment period it has motivated Europeans to rationalize human interaction, often to the horror and moral disgust of people in many so-called pre-modern societies and more recently also to the disillusionment of a growing number of people in societies of high monetarization, machinization and rationalization. The empirically interesting question is therefore no longer whether the simplified model of utilitarian agents holds or not, because it never does for the cases of practical life that anthropologists are normally interested in. Rather, the empirically interesting question is how the unrealistic idea of optimality affects practice and how exactly social relationships and social institutions are transformed in the process. The problem is not how to reconcile an abstract economizing behaviour with an abstract sociality. Rather, it is the incongruities that inevitably emerge because those who are economically active live within the limited repertoire of relations that position them socially.

In the "sharing economy" many people who consider themselves to be an avant-garde of postmaterialist society, express an uneasiness with a purely utilitarian view of the world. This counter-movement is sometimes reminiscent of ideas of pure, altruistic gifts that were already criticized by Mauss (see Chapter 1). However, the spectrum of ideas and initiatives that go under this label is very broad. Paired with a longing for human modes of transfer that bring relationships and meaning back into the exchange of goods and services are very concrete strategies of co-consumption, of recycling and circulating goods, and of new modes of providing and gaining access to goods and services. The remainder of this chapter considers some of the cases of the "sharing economy" (car sharing, music swaps and other forms of co-consumption) in the light of these considerations, before turning to Basic Income schemes which are not commonly included under the label "sharing economy" but which constitute developments that would deserve that name.

When "sharing" is renting (out)

One of the earliest manifestations of what is now called the sharing economy is car sharing that has grown out of informal casual carpooling (also known as ridesharing or slugging). In formalized car sharing schemes, registered customers use a pool of vehicles for a fee that allows them to use (or "possess") the car for a certain period but not to "own" it in the sense of permanent property. Car sharing is also a good example to show that much of what goes under the label sharing economy is in fact not sharing at all. Car sharing is above all the purchase of use-rights, therefore a straightforward case of buying and selling. Even though I may take the car into my possession for some hours or days, there is no question that the car remains the property of the company who set up the car-rental business and who can penalize me when I do not return it on time. And it is the rental company who can unilaterally determine what the fees are for this type of market-exchange because, after all, this is what it is. There may be good reasons for practicing car sharing, above all the fact that less immediate capital is needed than when buying a car, although it may turn out to be more expensive in the long run. Whether car sharing is less of a waste of resources, as it is often claimed, all depends on what is done with whatever money is saved. If that money is used to buy yet another car or vehicle which one otherwise would not have bought, then there is no resource-saving effect at all. In any case, calling it "sharing" is a euphemism at best and mystification of commercial market relations, at worst.[3]

I suggest that there are two main reasons for why the term car "sharing" got established. Firstly, "sharing" has positive moral connotations of generosity among many late-capitalist urban dwellers, the main targeted group of customers for car sharing contracts. Secondly, since it realizes access rights that are carved out of the larger bundle of property rights, it is indeed different from the simple equation of owning and using or indeed between ownership and possession. It is also slightly different from hiring or renting a car, but in car sharing even less rights are vested in the person renting. In sum, the differences between car sharing and renting are so limited that "long-term itinerant car rental" would be the most appropriate description for the latter. More recently, there are new manifestations around car sharing, namely "private cabs" (*UBER*, *Lyft*) which can be called via a mobile phone app and where the passenger pays a "tip" to the driver. The protests of establish taxi drivers show that despite the discourse of private people "sharing" their own cars we are in fact dealing with a competitive measure by the app business administrators seeking "a share" of the taxi market, and unqualified drivers seeking "a share" of income in a deregulated job market.[4] Far from being a case of "sharing out" goods and services, we are dealing with a case of underpricing through deregulated jobbing since the companies who broker "ride-sharing" have none of the costs and obligations towards drivers and passengers that registered and regulated taxi companies have. Moreover, what appears to be a bilateral agreement between car drivers offering a lift and passengers offering a "tip" in return is in fact mediated by an opaque but very powerful third party, namely the distributors of the app who become not owners of a fleet of cars (which could be a burden) but of something much more valuable: they are able to cream off a fee for every driver/passenger link that the app provides and they also generate and own an unprecedented amount of data. This data comprises not only the contact details but also masses of aggregated data about movements and patterns of supply and demand. Apparently, *UBER* executives had boasted that in densely populated areas such as New York City it is possible to discern (and predict) patterns of extra-marital affairs, when they take place and where, on the basis of this data.[5]

Old fashioned hitch-hiking and ridesharing among colleauges who form regular car pools when going to work would appear to be much closer to a sharing economy since it works on demands made by those in need of a lift to which a driver can respond by granting access to transport. The system may be less "efficient" since probably less successful shared hikes are realized this way at a certain place and within a certain time period. Correspondingly, ridesharing centres emerged long before the *UBER* app got invented. The reason that these were not commonly considered to revolutionize the economy is not because they were less about sharing (I would argue they were more like it than more recent phenomena) but because of the unprecedented size and the potential for accumulation in the new schemes. The sheer size of recent modes of ridesharing facilitated through technology increases the volume of brokered rides so much so that it threatens the established taxi companies. Maybe more importantly, the added value of accumulating mobility data makes the new scheme so much more attractive to the companies running them, and so much more intimidating for others. In other words, what drives the app-controlled ridesharing is their potential to boost accumulation and competition rather than sharing. The underlying strategy may be disruptive to the existing market and its dominant players but it is orthodox in the sense that it is reducing the operational fixed costs (by getting rid of a car fleet and workers on the payroll) while accumulating assets (in this data that can be sold on).

Although *Airbnb* and other lodging rental companies deal with a different domain, the pattern is very similar to what I have just described for *UBER* and other transport companies. In all these cases the digital platforms (apps or websites) that connect supplier and clients are at the centre. In the *Airbnb* case it is hosts and travellers who get connected by a largely invisible third party that runs the platform. The company need not own any properties itself but makes business by taking a fee from the users. The trend to "circumvent" established hotels through these platforms has generated similar hostile reactions from the hotel industry as *UBER* provoked from established taxi companies. And there are similar criticisms being raised against those who offer lodging in this way, not only in terms of undermining industrial standards but also by commercializing what used to be private. Drivers working for ridesharing platforms offer their private cars, often in an attempt to make the income that they need but which they cannot achieve through a "regular" job. Similarly, many flats or houses offered by private persons on the lodging platforms are vacated by their occupants who move into cheaper or smaller places while they rent out their houses to others. Often they leave private belongings in their home and often the motivation is that they cannot afford the expensive rates for homes in metropoles like London. The sharing of one's own flat is then in effect a desperate attempt to raise rent as an extra income in order not to lose the property – or in order to be able to cover other expenses such as the education of one's children. The relation between landlords and lodgers is a commercial one and so is the relation between house owners and municipalities, insurances, banks and other corporations that are implicated in owning a house in metropolitan areas.

When "sharing" means having and insisting on keeping

There are other instances of the "sharing economy" which may seem to be less obviously a market-driven misappropriation of the term "sharing", for instance music download services. These often began as peer-to-peer barter schemes and are occasionally referred to as the "musical gift economy" (Layshon *et al.* 2005: 181, see also Giesler and Pohlmann 2003). The growing digitization of music and the emergence of internet platforms allowed swapping titles through internet sites that transformed the whole music industry and led to large scale "file-sharing".[6] Those who uploaded files for others could in turn download what others had uploaded. Today, after a series of disputes with the established industry that was selling CDs and other media, many of the platforms work as subscription schemes, in which the user is paying a fee for streaming – temporarily "using" or accessing music – without materially owning the music in the full sense of an unlimited usage, its alienability etc. In this typical manifestation we are dealing with another straightforward commercial case that is part of a larger market set-up. Discursively, these forms of use are sometimes advertised as constituting a paradigm shift from "having" to "being/enjoying" a move toward a post-materialist society (see Fromm 1976). However, we are dealing not only with a euphemism but actually with a mystification. In fact, the amount of music at one's disposal actually increases as one becomes a subscriber. Language is deceptive here. What may appear to be a shift from "having" a CD collection to "being" a subscriber to a music provider can easily be depicted inversely: after all, "having" a CD collection makes you "be" a successful collector – and you "are" someone from whom others may borrow disks, for instance. By contrast, "being" a subscriber allows you to "have" access to a huge collection of music – and relieves you of any pressures to share because you only have ephemeral rights in music pieces that you cannot (easily, legally) store and hand on.

Music swap portals, where they continue to operate, are somewhat closer to barter but only to some extent. In this case, whatever you upload for others to use is not lost to you, strictly speaking it is not a swap of music but of access rights, and consequently it is not tantamount to a decreased interest in "having". As with the private cab drivers and flat lessors it is a case of competitive moves, here between music companies and individual "entrepreneurs" trying to make more profit in terms of market value of the music they have purchased for themselves. And consequently we see the same hostile reactions and legal protections on the side of the established market players. Contrary to the discourse, music "swaps" may therefore be considered a case of "having more", even a sign of greed or at least of the desire to have ever more and ever newer things at any point in time. This point has been aired recently as a critique against such manifestations of the sharing economy hype. But on the basis of a comparative perspective some caution is in order. The hunter-gatherers who share are also not disinterested in things. As we have seen in previous chapters, they try to protect what they have from the sharing pressure that is on them, for instance by hiding and by trying to deflect demands. Since demand sharing is the prototypical form of sharing in these settings, it is fair to say that sharing in many places is driven by other motives than generosity. What it does require, though, is the preparedness to part with something, the ability to let go, a sense of renunciation and of giving up accumulation (see Chapter 7). Key to sharing is the general acceptance that ownership is transient and not constant and that it is relational in the sense that it is limited by the legitimate claims by others and not just by a single owner like the companies that set up streaming services. In other words the fact that some people enjoy having things and are reluctant to part with them is not incompatible with sharing. What is incompatible with sharing is the default expectation that one will be able to keep them and that someone is justified in insisting on hanging on to things under all circumstances and against everyone else. The difference between sharing and co-consumption is not the "wanting to have" but the "insisting on keeping" – and the social conditions that support this insistence.

With regard to music swaps and similar schemes it is also important to note that although they may look superficially like gift exchange or sharing, there is much less social commitment involved. Those who offer things and services on swap sites can do so at their own whim and those who use the platforms decide how much and for how long they get involved. A quick exit option is available as there are often no long-term contracts. Competition between different platforms allows quick movement to where the best deal is to be expected. Game theorists are always worried about free-riders (see Chapter 2) but to some extent these schemes are exclusive populations of free-riders who as a collective, and with the appropriate technology, seek to exploit those who have initially produced the music. Many forms of downloading from the internet are akin to what ethnographers have described for cattle raids.

These "raids" are often considered to be morally justified because they are directed at "the others", in this instance the rich companies and artists who were able to accumulate riches. This accumulation by artists, and their agents, is in itself rather recent because it relies on modern mass-media technology of reproducing artworks. This technology decouples the performance from the product which gave the music industry, in particular, an advantage in comparison to previous "breadless" artists who used to be paid like craftspeople in other domains. But note that for internet pirates these are ex post justifications based on the assumed riches of those who are considered to be outside one's own group. The anonymity of those who take by downloading from the internet, and the anonymity of those in the complex producing industry from whom things are taken, marks a considerable difference to the sharing schemes (and the gift-giving schemes) that have been discussed in the previous chapters. The "hidden" third party in this constellation are the internet platform providers, the software companies that allow for this particular form of anonymity to be upheld and to be managed. After all, the givers and takers may not know one another personally but the providers as the mediating third party can trace and record all movements and transactions on the net. They may use that knowledge to consolidate their own position against those with less knowledge, and they may in turn sell that knowledge as data. While participants in gift giving and sharing benefit from in-depth knowledge about who owns what and how best to elicit things under changing conditions, those running internet platforms benefit from the large quantities of data on transfers that no-one but they themselves can trace. The scope of the information (the sheer number and repetitiveness of recorded surfing behaviour) compensates for the fact that individual participants need not be known as individual persons. In most of these schemes it is the average, fractal person that matters (see Chapter 5). There is no need to know particular individuals as long as the probabilistic predictions allow anticipation of what participants, with a probabilistic profile made up of certain averages, are likely to do next (i.e. what they buy or sell). This aspect is not limited to schemes such as music swaps but it extends more widely into fields such as insurance brokerage and financial "swaps" of risks and rents. In the preceding chapter we have discussed the changes taking place in financial markets. Where there used to be one person owning a share of one company or being indebted to one bank we now have funds of shares (with average performance and average risks) and derivatives in which the likelihood of individual debtors to repay, or to be unable to repay, is pooled and bundled up in many ways. Many internet portals are similar kinds of "funds" and "pools". Unlike "holistic" human persons, they are fragmented and do away with personal needs that one could relate to through empathy, through direct interaction and personal experience. Modes of relatedness and exchange that were trained in interpersonal encounters seem no longer to have any purchase in a situation in which one never deals with counterparts but only with fractions of persons that are fused with other fractions beyond recognition and beyond the ability to oversee the consequences of acts of exchange.

Apart from the pooling processes that are very complex and diffuse, there are also examples of co-consumption and pooling at the other end of the spectrum, as it were, namely among those who do not operate in the world of high finance and derivatives but those who are to some extent cut off from monetarized exchange, either by exclusion or by choice. These schemes are generally known under the acronym LETS (Local exchange and trading systems). In these schemes co-consumption is realized through establishing a collective pool of goods and services, often with the support of a special-purpose parallel currency (see Figure 6.1). They are attractive in particular for people who are short of money and who cannot satisfy all their needs through commercial exchange. They are also attractive to those who like to organize at least part of their exchange locally, decoupled from the formation of prices and the collection of taxes (such as VAT) through the state or from the vagaries of the wider market. In some cases this is similar to collective pooling in associations or clubs,

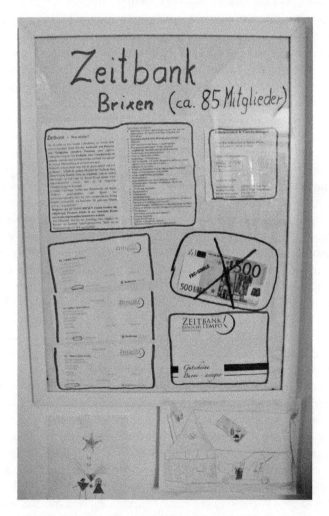

FIGURE 6.1   A LETS (Local Exchange Trading System) with 85 members in Bozen (northern Italy, 2015). Photo: Th. Widlok

for instance, when expensive garden tools are shared by an association of garden plot owners (see Chapter 5). While such associations that collectively manage their allotments have been around since industrialization began they have recently received a boost in what is called "urban gardening", projects in which urban dwellers join forces to cultivate communally owned land in their neighbourhood. Most LETS are not limited to a particular economic domain such as gardening or household services but try to foster non-monetary exchange across different domains involving household tasks, private lessons, babysitting, looking after pets and so forth. The schemes consist of barter governed by supply and demand. In larger schemes participants are rated (just as with *Airbnb* and similar platforms) and they often have to earn vouchers in a local alternative currency before they can benefit from the services of the network (see Hart 2000).

Occasionally such "pooling" of resources is confused with sharing but it is important to point out that most pooling systems work without sharing and that most sharing works without collectively pooling or storing. The more organized the LETS schemes are, the more reliably participants can calculate, offer and claim services, comparable to monetarized systems but without interferences from the wider economy or the state. The alternative currency of vouchers constitutes a collective storage that has some degree of guarantee and control through the local community. Several internet phenomena, such as wikipedia.org and other "mutual help" sites, show similarities to LETS schemes, except that they are not local in a spatial sense but rather with regard to a particular community of like-minded people who "meet" on the web. There are some limited similarities with sharing if we concentrate on the flow of goods, i.e. a move from individual possession into the open where things potentially can then be spread out in all directions. However, the similarities disappear when we concentrate on the relationships involved: sharing, in the ethnographically documented cases, does not create a collective pool which then gets redistributed. Polanyi (1944) rightly points at the difference between redistribution and other forms of transfer. Insofar as such a collective pool requires a socially institutionalized position of redistribution, it very much differs from sharing. In LETS schemes the collective setting up, demarcating and running of the scheme is invested with considerable power which provides both some stability but also some danger of an abuse of power. Sharing, by contrast, is typically more open and not predicated on a corporate collective. In some ways it actually works against the notion of an organized collective because it fosters individual autonomy and the levelling of power. Collective pooling in so-called alternative currency exchange schemes is more akin to exchange circles either with a central steering board that gives out a "currency" or fixes the exchange rates (as in internet currency) or with a "constitution" that sets the locally applicable rules. These are therefore less like sharing schemes and are appropriately labelled "Local *Exchange* and *Trading* System" because they facilitate exchange and trade. Whoever contributes to the system in return retains specific entitlements that are recorded together with a record of complying with the rules and of being a trustworthy member of the scheme.

As was discussed in Chapter 1, all exchange schemes can be said to be by definition not sharing systems because the latter lacks the specific mutuality of returns that constitutes the notion of reciprocity (Gell 1999). Sharing comprises uneven, unbalanced, one-way transfers. But more importantly than the question of actual balance or non-balance is the question of whether participants can keep track of the specific balance, and can bank on it. Exchange systems work because there is a record of specific obligations held by particular people against particular others, a *do ut des* logic. This is often facilitated through the alternative currencies that provide some means to keep that record (see vouchers in Figure 6.1). When some rating system of providers is added to the record of past exchanges, it influences future exchanges, not only in terms of comparing quantities but also for the qualities of what is being offered by specific individuals who may become reputable and preferred partners in the scheme. Sharing is organized in ways that limit such specific obligations and entitlements. As we have seen in Chapter 3, in many hunter-gatherer settings both the provider and the taker aim to circumvent specific obligations by decoupling the giver from what is being given and by distancing the act of giving from that of receiving. This is achieved through a number of strategies, for example by making the receiver initiate the transaction or by including go-betweens in the transaction, and by making depreciating remarks about what is being provided. Some of these aspects are emulated in other new institutions that are found in the urban settings of the industrial world on which the current chapter focuses. "Give boxes" are such an institution to which I shall now turn.

When "sharers" insist on giving

Many manifestations of the "sharing economy" look very different from sharing elsewhere because they are mediated by the internet or other digital tools such as apps. There are, however, also some that emulate more direct forms of interaction, or a mix between the two. "Give boxes" (see Figures 6.2 and 6.3) are new institutions that try to emulate some of the aspects of sharing that I have discussed. They respond to some of the problems that exist with the distribution of goods and services in a capitalist market system and seek to optimize the use of resources. Since most of these initiatives are instituted from the bottom up, they seem to fill gaps in the wider economy in more or less haphazard ways. In many countries of the West give boxes are set up by residents from a local neighbourhood. In these little booths locals can place items they no longer need so that others can pick them up. It probably began with book exchange boxes but has since been extended to boxes of general household items or clothes and boxes with vegetables and other food items. In previous decades most of these things would have been sold in jumble or car-boot sales or some other forms of informal markets. Since then many jumble sales have either become "gentrified" as antique markets or they have been converted into non-food consumer markets with cheap products. Instead of leaving things out on the street or in the front yard many cities have allowed designated "boxes" to be put up in public squares, often the visible emblems of the arrival of the "sharing economy". Two important features of these boxes need to be pointed out. One is that there is usually one person or a group of individuals or an association who have taken responsibility for the box in the sense that they try to prevent it from being vandalized or more generally from declining into a disorderly state. The other feature is that, not coincidentally, many of these boxes are in public spaces where there are also other "boxes" for recycling, e.g. glass, clothes and paper containers, and more recently containers for recycling electronic parts. In other words, the initiative for these boxes originates from the givers who own things they no longer need, that they find too cumbersome to sell (or which would not get a good price anyway) but which they feel are "too good to throw away" and which they therefore would like to hand on to someone else. Since most of these boxes are in the public realm, they do need to be recognized, and to some extent regulated, by the municipal bureaucracy, which warrants calling them new forms of institutionalized transfer.

FIGURE 6.2 A Give Box in Mülheim/Ruhr (Germany, 2015). Photo: Th. Widlok

In many urban centres of Germany and neighbouring countries there are three types of give box. The first type is that of book exchange boxes that were often put in place by cultural institutions such as public adult learning centres, music schools, museums or libraries. They are often run by the municipality or by welfare organizations or church-based organizations. A more recent type of box is give boxes for non-perishable household items such as toys, clothes, cutlery and crockery or decorative items. These boxes are typically on public ground and they, too, require public permissions. Regulations are particularly rigid with regard to the third type of box, food boxes. The so-called "fair-teiler" system (a pun on "verteilen" ("to allocate") and fairness, fair trade) is highly organized. In order to become a recognized distributor of free foodstuffs one has to register and undergo a test period before one is allowed to receive excess foodstuffs from supermarkets or canteens and to become an active node in the redistributive system (see www. foodshare.org and www.foodsharer.de). The "licence to give" is a quasi-bureaucratic act necessitated through regulations to do with the safe handling of food. With non-perishable, non-food items things are much easier once a box is in place.

I have conducted participant observation around such a give box in my home town (see Box 13). Visiting the box regularly to place things there and to take stock of what was inside, it quickly became clear that there was someone from the neigh-bourhood who looked after the box. There were instructions on what to do and not

FIGURE 6.3   A foodsharing box in Mülheim/Ruhr (Germany, 2015). Photo: Th. Widlok

BOX 13 PUTTING UP A GIVE BOX

The give box is a small wooden booth of about three square metres (see Figure 6.2). Like many others it is constructed and decorated in a do-it-yourself manner (plans for making a booth are circulated through the internet). It has a shelf on which books, CDs, children's games and a diversity of household goods such as candles, plates, mugs etc. can be placed. It also has a coat rail where clothes of various sorts are placed. On the floor of the box there is room for slightly bigger items such as lamps, children's toys and such like. When visiting the box on a daily basis over several weeks there was usually one person in sight who either paid a short visit or who was placing or taking things, i.e. considering how small the box is, it does get a lot of attention by locals. Correspondingly, most of the items that get placed here are gone within a day or two. Occasionally, things that do not get taken and that seem very unattractive do get removed by the individuals in the neighbourhood who are "guardians" of the give box and who also tidy up the place at regular intervals.

It is easy to get into conversation with visitors of the box, about the objects found, but also about other users of the box. In larger cities there are online platforms for discussing events surrounding the boxes and their use(r)s. Although the general comments I collected were positive about the give box itself, there were also negative comments, in particular about some of the users. The negative statements refer either to those who are said to "dump" things in the box that really belong in the rubbish bin but also to those who frequent the box not because they want to use some of the items themselves but because they take things to sell them elsewhere, e.g. at jumble sales.

Those who place items in the box often drive up to the box, which is next to the road on a little square of green, get out of their car, just to drop things off and then move on. Others who sit on a bench next to the box or who stroll around it are usually potential recipients who check more or less regularly whether new things have arrived which they may find attractive. There is usually no interaction between givers and receivers although some individuals are both or claim to be both providers and occasional takers. Also, some items disappear from the box but reappear some days later, which suggests that they have been taken home but returned later. Some types of items seem to be in higher demand (office and school requisites such as paper notebooks for instance) while others stay for longer (many of the books, for instance). Unlike with classified ads which fall into "wanted" and "offered" categories, there is no way for the potential recipients to express their demands. The only act of demanding that I have experienced when visiting the give box was when someone who had observed my placing of things had spotted the camera which I used to document changes in the box and about which he asked whether I was planning to put it into the box as well. This was an exception since for most other intents and purposes "give boxes" are exactly what the name suggests, a way of giving things away that one no longer wants but for which giving away seems more appropriate than disposing of as waste. They also typically decouple giving from taking.

to do (e.g. not to leave any perishable items) and things were regularly put into order and some items removed to the nearby rubbish containers if they were broken or in such a bad shape that they were unlikely to be picked up. Participant observation also revealed that although this giving was structured by the motives of the givers rather than by the needs of the receivers, the give box successfully filled a gap in the repertoire of (re-)distribution in at least two respects. Firstly, most items were gone fairly quickly, mostly from one day to the next. This indicates that there was a demand, after all. Secondly, the box successfully decoupled the act of giving from the act of receiving. Receiving alms, and the begging that goes with it, often makes people feel uneasy in societies in which everyone is supposed to work for what they desire. Most visitors whom I encountered and spoke to at the give box highlighted that they liked the box because they could give things away that were "too good to throw away", even though observation showed that these visitors were there to search for items to take rather than for the opportunity to place things. Hence, visiting the box and browsing in public was okay since it was not concomitant with being a recipient of alms. This way "giving through the box" reached many people who would otherwise not be recipients of public welfare either because they are too ashamed to register or because they were just above the officially recognized level of poverty but still in need of things. Another important point that was repeatedly made by visitors to the box concerns possible abuses of the box as a "dumping ground" but also attempts to (re)commercialize the contents. Such concerns are also echoed by online comments with regard to give boxes that have a presence on social media or local websites (see www.givebox.eu).

None of the "new" transfer modes that emerge with the "sharing economy" are isolated, they all get integrated into other transactions, most importantly into the framework of commercial market transactions. Thus, individuals who frequent the give box are not necessarily destitute or completely without money. Rather they seek ways of getting things for free which in turn frees money for other items or services for which there is no alternative but to pay for with money (e.g. energy bills, petrol, insurances etc.). This also holds for most of the transactions in the above-mentioned LETS exchange systems which carve out a domain for non-monetary exchange which allows the reserving of financial means for other domains. At the give boxes the integration into the wider economy of transactions is very visible in another way. At all give boxes that I have visited *in situ* or online, there were complaints about "hawks" who would patrol the give boxes for things that they then would sell at jumble sales or through other commercial platforms which continue to exist side-by-side with the new give boxes. In the context of give boxes such behaviour is usually scolded and complained about because it is said to be counteracting the purpose of the give boxes. This shows that for most people involved, give boxes are very much seen as being part of the register of giving of alms, giving to the poor and generosity. They are set apart from commercial exchange but also in practice from sharing which would leave more initiative with the receivers and which would highlight allowing access to goods and individual autonomy. In the view of most give-box initiators the establishment of a counter-domain that is not governed by market principles and utilitarian morality seems to be very marked.

More generally, it is important to note that even where there are no direct links between instances of the "sharing economy" and the rest of the "commercial econ- omy", the frame of market relations is so omnipresent that those transfers that are different will always be placed in relation to the commercial market, if only as a denial of market ideas and practices. Not surprisingly, therefore, give boxes and similar new institutions always also share some of the properties of other modes of transfer. In this particular case they share with gift giving the fact that they are again based on generosity and are initiated by the givers who often want to rid themselves of certain items. They also have a commercial dimension insofar as the items found there can be re-introduced into commercial exchange by trying to sell them but also because the items transacted through give boxes free funds for purchasing other objects or services.

When paying tax means enabling sharing

The preceding sections of this chapter have critically assessed a number of phe- nomena that use the label "sharing economy" with the overall result that there is a considerable degree to which commercial and reciprocal exchanges are misnamed as "sharing" either as a purposeful strategy of disguising dependencies or as a undeliberate case of misnaming and imprecision. However, the inverse also exists; that is to say there are contemporary phenomena that are facilitating and enabling sharing although the label is not used in these contexts. Proposals for a Basic Income Grant are a case in point to which I shall turn now.

Occasionally, sharing has been glossed as a form of taxation. Gregory Clark, for instance, talks of hunters being "taxed by the less successful" (2007: 36). Chakraborty (2007: 82) developed a formal mathematical model of sharing as tax according to which it works like a "high implicit tax rate" (of 76 percent and more) that successfully "avert[s] a 'feast and famine' pattern". Other authors, who want to reserve the notion of "tax" to state-based societies talk about "pooling" in this context (Price 1975). I have outlined in Chapter 1 that sharing was for a long time largely subsumed under reciprocity which in turn was set apart from redistribu- tion. However, as Price (1975) has pointed out early on, sharing is distinct not only from both reciprocal exchange but also from redistribution because the latter is associated with chiefs or states. However, he maintains that sharing, too, has a pooling function and therefore uses the notion of "allocation" for sharing. It is noteworthy that his definition of sharing can easily be read as a description of what happens in taxation. If sharing is the "allocation of economic goods and services without calculating returns, within a … social group, and patterned by the general role structure of that group" (Price 1975: 4) this describes perfectly well how taxation works from the perspective of those who pay. When I pay VAT on my daily shopping, or when I pay a 16-month period of my life as compulsory national service, I do that without calculating returns, I am not doing it out of choice at all but because it is "patterned" by what the "structure of the group" (i.e. the law of the state) requires me to do. I may not like it and the returns that I may or may not get out of this (e.g. protective infrastructure) are exactly the same for those who manage to avoid VAT or national service, either because they can dodge it or because it is not part of their "role" in the group. After all, companies often pay no VAT on their purchases and women, the infirm and the over 30 years old were not expected to do the national service that I was obligated to do. To express the obligation entailed in taxation, and to distinguish it from other forms of demand sharing, it may be usefully seen as a form of "mandatory sharing". It is not only obligatory but as soon as the tax is raised by a state that represents the population and that guarantees effective political participation, the obligation to give taxes is derived from a mandate to be allowed to ask for taxes.

Note, however, that in the above definition by Price the word that was bracketed out was "intimate". Price, like many others, noted that sharing becomes more difficult once it extends beyond "intimate groups" defined as groups in which the "changing identity of persons would change relationships" (1975: 4) because people know one another and have "inter-personal sentiments" for one another. I shall discuss in more detail below (see Chapter 7) that there are ways of having an "intimate" relation even in larger groups such as nations or professions. The precondition is a mutual awareness of how we need others and a sense of our own finiteness which enables sharing beyond a small group as Marten (1987) has pointed out. At this point it suffices to say that it is not easy to determine any demographic threshold which would turn the pooling of resources inevitably from sharing to obligatory taxation. As we have seen above (Chapter 3) sharing in many small-scale societies also includes those whom one may not know particularly well (or may even not particularly like very much). The conscripts who do military service in a nation state often do this with strong sentiments of being related to other members of the same troop and the same nation, whether personally known to them or not. Moreover, even in many large pooling schemes relationships are altered when the identities of persons change in critical ways, for instance if they become criminals, if they migrate or otherwise act in ways that can be interpreted as their quitting (or joining) the social group in question or as not complying with role expectations. The reason why we do not usually consider tax as a form of sharing, I argue, is not the size of the group but that typically those state agencies that collect the tax have a privileged position in the re-distribution as a third party between those who give and those who receive. The state calculates what they tax me (and others) on salaries and other social transactions and it calculates what others (and I) can hope to receive from the pool of collected taxes. The uneasiness that many people have about tax-paying is that they are unhappy about the particular calculus rather than with pooling resources in itself. There is disagreement and debate about what kind of service or good should fall under which type of tax (alcohol, cigarettes and pet dogs are often taxed differently from milk, pencils and pet hamsters) and whether or not and along which thresholds salaries should be taxed progressively and so forth. Similarly fierce disagreements surround the question as to when and to whom should the state pay social welfare, how much its personnel should be allowed to keep for themselves, and what falls into the domain of state tasks in the first place. Generally speaking, therefore, the debates are about whom and what is determining the modalities of the redistribution. What kind of abilities should make me a contributor and what kind of needs would make you a recipient.

This is the point where the suggestions for an unconditional Basic Income Grant (BIG) come in. The "unconditional" is central in this conception since everyone, it is suggested, should get the same amount that would enable a dignified life and there would not be any means-testing. This would largely eliminate the power from the state to use its payments as a reward system for particular people and for encouraging certain behaviours while discouraging others. It would also transform government payments from something that the recipients need to prove they are worthy of to something that everyone can rightfully demand from a shared pool. At the same time the BIG schemes are suggesting to eliminate the power of the state to decide which economic activities should be taxed (wage labour for instance) and which ones should not (looking after your own children or parents, for instance). Instead, the suggestion is to pool all taxation in Value Added Tax which combats tax loopholes and directly ties taxation to consumption. The link to consumption not only creates greater equality but it also connects tax to the same process to which the payment of government payments is tied – namely consumption – to the ability to feed, train and house oneself in a way that allows everyone to participate in the wider economic activities and exchanges.

BIG initiatives (see www.basicincome.org and Box 14) are very active in Europe, in Germany and Switzerland for instance, but also in Brazil and in South Africa. In these schemes income is considered a civil right that is a basic requirement for making a living. In most of these countries the majority of citizens receive their income from transfer payments rather than from their own paid labour. But both waged labourers and non-waged dependents receive their payments as dependents and as partners of an asymmetrical relationship with other family members, pension funds or the state. Those who receive welfare and pension payments, as mentioned above, depend on a positive evaluation by the state or their pension fund or, alternatively, they depend on waged relatives. Those who receive a wage, increasingly in times of rationalization, are in a weak position because their life increasingly depends on having secured employment from a dwindling number of job opportunities. There are very few, if any, opportunities for autonomous self-sufficiency and autarky anywhere. The employer depends less and less on human labourers, since there are increasing opportunities of replacing humans with machines. The main positive effect that the BIG schemes seek, is to strengthen the position of the individual and their power to decide as to how they use, pool and improve their guaranteed basic income. This social project of enhancing individual autonomy without (illusionary) self-sufficiency places BIG close to sharing practices that cultivate a similar combination of personal autonomy, the notion of a rightful share and an underlying basic reliance of people on one another.

BOX 14 GRANTING A BASIC INCOME

While the Basic Income Grant (BIG) initiatives are discussed worldwide, a BIG campaign in Namibia succeeded in running BIG as a test case in Otjivero (eastern Namibia) since 2007. BIG is a non-means tested basic "salary" that is paid out for every member of the village, independent of age or other income. Namibia, like many other countries, has a high Gini-coefficient that measures the discrepancy between highest and lowest incomes with about half of the population living below or close to the minimum income and, unlike in welfare states elsewhere, with insufficient means to administer the neediness of the population. The non-means tested BIG therefore promised a practical way of providing every resident of Otjivero (around 900 individuals when the project began) with a minimum monthly income of (initially) 100 Namibia Dollars, enough to subsist on basic rations of maize meal, tea and sugar. Beyond the practicalities of administering the BIG, the debates and ideological rifts that accompanied the Namibian project were parallel to the discussions elsewhere (in Switzerland: http://www.grundeinkommen.ch, Germany: /www.grundeinkommen.de, and worldwide: http://www.basicincome.org/basic-income/) and indeed intertwined with it since supporters, above all church groups and critics in the media and government, had built up coalitions that involved global, national and local players. In Otjivero the initiative was welcomed by the majority of the population. A first assessment (Haarmann 2009, Klocke-Daffa 2012) shows that BIG had considerable effects – some anticipated, others not. The living conditions in Otjivero improved through BIG insofar as there were less malnourished children, lower school drop-out rates and residents were in better health (Klocke-Daffa 2012: 6). However, some of the other anticipated results were not realized. Residents used the extra cash income not as start-up capital for their own businesses or as a way of building up personal savings and living without debts. When comparing the expenditure of Otjivero residents with those of nearby Witvlei (who had not received the BIG), Klocke-Daffa found that the pattern of spending was not much changed structurally, even though the volume had increased. In both villages most income transfers consisted of gifts, especially gifts of food, and mutual indebtedness continued. The BIG was integrated into the local system of norms and practices. Local Christianity emphasizes that everything people have is a gift of God and this conviction supports giving as a general practice. Local exchange patterns work in a way that lending and giving are seen as important ways of participating in a social network that provides security. The BIG was appropriated by the Otjivero residents as a means to participate more fully in this exchange system and to increase their basic general welfare. However, it was not employed by beneficiaries in order to reduce the need to ask their kin and neighbours for support, nor did it boost economic growth as it is generally measured in national economies.

Despite the largely positive evaluation of this pilot project there is currently little prospect for the BIG to be implemented at a national scale. The tendency to link access to labour, production and growth is very strong both among the political left and the political right with a strong subcurrent of meritocratic assumptions built into the dominant worldviews. At the same time there are indications that there might be a piecemeal realization of the BIG objectives in that an ever-growing number of groups in the population are considered eligible for non-contributory and non-means tested grants which turns receiving grants into a normal and non-transitory state of affairs for a large part of the population.

It is intriguing that the BIG initiatives can become strong under very different conditions. In countries of the North it is strong, among other things, because other modes of providing for oneself, through using wild or self-domesticated food for instance, are increasingly out of reach due to demographic and bureaucratic conditions. In some countries of the global South BIG initiatives are strong because it has become clear that a minimum support is necessary for people to become economically active in the process of social and economic transformations. Even development aid that is earmarked for the poorest is typically only within reach of those who have a sufficient basis, in terms of schooling, transport and so forth, that allows them to make claims effectively and use the funding and the projects that are meant for them.

There are differences as well as continuities across these cases. The pilot project in Namibia (Box 14) which has been investigated anthropologically, has shown that there is a clear effect of poverty reduction. It has also shown that people indeed use the basic income for more equitable participation but that the way in which they do it very much depends on the social and cultural conditions in place. While the expectation for European countries is that individuals will want to use the basic income strategically to become economically more independent from employees, the Namibian participants in the pilot study invested their basic income into strengthening their exchange network with neighbours and relatives (see Klocke-Daffa 2012). In both the North and the South, BIG initiatives are only strong in those places that do have a state in place that is reliable in the sense that citizens have enforceable rights. Again, this is similar to situations in small societies dominated by sharing because the "rightful share" under all of these conditions is above all that of a share that everyone can enforce and that can be enforced on everyone. We could argue that the basic income grant is the continuation of sharing by means of the state. Or to put it differently again, if there is the potential of a "sharing economy" to re-emerge at the scope of large-scale societies it is in schemes like the Basic Income Grant rather than in the various self-acclaimed notions of the "sharing economy" that I have covered at the beginning of this chapter.

Despite these open questions, does the BIG proposal illustrate how innovations in complex state societies can receive inspiration and guidance from the anthropology of sharing in small-scale societies? Unlike previous paternalistic gifts in kind (e.g. food-for-work programmes) the BIG and related payments operate with a notion of entitlement that we also find in sharing among hunter-gatherers. When labour can no longer be considered the only way to participate in the wider national or global good, new modes of distribution and entitlements have to be discussed (see Ferguson 2015: 15-17). Social grants schemes developed in many southern African countries today are non-contributory, that is to say they are given out without calculating prior contributions which makes them, again, more similar to sharing and less similar to common insurance systems. Further similarities are the fact that the shares that are provided have an enabling effect, rendering people active while at the same time preserving the autonomy of the recipient as no moralizing preconditions are attached. It is taken for granted that recipients are not only entitled to a share in times of extraordinary crisis but rather as part of the normal state of affairs. All these properties link BIG and other social grants to sharing and separate both of them from previous modes of welfare payments or development aid. Moreover, when trying to suggest the future development of these social grants Ferguson suggests that we keep looking at what has made sharing in small-scale societies particularly successful. Many social grant schemes, in Africa as much as in the global North, face the problem of defining eligibility for services. There is a tendency to exclude migrants and occasionally this leads to xenophobic reactions against those who are not recognized members of the circle of beneficiaries which is typically drawn along national or even ethnic lines (Ferguson 2015: 212). Many redistributive systems that pool resources have to spend considerable effort on establishing who belongs to the group of beneficiaries. This is particularly striking in cases in which indigenous people have sought to realize their claims as legal claims against nation states or mining corporations. The lead that one can take from the anthropology of sharing is that presence is the basis of the right for a share and not membership in a fixed community. In other words, the rightful share can be claimed not as a citizen of a nation but as a denizen, an occupant of a place, a permanent resident (Ferguson 2015: 213). What is at stake here is nothing less than a new figuration of "the social" as something which is not defined by a social contract or by the integrative power of authoritative structures. The community of practice that is created through sharing is neither held together by strategic association of free agents nor by authoritarian verdict over unfree subjects but by "performed presence" between people who share their lives. The next chapter will spell out in more detail some analogies between sharing in face-to-face situations and conditions that involve social relations at a larger scale.

When "sharing" is just a button

The case of the Basic Income Grant may be mandated sharing at the click of a button. The social welfare payments work well in states that have the necessary technical infrastructure for automated distribution and identity recognition. As Ferguson (2013: 235) noted, many Africans consider these welfare payments as "cold" since they lack the relational qualities that even relations of dependency often have. This corresponds with the critique that is occasionally raised against the Basic Income Grant as a panacea, namely that it cannot compensate for the loss of employment opportunities. It is useful to be specific here as to what exactly is being shared in a Basic Income Grant. What is shared is income, in particular revenue that is generated at a large scale, for instance a state, through a complex division of labour and through tax collection. What is not shared are the many other things that people associate with work beyond its income-generating function, e.g. the opportunity to participate in a larger enterprise, to be productive and creative, to be tied into structurated social life, to receive recognition and so forth. Advocates of the Basic Income Grant argue precisely along these lines of decoupling work from the many other aspects that it has received as labour in a complex division of labour, above all being the main source of revenue for the state in terms of income tax.

The more general lesson to be learned is that in a complex economy, sharing practices (like gift exchange before) get overburdened with expectations of social improvement as if it was replacing all commercial exchanges that are going on. When sharing complements market transactions that continue alongside and when it is embedded and framed by market conditions, it often requires some careful unpacking as to which practice has what kind of effects. Take the *AirBnB* phenomenon already mentioned. As I have suggested, it should be considered above all as renting and a commercial transaction. If it is perceived as sharing, I suggest, it is because those who rent out their own flat and the visitors who rent it, share the extra money that they have "saved" by not having used the regular market of hotel accommodation and by not renting things out professionally respectively. Implicated in the transaction are other transfers, some realized and some prevented. For instance, by practising *AirBnB*, tenants who sublet flats may fuel a gentrification process because flats that are occupied by visitors paying a high price are no longer available on the market for local residents who need a reasonably priced place to live. A similar argument can be made with regard to many phenomena of the "sharing economy". The point is that sharing, if at all, is only realized between some participants in a connected economy in which everyone is tied together in numerous transfers. It would be wrong to attribute to the sharing element what is due to the market effects into which it is embedded. One and the same object (e.g. a flat) features in several parallel transfer arenas, some of which are in the background. This is not a new phenomenon. As mentioned before, the rise of many modern industries and markets is typically made possible by the non-market transfers into which they are embedded. Small shop owners and many waged labourers would not be able to engage in marketing their products and workforce if they were not embedded in social networks of non-commercial support, usually through family members. The larger part of the debates surrounding the "sharing economy" concerns the articulation of modes of transfer with regard to one another. As John (2012: 177) pointed out, the notion of sharing has developed considerable "rhetorical power" over the last decade with regard to the "Web 2.0" industry where it "serves to paper over the commercial aspects" of social network sites. In other words the notion of sharing has been instrumentalized by sites like *Facebook* in what he calls "mechanisms of mystification" (John 2012: 178). When "sharing" is considered "disruptive" to the existing economy, or when sharing practices are said to be "co-opted" back into the market with its own rules of commodity exchanges (Cammaerts 2011: 4), we are always dealing with complex effects that cannot be explained with regard to only one of the modes of transfer that are involved. The best-known case of such complex embedding is the case of software development. What began as sharing between a very small circle of information technology scientists quickly turned into commercial software engineering which repeatedly got disrupted by an active community of "hackers" who in turn are partially co-opted into the market economy and partially operate in explicit opposition to it. In the course of these transformations bits of code are shared, others are sold and, as Zeitlyn has shown, a considerable part of the open source software development has characteristics of a gift economy that allows individuals to give for free what allows them to accumulate reputation and where "each software project is a kin group" with comparable exchanges and hierarchies (Zeitlyn 2003: 1290, see also Wasko et al. 2005 and Zhu et al. 2012). The common pattern of innovations in the software market seems to start with some degree of sharing (for some time or some basic functions) to stimulate the use and further development by practitioners and ultimately to generate a market with commercial business opportunities with various types of exchanges going on in sequence as well as in parallel (see Cammaerts 2011). The open software movement *ubuntu* (also known as *Linux ubuntu*) exemplifies this entanglement. The operating system *ubuntu* is the most widely used distribution of *Linux* which in itself consists of a freeware kernel linked to commercial software packages, in other words a hybrid between things shared and things exchanged and sold. *Ubuntu* derives its name from a key concept in African philosophy that is occasionally translated as humanity or as "I am because you are" (Lief 2015, see also Chapter 7). In other words, *ubuntu* connects to an African idea and practice of "sharing in", of creating a communal basis for mutual help, while, at the same time, as a software tool it originates in the initiative of a South African multimillionaire and a foundation that distributes and to some extent commercializes the product. Since version 12.2 (in 2012) *ubuntu* captures search data from users that is sold to the internet retailer *Amazon*, a feature which has caused protests within the free software movement and is said to be disabled again in version 16.04 (in 2016). Hence the *ubuntu* operating system exemplifies shifts between sharing and exchanging/trading within a single product and within the community that has formed around this product.[8]

Other cases of what is sometimes called "the dark side of sharing" are also examples of this effect whereby individuals, and individual acts of allocation and transfer, are often (and probably increasingly) part and parcel of a number of relationships. Students at the University of Cologne and a number of neighbouring universities have attracted some attention in this respect. After the Cologne municipal public transport service granted regular customers the option of taking along a second person (in 2008) students started a *"Bahntrampen"* (hitch a tram ride) campaign. This is because students across the state were granted a rail ticket with the option of taking along another person as part of their package of being enrolled in state-owned universities. In the hitch-a-tram-ride campaign ticket-holders would use buttons to signal to strangers that they could hitch a free ride with them on the tram which raised the objection of the transport companies who felt that they were losing money.[7] In one celebrated case an estranged customer decided to take revenge on the transport company by taking along as many co-travellers as he possibly could. Similarly, left-wing activists started a (failed) attempt to bankrupt an opposing political party by donating micro-amounts that would incur high costs of receiving such donations through online payment services such as *Paypal* that incur a fee for each transaction. The point is that what appears to be "harm" caused by sharing is in fact a coupling of two (or more) transfers that go on at the same time, sharing (with fellow travellers, with the receiving party) that is framed by commercial transactions (between customers and transport company in the one case and between *Paypal* and the political party in the other case). An inverse form of coupling occurs, I would argue, when the collection of Value Added Tax is framed by sharing transactions as in the case of the Basic Income Grant.

Probably the most common case of such a coupling is the "share" button on new social media. Despite the name, pressing the "share" button can trigger a number of transfers at the same time, some of them sharing, others not. This phenomenon is not restricted to sharing. Think of "free gifts" for which people sign up, not being aware that they have also (and primarily) signed up for a commercial subscription for a journal or whatever the case may be – a gift exchange at the surface with a commercial transaction hidden. Think also of the "symbolic Dollar/ Euro" that is given in the transaction of buildings or other entities that have "negative value" in that they require enormous renovation or investment costs – an apparently commercial transfer which may be a hidden "gift" of a rich sponsor. I suggest that pressing the "share" button is a similar process, except that may be more frequent nowadays than many of the other examples and in that sharing on the internet has more potential for "hiding" transaction costs, as we shall see in the next chapter. Like the "gift" that may turn out to be poison, sharing wrong information through the social media can be a case of deception. I may be deceived (or deceive myself) in thinking that what is transferred is anything of value whereas it is in fact either useless or even harmful. In that case it would not count as sharing in the sense of "getting access to what is *valued*". Moreover, typically, pressing the "share" button is offering information that was not demanded, it is unsolicited giving, unless we are prepared to consider signing up to a social media service as a flat-rate demand for receiving any information whether useful and truthful or not. More generally, the sharing of information in these contexts is embedded in a host of other transfers with their respective motivations and implications. Handing on untrue or compromising information may appear to be an act of sharing between person A and person B while it is in effect structured by other modes of transfer, for instance stealing reputation from person C, accumulating prestige for person A, creating dependency for person B and many other possibilities. Moreover, offering a "share" button (or any other device to express likes) is a demand that may turn out to be like the "humbugging" in Aboriginal Australia (see Chapter 5). There is a demand to share which may be unwarranted because the contents are not worth sharing. As with any other demand, the skill of sharing is to recognize demands that are out of proportion or otherwise inappropriate. In this sense, sharing on the internet, often praised to be the driving force behind the "sharing economy" at large has not only become simpler, it has also become more difficult and intricate, as we shall see in the following chapter.

Conclusion

Comparing sharing across diverse cultural settings suggests that much of what goes under the notion of "sharing economy" is in fact an extension of the market economy into spheres of life that were previously exempted from the market. What has been summarized in this chapter for car sharing and cheap private cabs could be spelled out in parallel with regard to couch surfing schemes and other domains. In all these cases the driving forces are the economic pressures to make an extra income, especially in urbanized globalized places such as London and Berlin, from assets that were previously not capitalized. "Exchange" schemes in which members offer odd handicraft services, taking the dog out or looking after plants, are also services which were previously covered under non-monetized assistance among neighbours. The driving force here is often an attempt to create a parallel access to services that are decoupled from the vagaries of markets and cash incomes. Money may or may not be involved, but similar accountancy thinking that goes with money is involved (see Graeber 2011). Despite the discourse of "sharing" that sometimes accompanies it, we are actually dealing with a situation in which people try to have more, either more by paying less or by getting out more from their property – or more out of a skill they have. In some cases they may be trying to not have less, not to make any losses, when high rates force them to seek sources of income that they cannot provide with their labour. While it is useful to de-mystify much of the pseudo-anticapitalist rhetoric that goes with these schemes in the "sharing economy" it is important not to miss a key point: If this is indeed a capitalization of reservoirs that were previously exempted from capitalist and market thinking, it is noteworthy that it is couched in a rhetoric of sharing. There seems to be some very basic uneasiness with schemes that are "purely" utilitarian.

The situations of hunter-gatherers and urban dwellers in the globalized metropoles of today are different, no doubt. However, as the case of the Basic Income Grant suggests, there are also similarities. The motivation to maintain personal autonomy and relatedness without submission to a centralized authority, without bilateral quasi-contractual obligations or a forced collective is shared in both hunter-gatherer groups and among supporters of a Basic Income Grant. Moreover, there are striking similarities in the social implications of sharing in small-scale societies and in Basic Income Grants provided by institutions like the state. The remainder of this book seeks to spell out these differences and similarities in more detail. It revisits the main themes that I have outlined so far on the background of ethnographic work in small-scale societies but attempts to put these themes into a systematic comparative perspective of contemporary society.

Notes

1 According to its proponents, the sharing economy comprises all of the following: "swapping, exchanging, collective purchasing, collaborative consumption, shared ownership, shared value, co-operatives, co-creation, recycling, upcycling, re-distribution, trading used goods, renting, borrowing, lending, subscription-based models, peer-to-peer, collaborative economy, circular economy, pay-as-you-use economy, wikinomics, peer-to-peer lending, micro-financing, micro-entrepreneurship, social media, the Mesh, social enterprise, futurology, crowdfunding, crowdsourcing, cradle-to-cradle, open source, open data, user generated content" (www.thepeoplewhoshare.com).

2 For a balanced account of this debate see Juliet Schor's essay on http://www.greattransition. org/publication/debating-the-sharing-economy and her discussion of shared consumption (Schor 2010).

3 Some authors also speak of the "ideological forms of hijacking of this word" (see Wittel 2011: 8).

4 As I finalize the research for this chapter (early 2016) the *UBER* company is once again in the news since it is said to have driven the largest taxi company in the San Francisco area (*Yellow Cab*) into bancrupcy. The 350 drivers of *Yellow Cab* reportedly face 16,000 registered *UBER* drivers (see www.sfexaminer.com/yellow-cab-to-file-for-bankruptcy, accessed 7.1.16).

5 http://www.nytimes.com/2014/12/08/opinion/we-cant-trust-uber.html (accessed 7.1.2014). Tufekci and King, the authors of the piece "We can't trust Uber", give further examples of how big data accumulated by facebook and similar services allow to lay open and predict typical behaviour and preferences of users.

6 Consequently, there is a considerable literature today on file-sharing, in particular with regard to the music industry. It is noteworthy that many contributions deal with the legal and moral issues of the matter (see for instance LaRose *et al* 2006; contributions in Stalder and Sützl 2011), sometimes using sharing and piracy interchangably but underlining that this "culture of piracy" varies across time and space (Condry 2004). Dawdy and Bonni (2012: 695) found that the new forms of internet and file-sharing piracy attracted similar fantasies, ranging from greed to a sharing ethos, that had already been projected onto pirates in the past.

7 These events are covered in the local and regional press (see www.derwesten.de/politik/campus-karriere/bahntramper-veraergern-die-verkehrsbetriebe-id7963.html) including the case of "customer revenge" (www.zeit.de/1996/27/Alles_ist_voellig_legal) and of damaging the political opponents by donating small amounts of money to them (www.n-tv.de/politik/Mini-Spenden-sollen-die-AfD-ruinieren-article16550941.html.).

8 For a summary of the debate about *ubuntu* as spyware see: http://www.omgubuntu. co.uk/2016/01/ubuntu-online-search-feature-disabled-16-04 The career of the notion of *ubuntu* from an everyday concept in southern African Bantu languages to a pivotal figurehead of African communalism is captured, for instance, in interviews with Nelson Mandela portrayed as the "personification of *Ubuntu*" (in https://www.youtube.com/watch?v=HED4h00xPPA) and with Desmond Tutu (see https://www.youtube.com/watch?v=0wZtfqZ271w). Their interpretations of the term covers a wide range of translations including "respect, trust, helpfulness, sharing, caring, community, unselfishness" (Mandela) and is best summarized in the realization that "you cannot be human on your own" (Tutu). [All webpages accessed 7.6.2016.]

7

THE TIME TO SHARE

Introduction

Considerable preconditions have to be in place before sharing can be successfully practised in face-to-face situations. One of these conditions entails that the situation is transformed so that it is in fact no longer of a face-to-face kind in the narrow sense. To prevent either the act of giving or that of receiving as a "face-threatening act" (see Brown and Levinson 1987), the two actions are often decoupled and transformed. The gift-giving sequence is inverted since the transfer is initiated by the recipient and "handing over" typically gives way to "allowing to take" so that the transaction does not affect the "face" of the people involved in the way that gift-giving does. It should not lead to the donor gaining face or the recipient losing face. The main modalities involved in the sharing transfers have been discussed in the first chapters of this book.

When sharing is to be successfully transposed into complex settings of corporate agents (see Chapter 5) or to national and transnational settings (see Chapter 6) further preconditions have to be met. Much of the so-called sharing economy has only become possible through the use of computers linked in a network creating new forms of practical but fragmented presence. But what are occasionally praised as unprecedented opportunities for exchange also create unprecedented problems. Maintaining sharing relations is being challenged as the new technology can also amplify accumulation and can destroy the level playing field that characterizes sharing in small-scale societies. As I will discuss in this chapter even the "personal" computer in front of me is a site of many uneven social exchanges, of alleged and aborted sharing, beyond direct file sharing (see Box 15). The analogies between patterns in the sharing practices of small-scale societies and in the newly emerging distributive systems at larger scales of complexity throw a sharp light on the problems of accumulation in digital environments. It is not that sharing practices of the past are inevitably ill-suited for the situations of present-day digital networks. As I shall show in this chapter, some critical reflection is in order when we seek to develop new sharing regimes. There is more to it than an individual right to a share – above all, the ways of establishing the right time to share and the right time to keep. Unlike with gift giving where subjects are sometimes said to share substance with one another through their exchanges, sharing ties people together who limit one another by realizing that they are not everyone, not owning everything and forever. Sharing is conditioned by the experience of living a finite life, limited by others who are in turn limited by me and by the fact that what is gained is also lost in the end.

Oversharing – sharing all over?

Much popular discourse assumes that sharing is good because it is imagined to follow rules of altruistic generosity. And much scholarly discourse assumes it is good because it is thought to follow the necessities of food security. As we have seen in the preceding chapters, both may appreciate sharing for the wrong reasons. However, there are also negative evaluations of sharing, out of other but equally wrong reasons. The most recent manifestation of this view can be found in the notion of "oversharing" (Agger 2012). "Oversharing" is not a word that most speakers of English would know, at least not those who have left their youth behind them. The reason why it has been elected word of the year by the editors of Webster's Dictionary in 2008 and by Chambers Dictionary in 2014 is due to a widespread phenomenon in the social media. By "oversharing" we mean voluntarily providing more information about one's person on the internet, more than one would disclose in a face-to-face relationship, often with detrimental effects for the person who "overshares". Although the popularization of the notion of "oversharing" is not part of the sharing economy discourse, it may also not be coincidental that the two are co-emerging at the same point in time. Many of the phenomena that were discussed in the previous chapter under the heading "sharing economy" have become amplified through the emergence of computers that are connected in a network, above all the internet.

Price suggested as early as 1975 that the emergence of the "personal computer" may allow sharing systems to grow beyond the band-size group in which humans are able to remember and handle face-to-face interaction (1975: 7): "[a] much more intelligent computer brain can in certain ways be sensitive to the individual differences (and in this sense can be 'personal') of a much larger number of people", he suggests, and "[c]omputer dating services, like intimate sharing systems, help us to integrate people in terms of abilities and needs, but the similarity seems only analogical." It is interesting that Price names dating services because the notion of "oversharing" extends in a similar direction. When young people share personal information and photos through electronic media, this constitutes a prototypical case of "oversharing". Concerned parents and sociologists tend to consider it to be part of pathological personality disorders and as a problem (see Agger 2012). While sharing means "splitting your dessert", they contend, oversharing means "spilling your guts" (Agger 2012: 3). While the first is considered virtuous, the second is considered a vice. The underlying "bourgeois" assumption is that sharing should be limited to intimate family and friends but should not go beyond. Sharing within the family, it could be argued, has been an essential element of rising capitalism. For the elites, think of rich families owning property, pooling resources was essential for creating powerful corporations. For the "superexploitation" of the poor, in the industrializing North as much as in the mines and plantations of Africa, being able to lay off the costs of social reproduction, caring for the children and the old, onto family bonds were also key (see Ferguson 2015). Thus sharing is okay with "significant others", while oversharing typically involves posting to a large and non-intimate group of others. The problem that "oversharing" suggests is not simply that too much information is shared but rather that it is shared with too many people and with too many beyond the circle of where it belongs.

This sharing of personal information is not provoked by scarcity, at least not on the side of the oversharers.[1] There is a parallel here in a sense between give box and internet postings, the first consisting of superfluous objects the giver wants to give away (see Chapter 6), the second consisting of comments and sentiments that the person posting on the net wants others to have. However, while gift boxes are considered morally acceptable, oversharing typically is not, even though the exact boundary between being active on the internet and oversharing is subject to debate. The notion that there can be "too much sharing" is, however, not new and it is not limited to phenomena related to the internet. The editors of Webster's Dictionary are quoted as saying that oversharing is "a new word for an old habit" because the practice underlying digital oversharing existed before. At a very general level Brown and Levinson's politeness theory provides many cross-cultural examples for oversharing if it is understood along the lines of violations of the Gricean universal conversational maxim of "don't say more than necessary" (see Brown and Levinson 1987). More concretely, oversharing existed in a number of ways prior to the internet, for instance at dinner parties and similar events. What made it word of the year, repeatedly, is that in a digitally connected environment any instance of people disclosing more of their life than is good for them now has the potential of being amplified in unprecedented ways. A single tweet or a *Facebook* posting can create a "shit storm" ruining personal lives in a keystroke. While the technological impact may be almost universal now, the question remains as to how universal the underlying notion of sharing is from which this notion of oversharing was derived. "Oversharing", in particular in the US, seems to go back to a Puritan practice of declaring your sins and failings in front of a community. In the analogue days this would typically take place within the confines of a church or community congregation as they were widespread across US-American history. Here you were supposed to share your personal failings and confront the judgements and forgiveness of your fellow church members. Arguably, the notion of "oversharing" is less widely spread in Europe where the default expectation for a long time has been that failings are to be judged by a royal, a noble or clerical power elite and are not self-declared.[2]

BOX 15 SHAREWARE: SHARE – WHERE?

The box in front of me is full of gifts that I did not ask for and that are hard to get rid of. The software of the first computer I had, consisted of files that I could see, that I could copy and delete as I wished. There were a few invisible files but there were ways of making them seen. It was easy to share programs because all one needed was a floppy disk onto which they could be manually copied and then carried to another computer onto which they were copied again one by one. This is also the way that the first word processing programs worked. Software had to be bought once but then got copied, while now software may be initially free or cheap but forces users into a subscription and everlasting dependency. When I install a program today, whether bought or not, it places little packages of software in various parts of the machine in ways that I have not asked for, that are beyond my control but that leave binding obligations. I am constantly asked to download and install updates and if I do not take these extra gifts (they are "for free") my computer may not work properly anymore, often I am left with no chance to say "no" once I have ticked a box.

Within the environment of many programs, too, I automatically get services that I have not asked for and that are cumbersome to switch off, various types of autocorrecting for instance. Then there are email attachments which promise gifts but bring viruses, dependency and destruction. To combat those programs I have to install an anti-virus protection program which, again, needs regular updates on which I am made dependent. Even for small programs, referencing tools for instance, I enter long-term dependency relations because having invested through data input make it hard to leave and go elsewhere. If it is so-called shareware or freeware, things often get worse. Shareware is only free for a limited time period, after that life is made difficult because I am asked to register and engage in a costly personal contract. The demands for entering such a contract can become so irritating that the only way out may be to de-install the program. Freeware often consists of very small programs with very limited functionality but with a tacit insatiable hunger for a counter-gift that is completely out of proportion with what I received in the first place. The "free torch app" for a smartphone demands access to all parts of my phone, including the personal data in my address book and my log book, information about my whereabouts and many things that are taken from me without me realizing it. The boundary between freeware and malware has become blurred. A small program for recording films from the internet is advertised as free but when I download it I also have to accept the extra search tool and explorer toolbar that comes with it. Once I have those, they prove to be difficult or impossible to de-install. Sometimes only specialized counter-software or a complete re-formatting of the hard disk drive can wipe out the "free" program. It constantly collects valuable data in the background as it traces and records my steps through the internet. It takes me to sites that I neither have asked to visit nor want to visit and it prevents me from going elsewhere.

I also inadvertently share information as soon as I call up a webpage. Providers and the software companies employ automated data grabbers and like most users I tolerate their thefts. They sell the information that they got from me for free to online dealers who in turn seek to sell their products to me. There is no easy way to evade any of this because I am not dealing with other human beings who have a limited memory and reaction time as I have. The machinery at the other end uses algorithms that I do not have at my disposal. For them it is little effort to get in contact with me whereas considerable effort is needed on my part to escape auto-completions, the placement of cookies and advertisements. It is not a level playing field. I do not know where my data is or who has opportunity to look at it but the internet sites know where my computer is. They may deny me access because I live in a country in which some videos cannot be shown or some services are not available. They may also increase the price for a product because they remember that I have shown interest in it before. The air of generosity lures me into obligations and dependencies. The open source movement has been very productive in that it allows many individuals to work cumulatively on one software solution. These software tools form part of a larger creative commons repository that I can access with my computer. In other words, there are things that can indeed be taken for free, if they are licensed for it by their creators, but in practice it is not the rule that this exchange is unconditional or non-contributory.

These instances of "oversharing" are therefore part of a more general theme of "overdoing" things that stretches beyond the transfer of goods. Welcoming guests may be considered a duty or of positive value in bourgeois society (or indeed in many other societies). But having them stay as an integral part of the family (a boarder) is often considered "overdoing" it since this may erode family boundaries. As a social practice this is typically attributed to proletarian households and a horrifying idea in many house-based societies. Visitors may be welcome as visitors (or accepted as temporary labourers or refugees) as long as this does not blur the boundaries between non-members and legitimate members in a nation. This is a common position in complex societies today while many foraging societies keep the boundary between visiting and joining a group much more flexible. Many comments on "oversharing" exhibit exactly this difficulty of establishing the right amount of sharing. Agger (2012), for instance, suggests that using social media to extend one's social network is useful, acceptable and desirable, but exposing yourself naked (physically or metaphorically) or half-naked (or drunk etc.) should be considered "oversharing".

For many ethnographers who are working with hunter-gatherers under conditions of change, the negative view on sharing as "oversharing" does not come as a surprise.

European employers and self-declared "developers" of indigenous hunter-gatherers have often looked upon sharing as a vice, and often continue to do so (see Macdonald 2000, Peterson 2013). They complain that sharing prevents accumulation and economizing. Labourers, they argue, are frustrated in their upward mobility because their surplus is divided by a large number of dependents. Pensioners and others who receive a social grant cannot budget with their monthly payments because the money is spent rapidly through their large social network once it has been paid out. As mentioned in Chapter 3, Altman (2011) has traced the career of the notion of "demand sharing" that was readily adopted by politicians (including some of Aboriginal descent) who identified it as a major impediment for modernization and improvement, leading to corruption and exploitation instead.[3] Narrowing down all kin-based transfers to specific forms of demand sharing which are again narrowed down to the "humbugging" of extreme demand sharing has led to a bureaucratic justification of the Intervention (of state force into Aboriginal settlements) and to a technocratic solution to the problem, namely prescribed "income quarantining" in which half of the welfare income is reserved for basic food purchases (Altman 2011: 196). This strategy against sharing as a "cultural failure" is depicted as a technical solution[4] for those who in principle are given enough income to live a life according to the minimal standards set by "developers" but who continue to be classified as vulnerable since their income is drained by kin obligations. There is a parallel here insofar as "oversharing" internet users are also said to make themselves vulnerable through their act of giving, vulnerable to exploitation, mobbing or whatever. However, they become vulnerable vis-à-vis those who can accumulate and use the information they provide. In other words here sharing does not operate as a levelling device that (re)creates symmetry but in effect new asymmetry is generated since internet oversharing grants an advantage to others, not only peers who want to gossip but also companies with an interest in consumption behaviour or authoritarian regimes who seek to control their subjects by spying on them.[5]

Thus, in the colonial and post-colonial period there are many accounts of Europeans who disapprove of the foragers' sharing behaviour. It is often considered "wasting" or being an indicator of insufficient planning and foresight. Instead of saving up for lean times, things are shared out among a large group of people including visitors and distant relatives. Some African farmers who employ San consider sharing as one of the main obstacles of their San employees breaking out of poverty. Up until today farmers and many expatriates working for development NGOs maintain a strong sense of an economy and society based on merits and performance. In their view, self-sufficiency and resilience against crises requires accumulation at the level of the individual worker and their core family or an otherwise clearly demarcated social unit. The social pressure to share is recognized as a threat and some employers, for instance, have started putting some of the salaries into bank accounts, instead of paying them out in cash, in order to allow employees to save up so that they can buy a bicycle, goats or any other item that requires accumulating money over several months. Experimental economists have recently started to carry out "sharing games" cross-culturally and they tend to present their research as a contribution that provides tools for those who face the "problem" of not being able to sufficiently accumulate due to an overwhelming social levelling mechanism. As Bob Layton noted, economists identify this "problem" not only for foragers but also for peasant societies in which entrepreneurs had difficulties accumulating because it would mean "sticking their heads out" (Layton personal communication). Sharing and pooling resources in this perspective is a problem, a deficit, and Western economics provides the seemingly neutral, culture-free tools for exhibiting this deficit and for taking action against it. Sharing, in such economic scenarios, is considered proper if it is either an investment (creating links of trust for future interaction) or if it is reciprocal (turning it into a balanced, commercial-like transfer). Importantly, it should not interfere with what is considered to be a necessary level of storage and accumulation. For the African farmer of European origin, in fact for most African farmers, and for the expatriate development worker, too, the sharing of foragers is *always* "oversharing" as soon as it leaves the confines of the core family because it is in conflict with accumulation and storage for bad times. Conversely, from the perspective of modern foragers, most wage earners and most of their bosses are *always* "undersharing" if they live beyond what they immediately need for themselves but refuse to share what is "extra" with those around them who have not reached that level of minimal provision.

The positions are culturally entrenched and seem to be irreconcilable. It is noteworthy that in all these debates around "oversharing" the focus has been on the amounts, the quantities of what is being shared. However, it may be more productive to think about the temporal dimension. Estimations of what is "too much" (see Robertson 2001) differ greatly since they are very much context dependent. We may therefore look more closely at the diversity of cases in terms of the temporal dimension, the "too early" or "too late" or simply "not the right time" for sharing.

Premature giving

If sharing is typically initiated by those who implicitly or explicitly make demands on something, that does not mean that all demands are being met. The recognition that some demands are out of proportion is also found among foragers, who tend to make fun of those who too readily respond to demands (Peterson 1993, 2013), including visiting anthropologists. One could argue that there are two types of prematurity: premature demanding and premature giving. Independently of what exactly is being shared, a demand may come far too early, for instance when the demander still has its own resources to use, or it may be complied with too readily. Offering too much and too early (i.e. before it is legitimately asked) can also be seen as an attempt to make others dependent. Putting off sharing demands is a legitimate response in such instances. We could also include the numerous ethnographic reports here which report the ways in which people (including foragers) try *not* to share. They hide valuable objects, they eat things before coming back to camp and so forth. Myers (1988: 59) depicts a case of (attempted but failed) hiding of meat from visiting neighbours as "polite rejection" of a demand.[6] The strategy that I have come across several times in the field in northern Namibia is that some ≠Akhoe Hai//om may carry two bags of tobacco with them, one with very little in it which they show to anyone who asks for a share and a full one that they keep out of sight. This seems reminiscent of the advice given to visitors of crime-torn US cities, namely to always have two purses of money on them, one to readily give away when being robbed and the more important second one that is kept separately. The similarity is not that far-fetched if sharing is considered "tolerated scrounging" or even "tolerated theft" (Blurton-Jones 1997, see Chapter 2). The difference is that when deflecting sharing there are often other options available while the robbing is a case of enforced presence that is hard to evade without loss of life or suffering violence. Consequently, the sharer who hides, as Myers reports, is found out "without any rancour" (1988: 59) and without any damage done to the friendship. More importantly, the tobacco owner often does eventually share with others, preferably at his or her own pace, which is very unlikely to happen in the case of robbery. Hiding is therefore more precisely an expression of the tension of keeping the personal autonomy to exercise a choice while enjoying the relatedness with others who may have legitimate demands, a tension that has a temporal dynamic.

As I have pointed out above, whether an act of sharing succeeds or not does depend on how things get pushed by those demanding the share and by those who respond – and not necessarily or primarily on a sense of duty or charity that is exhibited by the giver. Explicit charity or even the inner attitude of obligation is replaced by the practical skill of knowing what and when to demand and how to respond. If sharing is usefully considered a skill (Widlok 2004) then the core of that skill is to know when to pose a demand that is successful and to know when it is appropriate to comply with a demand and when it is not. As Ichikawa (2005: 155) writes about the Mbuti: "[n]ot everyone in the camp has equal access to the meat [...].While some people demand a share more easily, others find it difficult and may leave the place. [...] They may also get a portion afterwards from those who have received a share." Timing is a major part of a fully developed sharing skill. Not, or no longer, being able to handle timing is an instance of de-skilling.

How does this compare to current issues of sharing and "oversharing"? As long as we see sharing primarily as offering, then oversharing is tantamount to offering too much, and the problem is one laid down at the doorstep of those giving, e.g. young people posting on the web. However, if sharing is reacting to the demands of others, then cases of apparent "oversharing" may be reconceived of as demanding too much, more precisely as demanding when it is not the time to share. The current use of social media and smartphone apps provides some quick examples for what we may come to understand to be illegitimate demands: before I am allowed to install what appears to be a "harmless" app on my smartphone, say a "torch" app, I often have to grant the company offering the app access to virtually all my smartphone settings and its data. When registering for network platforms of various sorts, potential users are often forced to provide not only names and addresses but also other personal details such as their birth date and so forth.

Boxes that commit me to receive "newsletters" (or worse) are pre-ticked and adverts flood my mailbox if I am not alert enough to actively deny agreement.[7]

Premature giving is closely connected to receiving premature requests for giving. Those whom we call internet "providers" often prove to appropriate more than they provide. Cases of "oversharing" need to be reconsidered not only in terms of what is being offered but rather of what is being demanded, typically a prerequisite for any further interaction. Information that we may only want to release at a later stage of a relationship, once trust has been established, is prematurely demanded at an early stage. For those who are brought up in societies with extended everyday sharing, premature giving consists largely of undemanded giving that could create undesirable dependencies. It is deemed as unreasonable to accept demands too readily. For those who live in societies that put gift exchange at the centre, sharing in itself may be considered premature giving because it is usually given without a reciprocal return in sight and often without precondition. Finally, those who live in societies that allow market transfers to saturate all spheres of life tend to be unaware that there is an appropriate and an inappropriate time to give because sale contracts either prescribe the order of transaction (with penalty fees when defaulting) or they decouple the exchange of objects from the life trajectories of the giver and receiver and their transaction altogether. For all three groups things are somewhat different for situations in which there is belated giving, to be discussed next.

Belated giving

Belated giving is highly problematic in gift-exchange systems which are accompanied by an explicit ideology of circulation that prohibits taking items out of that circulation for a long time. In systems of bridewealth among African pastoralists, for instance, cattle theft can be punished harshly since it diverts the transfer of cattle that accompanies all important social and political ties (Taylor 1997: 563). There may be (violent) disagreements about who has the right to take what but there is usually wide agreement that the goods in question need to circulate. Similarly, while there are many uncertainties in exchange cycles like the *kula*, the need for necklaces and armshells to circulate is the bedrock of the system that is known to everyone. Foragers who share are less concerned about considerations of circulation. Contrary to a widespread stereotype it is not uncommon to store things. As mentioned before, the ≠Akhoe Hai//om of Namibia store meat by drying it in the sun and have storage facilities for fruit that is kept in the ground to allow it to ripen. I have commented in Chapter 2 on the problems that storage entails. Storage is not just a technical problem of making organic materials last but, if it is practiced at a larger scale and for a long period, storage invites a number of *social* problems which need to be taken care of. Storage as a form of belated giving provokes the need for inviolable property relations, for social sanction and obligations. Political authority and dependency on a larger group are therefore social side-effects of storage. The transfer is altered from a bilateral transfer between someone who provides and someone who receives, to a transfer that has at least a third party. Today it is often an opaque third party which can turn the stored items into a form of capital that can be pooled and invested for a variety of purposes. Elsewhere, stored food is elaborately exhibited as ethnographic accounts of many rural communities around the world attest. The Yam barns of Oceania or the large grain storage baskets in African rural homesteads not only exhibit storage (and wealth), they also put it up for public scrutiny. Digital data is hoarded in a much less visible way since it can do away with large archives of materials like papers and books. Despite its invisibility the micro-size digital data storage today also absorbs increasing amounts of energy and money for servers and newly developed carrier media. It is not only that the amount of data is out of public scrutiny but also the effective cost of maintaining it. Moreover, the social challenges that come with storage also do not go away with digitization. In a sense they can be said to be amplified today as they are hidden from scrutiny and allow unnoticed hoarding in hitherto unknown dimensions. The problem goes beyond the expenses that are incurred for pooling resources and for keeping things available, whether it concerns a guarantee of all fruit and vegetables across seasons or the migration of data to ever-changing digital formats. Rather, it is unresolved questions of access to stored items, of retaining and possibly monopolizing stored information. Privileged and uneven access to stored goods can not only undermine equality, peaceful social relations and individual autonomy, it may also enable power concentrations that are difficult to control.[8]

Digital storage allows a delay in giving to such an extent that unprecedented amounts of data accumulate and can be hoarded. Digital innovations reduce the technical costs for sharing *and* storing on a large scale. Advocates of the sharing economy argue that it is only because of the coverage reached by the internet, paired with GPS and mobile phone coverage, that the so-called new sharing networks have become possible (see Chapter 6). *Airbnb*, where people rent out their flats, would hardly work without internet data storage paired with increased mobility. When the *UBER* drivers offer paid lifts in their cars they need the new electronic infrastructure. Unprecedentedly (and to some extent unwittlingly) large amounts of data and information are stored in the process. The amount of digital data stored in the last year is said to surpass the sum of all previously stored data. The "sharing portals" mentioned produce a very powerful dataset on mobility and purchasing patterns that can provide market advantages to those who can analyse where and when people are likely to travel, stay away overnight or stream particular music. After initial costs of setting up the platform, all the data is collected "for free". Or to put it differently, accepting the technology tool that is offered entails a continual demand to transfer data for free for as long as the tool is being used. The accumulated data that allows statistical forecasting and predictions goes beyond what individual participants in market exchanges could master. The data is processed but not shared back with those who produce it – rather, it may belatedly be given back – for a price.

In the modern environment of globalization driven by the internet the central position behind a myriad of visible acts of contribution (postings, uploads) and distribution (clicks, downloads) are often hardly visible but they appear to be even more pronounced than in other storage systems. This is because of their invisibility and because of the sheer amount of what is being stored and of the numerous contributors that are involved. The most subtle use of time in this process is achieved by coordinating two different transfers and making them coincide. When we transfer an item, or merely search for it through internet platforms, there is a hidden transfer taking place at the same time: we also make data available to a provider who collects and hoards. The contributors and beneficiaries who share digital data tend to conceive of their exchanges as dyadic, not considering the distributive agent that allows, and potentially controls, their exchanges. The exchanges in blogs etc. indicate that this may be due to the fact that they are victim to a cultural bias that highlights reciprocal exchange and gift giving. If you take contents from my homepage and use it, either commercially or to enhance your prestige (if only by ridiculing me or "bashtagging" me), it may look like a conflict between me and you whereas there are third parties involved that allow the multiplication, that refuse to undo connections, for instance in auto-complete options when using search engines. Taking a wider ethnographic and anthropological picture on sharing and storing, I argue, can help resolve some of the underlying issues of property and access in the globalized internet economy. In sharing regimes individuals may readily shift their role in the process as the one who has received in the first wave of sharing is giving out shares in a second wave of sharing. By contrast, the position of distributor in large storage systems is hard to attain and correspondingly a matter of concern and subject to harsh competition. The conflict and competition is carried out not only between commercial corporations but also between the state and non-state corporations and in either case it is typically beyond the reach of individual agents. On the basis of a comparative anthropological perspective we may argue that the largely unreflected part of oversharing on the internet is not the problematic loss of personal information, but rather the concentration of knowledge and data in the hands of those who own the storage devices and who design and own the calculus that carry some agents to amplified heights (of the search list) and let others disappear into virtual oblivion.

Bringing together insights from the anthropology of sharing in non-digital and in digital environments can lead us to reconsider the way in which we evaluate the costs of sharing and of storage. Sharing has immediate costs for those who give up a part of what they possess. However, there are considerable belated or delayed costs that are involved in storing that go beyond the technical work to make things last. At the end of the day the benefits of sharing may turn out to be much higher than the benefits of storage. More fundamentally, the two are not independent and separate options but they condition one another to some extent. Shared information on the web is also stored. What may appear to be pooling is often in fact storage and often appropriation. Both sharing and storage may be said to make things available for future use but they differ radically with regard to the ways in which access is organized. While storage as accumulation has so far been advertised by developers as a remedy against sharing, sharing is increasingly considered the remedy for unwarranted accumulation. While the discussion has so far focused on "oversharing", there is increasing awareness about the problem of "overstoring", of a growing concentration of big data, and the ability to abuse it, in the hands of very few. The problematic appropriation of digitally exchanged data through a third party is often opaque and the negative effects of data concentration only show belatedly. The difference between sharing and storing regimes goes beyond the difference between immediacy and delay. It is not only the point in time that differs but also the different rhythms that characterize these transfers.

Picking the right time

The typical sharing scenario (as outlined in Chapter 3) has a guardian or owner of the meat who typically stays in the background receiving some of the prey but giving up some of it. Others are dividing and allocating the shares and yet others are receiving shares and allocating it further. The bigger the prey, the more people are involved in the chain of distribution and the more waves of sharing can be observed. In storage regimes, by contrast, the re-distributor takes central position in a double sense. Since storage is costly there is a tendency to create ever more centralized institutions that provide and organize storage. Many acts of contribution and distribution get centralized in one position from which redistribution takes place: the case of large land owners, chiefs or sovereigns, who reign from a central place or from computer platforms. However, they also reign from a central time, as it were. The sovereign controls calendars and clocks (see Bourdieu 2012) and the time for redistribution. To be able to determine *when* redistribution takes place becomes a more powerful position than the actual division and distribution which may easily be delegated.

Cliché has it that societies which give much room to sharing are "presentist", a view which is linked to the assumed incapacity for storing discussed in the previous chapters. However, the ethnography of sharing practice draws a slightly different picture. Sharing does not exclude a concern about the future (or about the past for that matter). There are clearly aspirations and apprehensions involved as people hope to find food, hope to get a share and as they talk a lot about events of eating well (or, as may be the case, of not having received anything). But above all, what is at stake here is not a difference between "cold" and "hot" societies, as Lévi-Strauss (1965) may have it. While many gift-exchange systems require elaborate preparations and follow-ups over an extended time period, sharing is all about picking the right point in time. What is of critical importance is not the length or depth of a period of mutual giving but the right moment in an ongoing process. Being at the right spot at the right time is the "secret" of successful sharing as indicated in Chapter 3. Sharing as a process links particular moments with specific opportunities.

Consider an instance from my field research in Namibia that is echoed in a number of other ethnographic accounts: after having killed an ostrich (from the back of my car) the successful hunter stands back and allows others to take over the distribution of the meat. The adult men separate some of the meat that they consider *soxa* (powerful) and which they want to claim for themselves (the scene is depicted in Figure 3.1 p. 66). Initially local men and local women cook their meat in separate pots while visitors sit in the back waiting for their share. Everyone starts eating bits and pieces while the slaughtering and cooking goes on. Cooking takes time and the time is filled with loud demands and repeated remarks about everyone's need to eat and, when the "men's meat" was finally ready to eat, the women had built up considerable pressure. Together with the children in the camp they had finished eating the larger part of the animal in the meantime. It did not take them long since their fires were already burning, pots ready at hand and many were eager to eat. The adult men take a little longer to get their fire at the *olupare* fireplace going which is only used on special occasions. When they start to eat, most of the others in the camp have finished but since the group is fairly large they are still hungry for meat. Some of the adult women, who have eaten their meat, now demand from the men to give up meat from their pot, calling out to them and joking about them. The men, some grudgingly, give up bits to the women who in turn share it with the young people.

In this instance, as in many others that I have observed, not everyone got the same portion and not everyone got a share right away. The hunter and visitors had to wait and the adult men attempted to keep some special parts of the meat for themselves. In the end they did not get any larger amounts than the others but could comfort themselves with the fact that they were able to separate some of the meat and hang on to it while everyone else had something to chew on – but not for much longer. This is in tune with other accounts of items that people attempt to exempt from sharing (see Widlok 1999): these are often small amounts but what is emphasized is the privilege to "taste first". As the distribution and consumption continues, the actual chance of keeping some "extra" meat for themselves is dwindling with time. In the above example, the women and children who had received some of the meat had eaten it all and were now nagging the men to share more of what they had in their separate pot. The longer the men waited, the louder became the complaints and social pressure rose. If we had hunted the ostrich on foot rather than by car the men might have had their fill before bringing the meat into the camp, but now that window of opportunity was closing. Those who happened to be away from camp this day and the day after did not get anything since the meat was finished by then. It is therefore misleading to simply record the amount of meat received by the various people who are present at a particular point in time. It does not do justice to what happens at such a sharing event since it disregards that unfolding in time matters.[9]

Debates about sharing are often conducted in terms of absolute proportions, the amounts contributed to the pool and the amounts given out. In a similar vein Hunt (2000) attempted to distinguish sharing from other forms of transfer in terms of it being overall "one-way" and "unbalanced" (see also Peterson 2013). However, apart from the overall amount or the direction of flows it seems highly relevant to consider the timing that goes with sharing and which sets it apart from other modes of transfer. As for commercial exchange, it may be said it basically collapses time (or tries to do so) since a sale contract makes the transaction immediate and complete by contract, in principle independently of whether it is the payments or the goods that are received first by either giver or recipient (see Gregory 1982). Gift exchange, by contrast, may be said to live off continual indebtedness, endless in principle since the exchanges are supposed to never even out (see Graeber 2011). Reciprocal gift exchange is fired by the rise of expectations and by the long term that ennobles a relationship and provides an additional value to the gifts. The time regime of sharing is yet again different since it is all about the right moment. As mentioned earlier, sharing is a stretched-out process with windows of opportunity opening and closing. The three waves of sharing have already been mentioned, one at the killing site, one when bringing the meat back to camp and one when the meat is cooked. The first moment is the point in time that is appropriate for the participants in the hunt and the owners of the hunting tools to make their claims. In many settings there are some strict rules that apply at this stage which are relaxed at the second moment in which the prominent members of a household or hearth make their claims and make sure that they are being included. The third moment then includes basically anyone who has not been involved up to that point, including visitors and others, however weak, young or old, who have little basis for their claims except their being there and being hungry for meat. The golden thread that runs through all of this is a sense of preliminariness. Those who receive in the first distribution will face demands in the second distribution by people who will hand on shares in the third distribution. In principle the chain can continue on since whatever is leftover is never "safe" in the sense that it would be immune to claims. As with all types of property that are subject to sharing, the "chances" of having to part with an object actually increases with the time that one owns it, or the time period that one has enjoyed it, if you will. Not having used an item for a long time, or having got a new one to replace it, usually puts pressure on people to give the object away. Just as hunger returns with time, so do demands for a share return to those who still have when others do not. Like gift exchange then sharing never quite ends but in a different sense. There is no sense of continual indebtedness, as with bridewealth or bloodwealth when there is a lifelong "debt" incurred by those who have received or taken a human life (see Graeber 2011). Rather, it is the continuation of life which constantly creates new demands (such as hunger) and which keeps the sharing process going.

Again, it is useful to search for analogue situations concerning transfers in the globalized world today. Consider the debate raging between copyright and copyleft activists. On the one hand are those who seek to transpose property regimes from a pre-digital era into the realm of digital media and, on the other hand, those who campaign for creative commons, open access and "pirating". When compared with the ethnography of sharing summarized above, the main opposition in this debate turns out to be a complementary opposition: a complementary opposition that does not provide an alternative but cries out for one. Copyright and copyleft activists on the internet usually portray one another as absolute opposites. But in terms of temporality they are not. The defenders of copyright have a notion of keeping rights in things over time, be it photos, text or any other creation in which labour was invested. The pirates of the internet argue for free access that allows an unlimited usage of these sources once they are in the public domain. Although being at opposite ends of the spectrum, both of these stances may be construed as operating with assumptions of eternity and timelessness that are ultimately cultural constructs or phantasies. In the first case it is the "eternal" right of the producer or creator in its product. As Kropotkin (1995[1892]) and others since (Ferguson 2015) have underlined, it is an illusion to assume that inventions are created out of nothing. For the major procedures or infrastructures that we enjoy, it is neither possible nor practicable to keep a total and endless record of those who contributed and to pay tribute to them without end. Modern railways, Kropotkin argues, are owned by "whole generations [who] have handed on this immense inheritance" (1995 [1892]: 14) so that "society's wealth properly belongs to all" (Ferguson 2015: 185). Its value does not originate in individual labour but it can be claimed by all members of a society that has brought it about. Hardt (2000) makes the same argument about the creation of advertising jingles out of a shared pool of music that constantly surrounds us, and both he and Kropotkin would certainly include the products of the internet in this notion of "all belongs to all" (Kropotkin 1995[1892]: 19).

The proponents of copyleft, one could argue, are also entertaining an omnipotence phantasy, namely that of having all knowledge and materials created at one's disposal all the time, often paired with an imperative of utilizing and spreading what can easily be copied and pasted. It is an illusion insofar as the amount of available information can easily block instead of enable creative or productive engagement. Arguably, being "everyone" and "everywhere" is the worst condition for any creative, productive life, or any human life for that matter. By contrast, being limited by others, being limited by one's own mortality and being limited by a world that is not perfect for humans seems to fuel human creativity and productivity. Moreover, skilful handling of knowledge and information is not a product of the available amounts of materials but of "legitimate peripheral participation", as Lave and Wenger (1991) have called it. Building up the necessary skill to do things with materials is a process that is limited through the embodiment and temporality of those who are involved and that cannot be unbound through universalizing access. Both phantasies have a lot to do with metaphysical claims of humans who aim to go beyond their limited personal lives, something to which I shall return in the concluding chapter.

A more general underlying conflict goes beyond literature, photos and similar objects of the "creative commons". Other instances where the conflict is being played out are, for example, police investigators and medical records. In police investigations information on the names of suspects and such like are restricted in an ongoing criminal investigation in order to prevent negative effects of pre-judgement. In medical and other person-related research the debate is not only about anonymity but also about the mandatory deletion of data. Should there be a right to allow things to fall into oblivion or is there a moral imperative to keep all data available because it may become important in the future? A true alternative against the "all-or-nothing" positions is to keep some human measure about the "right moment" in place with regard to disclosing or deleting information. One compromise that is often suggested to resolve the copyright conflicts is a delimitation of a moratorium for exclusive usage. In the copyright of books, for instance, this is already in place in many countries since literature ceases to be of limited access as from 70 years after the death of an author. Open access academic journals similarly reserve exclusive rights for a year or so before granting authors the right to distribute and download works freely. However, this compromise is about duration, and debate continues as to what the appropriate durations are for the various objects (or ideas) that humans create. Similarly, regulations of how much of an existing text an author may take over or how much of an existing song a musician may take over follows the same logic. The aim is to establish a period and an amount that can be set across situations and that can be calculated with. The problem remains that what may be appropriate in one case may be out of proportion in another.

In this situation, sharing practices offer a more fundamental alternative since it is not about duration and amount of time but it is all about the right moment, the *kairos* not the *chronos* if you will (see Marten 1993). If we transpose the observations from the ethnography of sharing to that of, say, sharing of contents on the internet the issue shifts from counting years to establishing what constitutes the right moment. What makes sharing work, and what makes it different from other modes of allocation, is that the transfers involved have an inbuilt shelf life, as it were. Things cannot be claimed "once and for all" and they are not given up unless it is "the right time to share". Many times ethnographers have reported how in sharing the "who gets what" is diffused to the extent that it becomes very hard, and very unacceptable, to collapse time and space and to connect acts of sharing across situations and across cases that are far apart. The "rightful share" is not an abstract entitlement. Or, rather, it is not effective as an abstract entitlement of "all towards all, and always" since it needs to be actuated through sharing one's life with one another. Because it is only through tuning in which actions of others, with what they have recently received, what they can be expected to demand at a particular point in time and by considering who else is currently around, that one can get a sense about the right moment. This applies to those making demands as much as to those who are facing demands and who are expected to react to demands.

We may speculate as to how this would work out with regard to publishing texts, for instance. Introducing temporality in this sense would mean that publishing (or reprinting) a piece of work that has intentionally brought suffering to many people (think of Hitler's *Mein Kampf*) would have to be considered differently from a piece of work that has encouraged many (think of Anne Frank's diaries). The fact that in both these examples just given we do already apply a differentiated view beyond fixed time spans is an indication that such a perspective can be feasibly put into practice.[10] The main point here is that the restrictions or regulations of sharing are not brought about externally but are raised from practice onto the legal sphere as "sediments of shared lives" (Marten 2009: 244).

Ultimate sharing: Sharing to the end – but not beyond

An important part of the temporality of sharing is that it has an end. There are good times and bad times for sharing and every person's sharing eventually comes to an end, a point to which I shall return at the end of this book. Windows of opportunity for sharing widen and they narrow but they also come to a complete close since life itself is finite. The end of sharing is implicated in what has been discussed above about the importance of physical presence in sharing (see Chapter 3). The most forceful instrument to generate sharing is bodily presence. Substitutes are possible but they are limited. A typical substitute is man-made objects, the tools for hunting, the arrows that are made by the old men that find their way into the quivers of the young men. Giving an arrow to another hunter is the most prominent way of aging hunters to become "owner" of the prey, or of parts of it, and to have some rights in overseeing the distribution of meat if that arrow hits the prey. Arrows create a practical presence at the hunt for those who do not directly participate because they are no longer agile enough. However, without such materialization, either in one's own presence or through the presence of objects that one has constructed, sharing claims become very weak indeed (see Box 16). Claiming a share "in the name of" someone who is absent becomes difficult if that person is away for a long time and far away. In such cases, relations of gift giving may replace sharing. Claiming a share on the mere basis of being a descendent of someone or of being of the right class or ethnic group, does not work in these contexts.

BOX 16 THE SKILL TO SHARE

Just before I left Namibia I had a text message on my mobile (see Figure 7.1) saying, "Thank you very much father but it's only hunger, I didn't have any food, please help me". The message came from /Abaro, a young woman of around thirty who lives in an "informal settlement" that residents ironically named Kuvukiland (a fictional place from a South African comedy film). I have known her since she was a little child (hence the address "father") and I had just forwarded her the remaining "airtime" that I had on my phone. Sharing airtime is a common feature in Namibia today. Many poor people now have access to a simple mobile phone but little or no money to buy airtime. They then send a "missed call" to friends or relatives who will recognize the number and who will understand that this is a "silent demand" for sending credit through the network since the sender of the text message has clearly run out of airtime but wants to get in touch. In East Africa the system is advanced further in that credit on the mobile phone can be converted to pay for grocery shopping at the main supermarkets. If I had a local bank account I could

FIGURE 7.1 Demand sharing through the text message service. Photo: Th. Widlok

send /Abaro a transaction number which she could use at a local ATM to draw money. All over Africa mobile phone technology allows money transfers for people who do not have bank accounts and little access to cash.

The new technology makes sharing easier. It is particularly highly in demand by the former hunter-gatherers who seek to elicit shares from friends and relatives. Before the use of mobile phones they would have given messages to people who go off visiting another camp in which they ask for things to be brought to them, or relatives to come and visit them. These messages were often not very effective given the importance of personal presence to underline such demands. In my early fieldnotes there is an instance where /Abaro, then around seven years old, had hopped onto our car to go along to a neighbouring camp. When her mother !Gamekha decided that she also wanted to come along I told her that the car was full but she could send messages of demand with her daughter. Her indignant response was "What is she going to get there?" indicating that a young child would only be able to elicit a small share of whatever it was that one could get at the other camp.

Hai//om can recount many stories of such missed opportunities – occasions where they were not present, could not get a lift or were unable to visit a place where some rich food was available. Bodily presence is a strong tool for demanding a share but the downside is that bodily absence makes it much harder, if not impossible to elicit shares. !Gamekha, like many adult women who had several children and partners in their lifetime, was renowned for her mobility, agility and serendipity that allowed her to elicit shares wherever she went. When she died recently her presence was missed by many but the sharing transfers that she maintained collapsed. I recounted to her family that I would do what was customary where I come from, namely having a mass read for her and visit her grave. This was noted but none of the close family members could point me to her grave since they had not been there. Those who had buried her had difficulties, too, because graves remain unmarked and are never visited. When we met, they told me about the loss they felt, as with all old people with whom one had shared a long life – but afterwards !Gamekha was not mentioned again.

It has been noted (by Nurit Bird-David and others) that scholarly discourse about sharing has been strongly influenced by "our bourgeois senses" (Bird-David 2005: 202). This includes, above all, a proprietary perspective on sharing that emphasizes the division of things between individuals. Such a "sharing out" sense, as Ingold (1986) has labelled it, is to be distinguished from a "sharing in" sense of individuals joined "in common action, experience, or usage" (Bird-David 2005: 203).[11] As I will discuss in more detail in the Conclusions, there is a sense in which common action and experience also involve some basic "division" in the sense that people in their joint action also experience one another as limiting "others" in a fruitful way. Experiencing that others' lives come to an end is the most direct way of realizing one's own finiteness. However, in most common usage today the permanent "proprietary" sense of sharing is dominant. While possession and joint usage can be temporary, and in fact often are, property relations are seen in their jural sense of excluding others and of extending across time and space. Property, unlike possession or joint usage, does not require any co-presence or proximity and it can be, in principle, eternal, as things can get inherited across generations. In that sense, property has a very different starting point than sharing but there is a tendency to think of sharing primarily in terms of objects changing their place but owners remaining stable and unchanging. Take "time-share" apartments as a case in point. These are precursors to the current phenomena of the sharing economy, then applied to "extra" holiday homes (see Bird-David (2005) for a discussion), now often applied to one's one and only home. In either case those who are co-using the flat (now called "co-consumers") typically never meet in person even though they are contemporaries. The shares in the apartment can move and "change hands" without one owner being in any way moved by other owners. This follows the logic of property according to which sharing is above all a division of objects. The other sense of sharing as bringing people together (subdued in the bourgeois world view, as Bird-David would put it) highlights sharing as a joined performance which in turn implies physical co-presence. It is an ethnographic question to find out which of these meanings of sharing are dominant with regard to particular cultural world views. The point of an anthropology of practice approach is slightly different: the aim here is to establish what practical (rather than ontological) possibilities and limitations are created through sharing as a social practice across ethnographic settings. If what I have argued elsewhere is correct (Widlok 2004), namely that sharing is an intrinsic realization of access to goods, then sharing is in the first place about the practice of sharing itself and not about the allocation of goods or the creation of social bonds. In a certain sense, sharing is good for as long as it lasts. It intrinsically realizes shared access and its termination immediately brings shared access to an end, while the allocation of goods or the creation of collective identities can be maintained in other ways.

Compare, for instance, attempts to share with physical co-presence and those without (see Box 16). Without embodied support the claims for a share can much more easily be ignored. Sharing meat sitting at the fire with others reinforces social bonds – stopping to share food at a joint hearth weakens the bond. In Chapter 3 I hinted at the ways in which changes in the architecture of huts and fireplaces, the permeability of space among ≠Akhoe Hai//om, affect the chances of personal encounters which in turn affect sharing. A closed palisade fence and an inner court yard, typical features in a modern farm labourer's compound, are sufficient to prevent seeing what others consume at their fire and to prevent passers-by accessing the fireplace as easily as in bush camps. But even before these changes occurred, the ordinary life cycle implied that enjoying co-presence is finite and as a consequence sharing was finite, too. People cannot be at all places all the time. They only receive shares where they are present somehow. And those who can no longer sit around the fire with us or otherwise assure us of their co-presence are not bound to us, and we are not bound to them as strongly as they were when we did enjoy their co-presence. This also applies to people who move away but also to the very old and frail and – ultimately – to the dead. Another way of looking at presence then is disappearance and absence. The living are freed of limitations and demands that may be ascribed to the dead because the dead cannot back-up their claims through a recognized form of bodily co-presence.[12] In comparative perspective this finiteness of personal presence is in fact a social achievement that seems to be an exception rather than the rule.

In forager societies sharing goes hand in hand with an absence of power for specific ancestors and for "bodiless" corporate groups. Although modern Western societies do not consider themselves as revering ancestors, they devote considerable thought and energy on ways of realizing presence beyond death, in monuments of stone as much as in digitally stored memories. Administering cultural heritage and personal memorabilia are an obsession of our current culture as the ever-growing number of heritage sites, biographies and so forth indicate. Debts and burdensome legacies for future generations are increasingly a problem, but even where there is a positive heritage it exerts power on the next generations that are bound to it. Inheritance, as we know from many complex societies, entrenches divisions of wealth, of opportunity and so forth – often for generations to come. By contrast, in most forager societies inheritance is a matter of those who are around (see Widlok 1998). With regard to material inheritance these are quite literally those who are around when a person happens to die. Those who are dead have little or no means of controlling the flow of goods and rights after they have gone, opening up new spaces for every new generation.

The opposite seems to happen in virtual reality. Here presence is multiplied or at least it is one of the main attractions of virtual reality that it promises the users to transcend the limitations of their ordinary embodied life. Telecommunication technology gives the impression of being at different places at the same time. Avatars in *second life* (and other virtual environments) allow us to design an identity according to our own wishes, to change age, gender, race and so on. Auction houses invented bid assistants that bid for me while I cannot be at the computer, i.e. allowing me to engage in several transactions on several platforms at the same time. Micro-cameras allow me to see and hear what happens in the children's bedroom, around my faraway vacation home and so forth. The tempting promise by virtual and mediated reality is to multiply presence and ultimately to extend presence beyond one's own lifetime. In this perspective, instances of "oversharing" discussed at the beginning of this chapter are not only about "disclosing too much" but also are an attempt "to stretch beyond the limits of one's presence". Those who overshare are not only innocent young people, victims of the internet (see Agger 2012) but they also seek actively to manipulate their presence. After all, oversharing has to do with the widespread internet obsession of presenting oneself not only in the best possible light but also as someone different. Young people boost their CV to make them look senior and experienced and older people tend to make themselves younger, emphasizing their flexibility and competitiveness. In a high-tech society we do this when trying to find a job or a partner and the new technology allows us to do this much more effectively than in the past. The phenomenon itself predates the internet but it is amplified and facilitated, paradoxically by the fact that digital encounters are reduced to a few communication channels. With media it is easier to deceive the other than in personal encounters, and it has become even more difficult to assess who one is dealing with. Accordingly, internet users get very alarmed when identities are forged. Attempts are made to develop means that allow internet users to tell the difference between an "authenticated buyer/customer" and the fake ones that are installed to enhance one's reputation and credits on the web. This uneasiness, I argue, is not only about wrong identities but it is uneasiness about people who try to be many different things at once, old and young, customers and sellers, claiming the authority of experts and the intimacy of peers at the same time, people who are overstretching their presence.

The peak of the phenomenon are attempts to create a form of eternal life on the web (Altena 2009, see also Altena et al. 2011). Often the webpages get created that commemorate the dead but increasingly they are put in place by people who see their death coming, for instance when they are terminally ill. They document the end of their lives and in a sense continue their existence after death. While there is no doubt a therapeutic element in this self-documentation, it is also an extension of one's presence, an attempt to extend if not life itself then at least life in the memories of others. These uses of the internet may be seen as a continuation of earlier attempts to ensure personal immortality through commissioning portraits, statues or busts, and through having streets, prizes or foundations named after oneself. From the perspective of sharing, all of these are manifestations of hoarding. The virtual presence not only allows accumulation of aggrandized identities but it also, by implication, multiplies the demands on others. It is a demand on the attention of others and for them to orient their lives with reference to the dead. Their capacity of maintaining a continuing (internet) presence and their capacity to engage with others is bound and limited by a virtual presence of those who refuse to let go. What some hunter-gatherers may occasionally lament, namely their inability to be present at several places where shared resources can become available (see Box 16), turns out to be an important measure against hoarding and against ways of fruitlessly occupying others. These processes are facilitated through virtual reality that increases the demands for the time and attention of the living without ultimately being able to expand the time that the latter have to create objects of attention in the course of their own lifetimes.

It is easy to see how demands for a "the rightful share" (see Ferguson 2015) may soon be extended to the field of digital media. Those whose data is collected and appropriated by software and internet giants may soon demand a share of that data and of the revenue that is generated from it. So far, the companies have been successful in keeping the public and the individual users at a distance from their data, the algorithms used and even the places from which they operate, creating a gigantic unevenness between individuals and corporate players. The question is whether the right to keep the accumulated data is given a shelf-life or whether it can be kept as corporate property for good.

Conclusion

The internet and digital communication technology is often presented as a precondition for establishing sharing at the level of large-scale societies. In this chapter I have outlined that there are also pitfalls in this process. Internet presence and virtual life can also be an expression of the attempt to discount time (and place) dependency and to have everything immediately and at once. In this sense the internet and related digital technology boosts the attempt to realize as many opportunities as possible in the limited time available. Personal lives are "front-loaded" and audited as if they were made up of market transactions. Being in touch with the many at any point in time instead of with selected few at the right point in time is one expression of this pattern. Such an accountancy approach to life ("the 100 places to visit before you die" etc.) is greatly facilitated by digital contacts and digital presence which gives people the impression of being in touch with their whole network all the time, of being in different places at the same time and as if condensing time and space. But being pre-occupied with self-perfection and maximization in practice often reduces the time and the inclination to think and act in relation to specific others in the actual surroundings that we occupy. What appears to be "oversharing" when people spend a good proportion of their time in perfecting their web-presence, and designing their various avatars in social networks, is therefore not sharing at all. It has none of the forager recognition that there is finiteness in possession, including the possession of one's own life. Oversharing in this sense is not so much innocent but often aggressive, it is an expression of a lesson not learned and of deskillment.[13] In principle, however, there is no reason why the millennia-old social practices of sharing should not be extended into a confrontation with new modes of data storage and data usage. The Conclusions will look at these possibilities in the light of the preceding chapters.

Notes

1 A constant release of personal details onto the web could be said to create scarcity on the side of those who are the potential recipients and whose time and attention is taxed by the unwanted offers and postings.

2 Within Europe we may see the notion of oversharing to be more widespread in protestant countries such as Holland. Here the cultural stereotype has it that members of the society are not supposed to have curtains in front of their living-room windows to allow other members of the parish to see that they have nothing to hide and are not doing anything sinful. The curtainless windows could be said to be analogous to setting all your Facebook-settings on public. As a Catholic in, say, nearby Limburg, again this is the stereotype, you only disclose your inner life to the priest in the dark. So where the congregationist puritan sets Facebook settings to public, it is as if the Catholic in the confessional box could be said to give his or her password to the clerical system administrator only, and only in an anonymized way. And, if we want to continue staying in the picture, traditionally this happened in Latin or in ritualized form, which to many is like sending an encrypted mail. Catholic churches have crypts, protestant churches are essentially assembly halls. In societies with dwindling church influences and high heterogeneity there is a growing tendency to alternate between these two modes of reconciling sharing with the public bourgeois order.

3 Examples given are those of Aboriginal checkout operators who "might feel pressured into giving the trolley full of goods to the relatives who haven't paid because it is more important to gain the approval of his or her social networks than to generate a profit within the business" (*Retail Times* quoted in Altman 2011: 195) and situations of addiction in which demand sharing transforms from a "valuable cultural tradition" into "a pathological culture" (Neil Pearson in *The Australian*, quoted in Altman 2011: 196).

4 Altman (2011) notes the parallel between interventions by the Australian state with development strategies in sub-Saharan Africa for which Ferguson (1994: 264) has diagnosed the attempt to gloss over struggles about political control by means of a technocratic imagery of betterment and rational technical intervention.

5 Other instances of apparently "harmful" sharing show a similar pattern because one transfer (in this case of sharing) is intimately tied up with other allocations (here data hoarding by others) with detrimental effects (see Chapter 6 above).

6 This is in sharp contrast to the cases of gift exchange in China reported by Yan (1996) who misleadingly uses "gift giving" and "sharing" interchangably. In the Chinese case there are strict obligations to offer cigarettes to visitors or colleagues as a gift and where

a violation of these normative expectations to offer gifts is met with an immediate and lasting loss of face not only for an individual but also for the larger family associated with that person (Yan 1996: 131). The resulting strategy for poorer Chinese who have few or low-quality cigarettes to offer is to refrain from smoking in public "in order to save money and face" (Yan 1996: 132).

7　It is easy to think of other examples that are not directly linked to the social media or the internet. For instance, one could equally ask how much information a bank can legitimately ask for before I can open an account there or how much I have to disclose to a health or other insurance provider before they give me insurance cover. Think of the debates surrounding the question as to whether prospective employers need to be told whether an applicant is pregnant, whether applications should contain photos or the real names of applicants which may raise prejudices among the employers by giving them "too much" personal information "too early". In fact, some uses of modern technology allow less disclosure of personal details because they "only" involve a virtual visit on a website where a visit in person may be completely out of the question.

8　Occasionally the unease about the loss of control also surfaces on internet groups. Here is a typical exchange found on sites where individuals post photos and information that regularly gets cut and pasted onto other sites:

> Contributor A: "The internet is all about sharing. If you don't want others to take things, then store them at home in a box."
> Contributor B: "Even if there is a new culture of sharing emerging, that does not mean that you should forget your good manners and not ask before taking something or not acknowledge that you have done so."

9　This point is echoed by Tim Ingold's critique of the "Sigma principle" (2011) of much research in economics.

10　Recent court decisions prevented copyright limitations of the Anne Frank diaries and prevented the lifting of copyright limitations in the case of *Mein Kampf*.

11　The distinction is reminiscent of the distinction between commodities (a relation between things) and gifts (a relation between people) that Gregory (1982) suggested. Like all dualistic distinctions these may be good to think with while empirical cases may not fall neatly into either of the two categories. Sharing game meat, for example, has been treated by most analysing anthropologists as a case of an object (meat) being distributed among independent subjects (human individuals) whereas arguably in most forager settings large game animals are more like other (human) subjects with whom one's life is entangled so that sharing brings together people and animals. The joint eating of meat may look like "sharing out" objects but it is in fact "sharing in" people and is reinforcing the bond between them. There is, however, no reason why one event should not have both dimensions.

12　In ancestor systems, by contrast, it is the back-up of the dead that is being conscripted, typically by the senior people alive. An example is the invocation of "founding fathers" in companies, corporations, academic disciplines and nations. A recent example is South Africa's president Zuma's threat that ancestors will curse those who do turn against his party (http://www.timeslive.co.za/thetimes/2014/01/27/zuma-stirs-up-ghosts-at-anc-poll-rouser/).

13　The extreme case of such a behaviour may be seen in a prominent figure in the modern cultural imagination, namely the zombie, a person who refuses to die but who lives off the living. They never get enough, as it were. The zombie is the end point of a career during which people have failed to practice sharing understood as training for giving up things that one values.

CONCLUSIONS

The limits of sharing and the finite self

The starting point of this book was the growing recognition that sharing is more than what the theory of gift exchange suggests. The preceding chapters have tried to put together a more appropriate understanding of what sharing is all about. The final piece in this emerging theory of sharing concerns death. Sharing ends with death. As I shall discuss in a moment, sharing may also be said to begin with death, that is, the recognition of human finitude. To establish that sharing ends with death is not banal. After all, gift giving and market exchanges do not end with the death of the exchange or market partners – or at least are not supposed to end. In fact, this is one of their characteristic features. With regard to market exchanges transfers are not necessarily terminated by death. Doing business with incorporated companies is the preferred way to buy and sell on a market that is ideally unaffected by individual human beings dying or defecting. This is most obvious with regard to credit agreements and debt. Contracts typically include succession in title so that debts are inheritable just as any other "positive" asset. A whole industry surrounding financial collaterals has emerged and over-indebtedness is a common phenomenon in so-called advanced industrial societies. Not only individuals but whole countries and nations are paying off debts over decades and across centuries. Germany finished paying its last war reparations for World War One only in 2010, 92 years after the war was over. Many African states, and Greece more recently, have accumulated debts that have to be repaid long after the death of any individual who was alive when the debts were incurred. The same is true for many municipalities in Europe where town councils have accumulated debts that future generations will have to shoulder and that already severely limit what they can do in the present. This has been a recurring pattern ever since humans switched from foraging to agriculture and from primarily relying on sharing to other modes of transfer. Debts often affect families across generations. This has led to modern forms of slavery whereby children are given as pawns for debts that families are unable to escape in their lifetimes. When Graeber (2011) points out that this has been more or less the pattern for the last five millenia, the anthropological challenge is to think outside the box of these 5,000 years.

Gift-exchange partnerships also typically extend beyond the death of a partner. This is true even for simple exchange cycles such as the *hxaro* exchange among San in which partnerships can get inherited. More elaborate exchange systems such as the *kula* rest on collectives like villages and lineages. Marriage and other exchange alliances derive their particular power from the fact that they continue to connect families beyond potentially disruptive incidents such as the death of certain individuals. In many societies death does not mark a major divide in relationships anyway. As Kopytoff (1971) has pointed out for Africa, the interaction with ancestors is driven by the fact that they are seniors, dead or alive, who deserve certain deference and being paid homage in return for their blessings and support. The seniority principle that dominates transfers in many agropastoralist societies extends beyond death, or to put it differently, when it comes to transfers the distinction between being junior and being senior is more relevant than that between being alive or being dead. This is very different among most hunter-gatherer groups in which sharing dominates. Most of these groups are not organized in lineages that ensure succession of title and property but have bilateral networks of kin. The dead are considered truly dead, there are no graves that get visited as burial grounds are best avoided (see also Woodburn 1982b). The dead cannot press for any shares because they are not considered ancestors to whom one needs to sacrifice. The whole notion of sacrifice that follows the logic of *do ut des* (I give so that you give) is conspicuously absent in the rituals and beliefs of most hunter-gatherers.

There is an interesting if inversed parallel here with what Kopytoff has observed for African agropastoralists: here the dead and the elderly are in a similar position vis-à-vis the young when it comes to transfers. For agropastoralists the young are dependent on both, the elders and the ancestors, who are often seamlessly and categorically connected since the elders are seen as mediators towards the ancestors. This contrasts pointedly with many hunter-gatherers where there is usually not a comparable dependency on ancestors. Jahai, for instance, distinguish sharply between the "primordial immortal ancestors" of long ago from "deceased mortal humans" (van der Sluys 2000: 433). While the recently dead are best to be avoided and play no significant role in everyday Jahai life, the former are like a "giving environment" (Bird-David 1990) that shares resources with all humankind, including the recently deceased (van der Sluys 2000: 434). These mythical ancestors do not request counter-gifts but they are seen as ultimately enabling sharing among living humans who "pass on" what they themselves have received, (van der Sluys 2000: 433). In the case of hunter-gatherers both the dead and the elderly are decreasingly involved in sharing because they are in a weak position to make sharing demands as their practical presence fades away and their specific demands are shared less by others. The fact that in many hunter-gatherer societies the old and frail are in some contexts left to their own devices has posed a puzzle for many observers. Why would this happen in a group that otherwise shares so widely in everyday life? The puzzle is resolved when we remind ourselves of the importance of demand in sharing and of sharing demands. As we have seen across many examples outlined in this book, the intensity and frequency of sharing declines if these transfers are not pressed for and not communicated appropriately. The old and frail are less in a position to do so because they lack the interaction with others in the camp. They no longer have the practical presence that would allow them to see who has which resources and they lose the discursive skill of demanding at the right point in time and in the appropriate way – in other words they lose gradually the presence that is a prerequisite for sharing (see Chapter 3) and that people build up steadily as they grow up (see Box 16).

In the settlement where I carried out much of my field research in Namibia, it was the evangelist from the neighbouring agropastoralist group who wanted to be photographed and seen as caring for the old by giving them food and washing them. Most of the local San found this behaviour strange. They did not think that it was appropriate to drag the senile out of their huts for special care unless being sufficiently prompted to do so. It interfered with their notion of personal autonomy and with their expectation that sharing food or care should be initiated through tacit or open demands by the recipients. They were extending "the right to be left alone" to include not only dead corpses (as in many legal traditions) but also to those at the end of their lives who may find it difficult to fend off interference by those who impose their gifts on others – a matter that is now debated in the international medical system with its tendency to prolong life at all costs irrespective of the situation and intention of those whose life they are prolonging. Following this logic, the dead are even less in the position to make any claims than the senile elderly. Everything possible is done to avoid any claims that the dead may possibly be able to make. At funerals rituals are performed to ensure a "cool death", i.e. one that basically makes the dead leave the living alone. They may live on elsewhere but their earthly life has come to a definite end. When the first death occurred while I was doing field research, one of my Hai//om interlocutors made a strong point by explaining to me that this person was now dead, knocking on an old piece of wood on the ground that was about to be burned and said: "He is as dead as that, and that is it." What I have outlined in Chapter 3 and elsewhere (Widlok 2012) about the importance of presence in sharing has a correspondence in the effects of absence. Absence means not making any effective demands or no longer being able to make demands in the appropriate way. If someone is not present when things are shared, this frees the others of the obligation to reserve a share for the absentee. This is true for temporary absence but also holds when a person has died. The inability of the dead to have power over the living is, positively speaking, the space that the living gain. They can respond to the demands of the situation among those who share that situation – and only among them. If they decide to consider those who are absent, it is their decision and initiative to do so. They are not pressed into it by the mode of transfer.

How is it possible that finiteness as such a highly relevant and distinctive feature in sharing, has been overlooked for such a long time? My argument throughout this book has been that the circle of societies that are regularly considered when exploring the spectrum of social possibilities of transfers has been drawn far too narrowly. Moreover, there is considerable cultural baggage with which we look at sharing. Societies of hunter-gatherers, in particular, but also new phenomena of accessing resources, have been pressed into templates that either make important differences disappear or that overdraw the cultural distance. An acceptance of human mortality and finiteness is cultivated in many hunter-gatherer societies but not in the civilizations that have brought about Western science, nor in science itself (see Marten 1987). The sociology of Emile Durkheim, which also informed the gift exchange theory of his nephew Marcel Mauss (discussed in Chapter 1), is a case in point. Durkheim stated that those religious individuals who perceived something larger than themselves were actually not entirely wrong, except that they misinterpreted that "something larger" as God, whereas it was, in Durkheim's view, society itself (Durkheim 1912). With regard to research on sharing and other modes of transfer this placed transfers not in reference to the finite lives of human agents but with regard to the eternal life of supra-individual entities, i.e. societies. For the society at large, sharing appears to have similar functions as gift exchange and other social interactions: it provides the necessary social glue for keeping societies together, it facilitates cooperation, it provides an insurance against resource variability and so forth. The main insight that Mauss offered with his theory of exchange (see Chapter 1) is that such gift transfers can provide sufficient stability for a society to continue to exist – without the contractual legalistic bonds or the coercive authoritarianism that characterize many market-exchange societies. The fact that individual lives are finite matters little in this scheme of things because individuals only fill social roles and in principle everyone can fill any of these roles at any point in time. Those engaged in sharing, however, do not have such a sociocentric view as a default. The perspective that is realized in their social practice goes against the mainstream of philosophies and ontologies in the written traditions of the last 5,000 years (see Marten 2013): sharing life with others is, above all, experiencing through the presence of others and their demands that "one is not everyone" and that "one is not everywhere and at all times" but that one's presence as a human on earth is limited and finite. The presence of a person is distinctly influenced by a particular, aging body and a particular set of social relations, above all with fellow humans but also with other living beings. My hunting luck and skill as an individual person is always limited and so is my capacity to always, at all times of my life, secure the goods I need or want. And the same is true for you. The ultimate reason for the practice of sharing in these societies is the practical realization that others, due to their finite lives, can make legitimate demands on what I have and that I, due to my finite life, going through specific times myself (either favourable or less favourable), can respond to these demands when it is time to share. I can practically respond by granting others access – or I can miss the opportunity to do so. If I had no sense at all of finiteness and of which times are appropriate for what, sharing would not occur. The only other options left, one could argue, would be to either only engage in instant selling or in endless loops of gift-exchange – or we would not bother about transfers at all since there would always be a second chance.

Evolutionist approaches, discussed in Chapter 2, only need to take account of death as a general possibility, not as an individual certainty. In this conception any one only needs any others for transmitting one's own genes into future generations. Or, more precisely, for some genes to be transmitted across generations they require some humans who carry them and who die in the process, while it does not matter who these carriers are and who exactly dies at what point in time. But the most striking feature of the evolution of sharing is not so much that it has emerged but rather that it has become so variable and versatile in human culture. It is not that sharing was an invariant part of the biological essentials of humans because sharing *can*, indeed, be reduced at times, depending on the context. After all, other primates have survived into the present without (much) sharing and in many societies in human history sharing is suppressed or sidelined in the face of market exchanges and the giving of alms or gifts. If there is anything essential here it is the fact that humans "essentially" live in non-essentialized existences, because they always encounter one another in particular relations, namely as a child vis-à-vis a parent (and other children, younger or older), as a husband vis-à-vis a wife (and vis-à-vis those still or not yet married), a teacher vis-à-vis a learner, a Dutchman vis-à-vis a German, an owner of an object vis-à-vis someone in need of an object and so forth. Whether a demand for a share is made, how it is being received and whether we let go of a share is not a unified essential human property. Rather, it depends on these specificities, the ways in which we relate to others at particular points in time. The human capacity to distinguish one another along these specificities is the reason why sharing varies in social relationships. It also explains why it grows exponentially when crossing the threshold to humanity. It is not only an extension of the person beyond the individual (see Belk 2010) but also establishing a notion of personhood and personal relations in the first place – primarily through realizing that persons and relations are finite and do *not* extend endlessly. Sharing depends on the ways in which we are able to distinguish and understand relationships and lived practice. It is not a strategy that is hard-wired in genetic, cognitive or behavioural programs but a skill that is built up across a multitude of sharing events.

As I pointed out in Chapter 3, Mauss' tripartite scheme of the obligation to give, to receive and to return assumes the perspective of someone who owns something and who takes decisions about allocation and transfer. Mauss is here not far away from Rousseau and his critique of the social ills created through property after "the first man who, having enclosed a piece of land, thought of saying, 'This is mine' [and] came across people simple enough to believe him" (Rousseau 1994: 54, see Widlok 2005:1). The ethnography of sharing compiled in Chapter 3 shows that Rousseau was misled in a very interesting way. The social process of developing a sense of self is set in motion by demands that others make for something that I *thereby* may start to consider to be "mine". A man or a woman can only gain a sense of self and act meaningfully on the basis of this sense of "me and mine" when he or she is limited by others and their demands. The practice of demand sharing and sharing demands is therefore in a sense prior to establishing who "me" is and what is "mine". The prerequisite of developing a sense of self, of being someone in particular who is limited by others who are equally particular is a two-fold finiteness, namely being finite with regard to others and being finite with regard to the extension of one's life – and that of others (Marten 1987). Finiteness in both senses enable the scheme that I have suggested for sharing, namely perceiving the opportunity to ask (others), the opportunity to respond (to others) and the opportunity to let go (for others). It enables these opportunities but it cannot enforce them since in all of these cases there is also the "opportunity not to care" or more precisely to let the opportunity pass. It is therefore appropriate to talk of "opportunities" instead of obligations (as in Mauss' scheme). They are temporary windows of opportunity and not the eternally valid laws of reciprocity. We are not dealing with an abstract space of weighing risks against benefits, utility against effort but with moments in a personal life that are apprehended and seized – or not, as the case may be. Conversely, not having the same sense of double finiteness can be said to prevent other species from developing the same rich repertoire of sharing and other modes of transfer that humans have. Sharing decreases when we are culturally less exposed to our own finiteness and to that of others, either because of a lack of reflective depth or due to ideologies that deflect and bracket out this finiteness. If the good that really counts is to be found in an afterlife or at the level of abstract groups or nations, then the realization of goods through sharing in the here and now can easily take second place.

Chapter 4 has traced the way in which sharing is practiced with regard to particular manifestations of objects that lend themselves to sharing, some more or more often, others less so or less often. In that chapter I have argued that sharing is best considered as a product of a community of practice that involves people as much as objects and the settings in which they are being transferred. Learning to become a skilled sharer is not simply a matter of socialization in early childhood. Rather, the training continues in a lifelong way and it culminates in the ability to be able to let go of what one accumulates in the course of a lifetime and ultimately to let go of one's life itself. In Chapter 4 I have suggested that the daily routines of sharing enable individuals in these societies that cultivate sharing to also cope with the fact that "shrouds have no pockets". However, the logic works both ways: A society in which the recognition of human finiteness is appreciated and cultivated also provides fertile ground for the development of sharing practices in the everyday. These practices then extend beyond big items and beyond the domain of material objects and can involve sharing time (e.g. in visits) and sharing infrastructure (e.g. pathways). In many of these cases sharing improves the "things" that are being shared so that there can also be an added value in sharing.

Chapter 5 reflected on the emerging global society of associations and corporations that explicitly take countermeasures against the finiteness of human life. Pooling resources in corporate bodies allows for much greater pools of resources than a single person could amass in a lifetime. It also allows for the management of these pools beyond the lifetime of those who have set up the corporation or who run it at any particular point in time. As I have pointed out, the pool may indeed grow but accessing the pool becomes increasingly problematic since membership boundaries tend to be rather permanent and non-permeable to individual actions. If interpersonal engagement is conditioned by recognizing one another as social beings who are aware of their finiteness, this is likely to change with the large-scale spreading of "eternal" bodies. When persons die, they do not just die for themselves but can be said to die for one another, the death of others being a constant reminder of one's own finiteness and mortality. When faced with corporations and associations that can claim "eternal" life, that balance is tilted. Associations may hold property forever, they can also survive a complete loss of property and they, in principle, can do all that without being tied to particular individuals. When assets and resources come to lie in the hands of such corporate bodies, the individuals who want to access these assets enter an asymmetric relationship and they become dependent. Moreover, what they own, what they receive and what they give away is heavily conditioned by their position within (or outside) such corporate groups. The emerging inequality is of a very different nature than the inequalities that participants in a sharing system may have to tolerate. The corporatist capitalist system is based on a very specific idea of "shares" and the practice of "shareholding". The question as to whether or not more egalitarian ways of accessing shares can be established within this system seems to very much depend on the way in which a sense of finiteness can be reintroduced. In practice, many associations and corporations are not living much longer than humans, but they continue to make claims as if they did and enjoy privileges on this basis. The possibility of accumulating enormous wealth is amplified through the creation and domination of corporations and through being a shareholder in a multiplicity of ways.

The shareholding world is the framework for the emerging trends in what is called "the sharing economy", discussed in more detail in Chapter 6. Many of these developments appear to be a straightforward continuation of market exchanges in which sharing is used as a label. That label is either strategically or unwittingly employed to expand the market rather than sharing in the sense of providing access to goods. There are exceptions, however, since some initiatives like the Basic Income Grant do provide the opportunity for a different sense of the social than that of being a member of an incorporated unit, be it a business corporation or a corporatist state. The importance of presence, which I have repeatedly emphasized throughout this book when describing and analysing successful systems of sharing, plays an important role here. The basic income is granted unconditionally, non-contributory and primarily according to being present at a particular place at a particular time. In this sense it is similar to sharing as it is practiced interpersonally by people whose presence is limited to a certain place and time. So far, the distribution schemes that are being developed for social grants, in particular in the global South, are still based on largely territorially defined membership categories. They are also not yet responsive to the fact that human presence is performative and time-dependent rather than categorical and once-and-for-all, an issue that is discussed at more length in Chapter 7.

Many of the new initiatives discussed in Chapter 6 rely on technical innovations through which the interpersonal character of sharing as we know it from small-scale societies is being transposed onto larger scales. Internet platforms and other communication technologies are at the heart of these developments that have been investigated in the last chapter. As it turns out, many of the problems and the, often unintended, side-effects in that process have to do with an insufficient recognition of the specific temporality as it is built into successful sharing practices. This temporality is in turn an effect of the recognition of personal finiteness, the fact that humans do not just face abstract time but rather good times and bad times and that they need the appropriate ways of dealing with such times. It is an important feature of sharing that it ends, namely when demands on sharing come to an end and the sharing of demands as living beings comes to an end. This implicates the opportunity for starting afresh and introducing something new, or – as the case may be – to decide to continue the old. It is also a "thinking from the end" which enables sharing in the way in which we find it practised in human culture.

Many worldviews suggest that individual lives, however miserable, gain their meaning through membership in a larger metaphysical body, be it the "house", "clan", "nation", a "church" or "the scientific community". I have emphasized the importance of an explicit recognition of the finiteness of life in many hunter-gatherer societies. I argue that it is also indispensable as a condition for establishing sharing in globalized complex societies. Hunter-gatherers are often considered a "cultural failure" precisely because their sharing practices are said to prevent them from creating corporate entities that promise individuals an eternal existence when they subsume themselves under the larger social whole or the "high culture" superseding the life of individuals. By contrast, the chapters of this book suggest that complex globalized society today is well-advised to turn to these societies and their social practice for inspiration. To be sure, social practices cannot be transposed across contexts and scales in a willy-nilly fashion. However, if we are searching for alternatives to the current regimes of distribution that leave many people destitute and excluded (see Ferguson 2015), it is a good idea to turn to those societies in which sharing has been successfully practised for millennia and under a host of changing circumstances. Hunter-gatherers are renowned for their insistence that the dead are truly dead, that they have had their life. The living do not "owe" them anything in that sense, at least not more than they owe to the social beings with whom they continue to share their lives on a daily basis. In their practices giving up life in death is not "traded in" for a better life in the way that we find in many book-based religions or political ideologies. There is also no attempt to convince oneself (or others) that the value of giving up things in sharing is compensated for by the prospect of a utopian future where one has everything. Sharing realizes its intrinsic good of extending the circle of those who can access a good, nothing more, nothing less.

This is where we may find the most radical interpretation of what it means to rely on your bodily presence for successful sharing. "Sharing a life" is all about being able to be young when it is your time and to be old when the time lapses, to be alive while it lasts and to be dead when the time comes. Being old and frail provides you with a different type of share than being young, typically at a later wave of sharing distributions, for instance. This may easily be misunderstood as a kind of "survival of the fittest" but this is not what is implied. Rather, it is the realization that no lifetime is perfect or privileged. Just as those who need something can make rightful demands against those who do have things to share, we may say that those who have their life in front of them can make claims against those who have had their life to the full. Or, from the perspective of those who are living among the have-nots: just as one has to learn to part with things, to give up things that others may need, ultimately one has also got to learn to give up one's life. Children and "the relative youth" are often privileged recipients of sharing (see Betzig and Turke 1986: 396) but a young person has no right to keep the benefits of the young once he or she has become older. The successful hunter today has no right to insist on privileges, because someone else could be the successful hunter tomorrow. The person who has just received a share is immediately the potential subject of demands by others who have got even less. The person nearing death has no privileged rights, being at a different stage of life than the ones that have their life in front of them. Just as everyone is potentially a recipient of a share and a provider of a share, depending how much the others have that one encounters, we could say that everyone is young or old with regard to others, not with regard to some abstract measure. As humans live their particular lives, there is no metaphysical point of reference to which some of these lives can be granted privileges vis-à-vis others. At different points in life we make different demands towards one another and we demand different things from life.

The sharing relations that we find practiced across the world are not between abstract humans that are all alive in the same general sense of being part of an unfolding live process. *Pace* Ingold (2011), it is all about "being mortal" rather than about "being alive". Sharing relations exist between those who are at one point in their finite personal life and others who are at other points in their finite personal lives. These are not points on predictable linear lifelines but are distinctly personal and unrepeatable. Sharing is not a relation between things in the abstract but rather between the things one has got and the things one will need to give up at certain times of one's life. We are here not talking about the universal fear of death in living beings or the philosophically constructed fear of existence in abstraction but about the concrete good times and bad times that each person experiences. People who face their mortality may attempt to ensure that survivors keep them alive in their memories. They demand a share in the collective memory of the survivors knowing that after death there are very limited or no means to do so. Survivors in turn give presence to the dead and they design many strategies to evade the demands that the dead may make on them. The issue of presence in the sharing process, already alluded to in earlier chapters, takes centre stage in this context. Just as much as death is about letting go, so is the acceptance of change. When things change, those who have grown up with the older ways need to let go of the world that they have lived in, in partial ways during their lives and in an ultimate way when they eventually die.

For a long time in human history, being mortal seemed to be self-evident and mortality was declared the "problem". Death was the enemy that humans set out to fight with their cultural repertoire of life-extending means and life-transcending imagery. Maybe it is one of the most important, if unintentional, lessons that sharing practices can teach: they provide an appropriate and much needed training for humans who are bound to deal with this finiteness in their social relations. Sharing in the form of allowing others access to skills, knowledge, and positions also invokes the notion of replacement and of giving up space for others, ultimately by giving up one's own life and by making room for others. People may give up personally owned things for others, they may love or hate one another, but "to die one another" (see Marten 1987) is of a different quality: the survivor determines how much the dead person is still present (in the memory of the living). Sharing life with others is about allowing them to have access to the developmental opportunities that would not be there if every generation would be able to secure their life beyond their own death. Those who are given the opportunity may still choose to reproduce the life of the elders but they are not forced to do so. They have alternatives.

BIBLIOGRAPHY

Adloff, Frank, and Volker Heins, eds. 2015. *Konvivialismus. Eine Debatte*. Bielefeld: Transcript-Verl.

Agar, Michael. 1994. *Language shock: Understanding the culture of conversation*. New York: Morrow.

———. 2008. *The professional stranger: An informal introduction to ethnography*. Bingley: Emerald.

———. 2013. *The lively science: Remodeling human social research*. Minneapolis: Publish Green.

Agger, Ben. 2012. *Oversharing: Presentations of self in the internet age*. New York: Routledge.

Aikhenvald, Alexandra Y. 2013. "The value of language and the language of value: A view from Amazonia." *HAU: Journal of Ethnographic Theory* 3 (2): 53–77.

Altena, Marga. 2009. "Agencies of the afterlife: weblogs and television shows on death in the Netherlands." In Dennis Cooley and Lloyd Steffen, eds. *Re-imaging death and dying: Global interdisciplinary perspectives*. pp. 183–190. Oxford: Inter-disciplinary press.

Altena, Marga, Catrien Notermans, and Thomas Widlok. 2011. "Place, action, and community in internet rituals." In Ronald L. Grimes, Ute Hüsken, Udo Simon, Eric Venbrux, eds. *Ritual, media, and conflict*. pp. 133–163. Oxford: Oxford University Press.

Altman, Jon. 2011. *A genealogy of 'demand sharing': From pure anthropology to public policy*. In Y. Musharbash and M. Barber (eds), *Ethnography and the production of anthropological knowledge: Essays in honour of Nicolas Peterson* pp. 187-200. Canberra: ANU E Press.

Altman, Jon, and Nicolas Peterson. 1988. "Rights to game and rights to cash among contemporary Australian hunter-gatherers." In Tim Ingold, David Riches and James Woodburn eds. *Hunters and gatherers. Vol. 2. Property, power and ideology*. pp. 75–94. Oxford: Berg.

Andersen, Steffen, Seda Ertaç, Uri Genîzî, Hoffman Moshe, and John A. List. 2011. "Stakes matter in ultimatum games." *The American economic review* 101(7): 3427–3439.

Antweiler, Christoph. 2007. *Was ist den Menschen gemeinsam?: Über Kultur und Kulturen*. Darmstadt: Wiss. Buchges.

Appadurai, Arjun. 1986. *The social life of things: Commodities in cultural perspective.* Cambridge.

——. 2016. *Banking on words: The failure of language in the age of derivative finance.* Chicago, London: The University of Chicago Press.

Bahuchet, Serge. 1990. "Food sharing among the Pygmies of Central Africa." *African Studies Monographs* 11(1): 27–53.

Barnard, Alan. 1983. "Contemporary hunter-gatherers: Current theoretical issues in ecology and social organization." *Annual Review of Anthropology* 12: 193–214.

——. 2002. "The foraging mode of thought." *Senri Ethnol. Stud.* 60: 5–24.

——. 2011. *Social anthropology and human origins.* Cambridge: Cambridge University Press.

Becker, Gary S. 1991. *A treatise on the family.* Cambridge, Mass: Harvard University Press.

Belk, Russell. 2007. "Why not share rather than own?" *The ANNALS of the American Academy of Political and Social Science* 611(1): 126–140.

——. 2010. "Sharing." *Journal of Consumer Research* 36(5): 715–734.

Benjamin, Geoffrey. 2011. "Egalitarianism and ranking in the Malay World." In Thomas Gibson and Kenneth Sillander eds. *Anarchic solidarity. Autonomy, equality, and fellowship in Southeast Asia.* pp. 170–201. New Haven Conn.: Yale University Southeast Asia Studies.

Benkler, Yochai. 2004. "Sharing nicely: On sharable goods and the emergence of sharing as a modality of economic production." *Yale Law Journal* 114(2): 273–358.

Béteille, André, ed. 1969. *Social inequality: Selected readings.* Harmondsworth: Penguin Books.

Betzig, Laura, and Paul Turke. 1986. "Food sharing on Ifaluk." *Current Anthropology* 27: 397–400.

Biesele, Megan, and Steve Barclay. "Ju/'hoan women's tracking knowledge and its contribution to their husbands' hunting success." *African Study Monographs* Suppl. 26: 67–84.

Biesele, Megan, and Robert K. Hitchcock. 2013. *The Ju/'hoan San of Nyae Nyae and Namibian independence: Development, democracy, and indigenous voices in Southern Africa.* New York NY: Berghahn.

Bird-David, Nurit. 1990. "The giving environment: Another perspective on the economic system of gatherer-hunters." *Current Anthropology* 31: 189–196.

——. 2005. "The property of sharing: Western analytical notions, Nayaka contexts." In Thomas Widlok and Wolde Gossa Tadesse eds. *Property and equality. Volume 1: Ritualisation, sharing, egalitarianism.* pp. 201–216. New York: Berghahn.

Bliege Bird, Rebecca, Bird Douglas, Eric Alden Smith, and Geoffrey Kushnik. 2002. "Risk and reciprocity in Meriam food sharing." *Evolution and Human Behavior* 23(4): 297–321.

Bliege Bird, Rebecca, and Douglas Bird. 1997. "Delayed reciprocity and tolerated theft: The behavioral ecology of food-sharing strategies." *Current Anthropology* 38: 49–78.

Bloch, Maurice. 1992. *Prey into hunter: The politics of religious experience.* Cambridge: Cambridge University Press.

——. 2005. "Where did anthropology go?: or the need for 'human nature'." In Maurice Bloch ed. *Essays on cultural transmission.* pp. 1–20. Oxford: Berg.

Blurton Jones, Nicholas. 1984. "A selfish origin of human food sharing: Tolerated theft." *Ethology and Sociobiology* 5: 1–3.

——. 1987. "Tolerated theft: Suggestions about the ecology and evolution of sharing, hoarding, and scrounging." *Social Science Information* 26: 31–54.

Bodenhorn, Barbara. 2005. "Sharing costs: An exploration of personal and individual property, equalities and differentiation." In Thomas Widlok and Wolde Gossa Tadesse eds. *Property and equality. Volume 1: Ritualisation, sharing, egalitarianism.* pp. 77–104. New York: Berghahn.

Boehm, Christopher. 1999. *Hierarchy in the forest: The evolution of egalitarian behavior.* Cambridge, MA: Harvard University Press.

Bohannan, Paul. 1967. "The impact of money on an African subsistence economy." In George Dalton ed. *Tribal and peasant economies: Readings in economic anthropology,* pp. 123–135. Garden City, New York: Natural History Press.

Bourdieu, Pierre. 1977. *Outline of a theory of practice.* Cambridge, U.K, New York: Cambridge University Press.

———. 1979. *La distinction: Critique sociale du jugement.* Paris: Les Éd. de Minuit.

———. 2012. *Sur l'État: Cours au Collège de France ; (1989 - 1992).* Paris: Seuil.

Bourdieu, Pierre, and Franz Schultheis. 2010. *Die zwei Gesichter der Arbeit: Interdependenzen von Zeit- und Wirtschaftsstrukturen am Beispiel einer Ethnologie der algerischen Übergangsgesellschaft.* Konstanz: UVK-Verl.-Ges.

Brody, Hugh. 2001. *The other side of Eden: Hunter-gatherers, farmers and the shaping of the world.* London: Faber.

Brown, Penelope, and Stephen C. Levinson. 1987. *Politeness: Some universals in language usage.* Cambridge: Cambridge University Press.

Brunton, Ron. 1989. "The cultural instability of egalitarian societies." *Man: The Journal of the Royal Anthropological Institute* 24 (4): 673–681.

Busby, Cecilia. 1997. "Permeable and partible persons: A comparative analysis of gender and body in South India and Melanesia." *The Journal of the Royal Anthropological Institute* 3(2): 261–278.

Cadeliña, Rowe. 1985. "Comment on H. Kaplan and K. Hill, food sharing among Ache foragers." *Current Anthropology* 26(2): 239–240.

Calvino, Italo. 1981. *If on a winter's night a traveler.* New York: Harcourt Brace Jovanovich.

Cammaerts, Bart. 2011. "Disruptive sharing in a digital age: rejecting neoliberalism." *Continuum: Journal of Media and Cultural Studies* 25(1): 47–62.

Chakraborty, Rabindra N. 2006. "Sharing culture and resource conservation in hunter-gatherer societies." *Oxford Economic Papers* 59: 63–88.

Christensen, Lisbeth. 2010. "From 'spirituality' to 'religion' – way of sharing knowledge of the 'Other World'." In *The principle of sharing.* Segregation and construction of social identities at the transition from foraging to farming; proceedings of a symposium held on 29–31 January 2009 at the Albert-Ludwigs-University of Freiburg. ed. Marion Benz, pp. 81–90. Berlin: Ex Oriente.

Claassen, Rutger. 2004. *Het eeuwig tekort: Een filosofie van de schaarste.* Amsterdam: Ambo.

Clark, Gregory. 2007. *A farewell to alms: A brief economic history of the world.* Princeton: Princeton University Press.

Coleman, James S. 1982. *The asymmetric society.* Syracuse, NY: Syracuse University Press.

Collings, Peter, George Wenzel, and Richard Condon. 1998. "Modern food sharing networks and community integration in the central Canadian Arctic." *Arctic* 51(4): 301–314.

Condry, Ian. 2004. "Cultures of music piracy: An ethnographic comparison of the US and Japan." *International Journal of Cultural Studies* 7(3): 343–363.

Cooper, Paul. 2004. "The gift of education: An anthropological perspective on the commoditization of learning." *Anthropology Today* 20(6): 5–8.

Csordas, Thomas. 2005. "Intersubjectivity and intercorporeality." In Kazuyoshi Sugawara ed. *Construction and distribution of body resources. Correlations between ecological, symbolic, and medical systems.* pp. 126–135. Tokyo: Research Institute for Languages and Cultures of Asia and Africa, Tokyo University of Foreign Studies.

Dahlberg, Frances, ed. 1981. *Woman the gatherer.* New Haven: Yale Univ. Press.

Dahrendorf, Ralf. 1969. "On the origins of inequality among men." In André Béteille ed. *Social inequality. Selected readings.* pp. 16–44. Harmondsworth: Penguin Books.

Damas, David. 1972. "Central Eskimo systems of food sharing." *Ethnology* 11(3): 220–240.

Därmann, Iris. 2005. *Fremde Monde der Vernunft: Die ethnologische Provokation der Philosophie.* München: Fink.

Dawdy, Shannon, and Joe Bonni. 2012. "Towards a general theory of piracy." *Anthropological Quarterly* 85(3): 673–699.

Day, Sophie. 1999. "Hustling: Individualism among London prostitutes." In Day, Sophie, Euthymios Papataxiarchēs, and Michael Stewart, eds. *Lilies of the field: Marginal people who live for the moment.* pp. 137–157. Boulder: Westview Press.

De Waal, Frans de, and Michelle Berger. "Payment for labour in monkeys." *Nature,* 404: 563.

Deacon, Terrence W. 2012. *Incomplete nature: How mind emerged from matter.* New York: Norton.

Dentan, Robert. 2011. "Childhood, familiarity, and social life among East Semai." In Thomas Gibson and Kenneth Sillander eds. *Anarchic solidarity. Autonomy, equality, and fellowship in Southeast Asia.* pp. 88–118. New Haven Conn.: Yale University.

Descola, Philippe. 2011. *L'ecologie des autres: L'anthropologie et la question de la nature.* Versalles: Quae éditions.

Dowling, John. 1968. "Individual ownership and the sharing of game in hunting societies." *American Anthropologist* 70: 502–507.

Drucker, Peter F. 1972. *Concept of the corporation.* New York: John Day.

Duerr, Janina. 2010. *Von Tierhütern und Tiertötern: Mythos und Ethik der Jagd im kulturhistorischen Vergleich.* Bonn: Habelt.

Durkheim, Émile. 1912. *Les formes élémentaire de la vie religieuse: Le système totémique en Australie.* Paris: F. Alcan.

Duschek, Klaus-Jürgen. 2006. *Leben in Deutschland: Haushalte, Familien und Gesundheit - Ergebnisse des Mikrozensus 2005.* Wiesbaden: Statistisches Bundesamt.

Earle, Timothy K. 2002. *Bronze Age economics: The beginnings of political economies.* Boulder CO, Oxford: Westview Press.

Edel, May, and Abraham Edel. 1968. *Anthropology and ethics: The quest for moral understanding.* Cleveland: The Press of Case Western Reserve Univ.

Eriksen, Thomas H. 1995. *Small places, large issues: An introduction to social and cultural anthropology.* London: Pluto Press.

——. 2004. *What is anthropology?* London: Pluto Press.

Ferguson, James. 1994. *The anti-politics machine: "development," depoliticization, and bureaucratic power in Lesotho.* Minneapolis: University of Minnesota Press.

——. 2013. "Declarations of dependence: Labour, personhood, and welfare in southern Africa." *Journal of the Royal Anthropological Institute (N.S.)* 19: 223–242.

——. 2015. *Give a man a fish: Reflections on the new politics of distribution.* Durham, London: Duke Univ. Press.

Fortier, Jana. 2001. "Sharing, hoarding, and theft: Exchange and resistance in forager-farmer relations." *Ethnologie* 40(3): 193–211.

Fox, Robin. 1967. *Kinship and marriage: An anthropological perspective.* Harmondsworth: Penguin Books.

Frischmann, Brett M. 2012. *Infrastructure: The social value of shared resources.* Oxford: Oxford University Press.

Fromm, Erich. 1976. *To have or to be?* New York: Harper & Row.

Fuchs, Thomas. 2008. *Das Gehirn - ein Beziehungsorgan: Eine phänomenologisch-ökologische Konzeption.* Stuttgart: Kohlhammer.

Gell, Alfred. 1999. "Inter-tribal commodity barter and reproductive gift-exchange in old Melanesia." In Eric Hirsch ed. *The art of anthropology. Essays and diagrams.* pp. 76–106. London: Athlone Press.

Gibson, James J. 1979. *The ecological approach to visual perception.* Boston: Houghton Mifflin.

Gibson, Thomas, and Kenneth Sillander, eds. 2011. *Anarchic solidarity: Autonomy, equality, and fellowship in Southeast Asia.* New Haven, CT: Yale University.

Giesler, Markus, and Mali Pohlmann. 2003. "The anthropology of file sharing: Consuming Napster as a gift." *Advances in Consumer Research* 30: 273–279.

Gintis, Herbert, and Carel van Schaik. 2013. *"Zoon Politicon:* The evolutionary roots of human sociopolitical systems." In Peter J. Richerson and Morten H. Christiansen eds. *Cultural evolution. Society, technology, language, and religion.* pp. 25–44. Cambridge, MA: MIT Press.

Glaskin, Katie. 2007. "Outstation incorporation as precursor to a prescribed body corporate." In James F Weiner and Kate Glaskin eds. *Customary land tenure and registration in Australia and Papua New Guinea: Anthropological perspectives* pp. 199–222. Australia: ANU Press.

Gould, Richard. 1969. *Yiwara: Foragers of the Australian desert.* New York: Scribner.

Gowdy, John M., ed. 1998. *Limited wants, unlimited means: A reader on hunter-gatherer economics and the environment.* Washington, DC: Island Press.

Graeber, David. 2001. *Toward an anthropological theory of value: The false coin of our own dreams.* New York: Palgrave.

———. 2011. *Debt: The first 5,000 years.* Brooklyn, NY: Melville House.

Gregory, Christopher A. 1982. *Gifts and commodities.* London: Academic Press.

Grinker, Roy R. 1994. *Houses in the rain forest: Ethnicity and inequality among farmers and foragers in Central Africa.* Berkeley CA: University of California Press.

Gudeman, Stephen. 2001. *The anthropology of economy: Community, market, and culture.* Malden: Blackwell.

Guenther, Mathias. 2010. "Sharing among the San, today, yesterday and in the past." In *The principle of sharing.* Segregation and construction of social identities at the transition from foraging to farming; proceedings of a symposium held on 29 – 31 January 2009 at the Albert-Ludwigs-University of Freiburg. ed. Marion Benz, pp. 105–135. Berlin: Ex Oriente.

Gurven, Michael. 2001. "Reservation food sharing among the Ache of Paraguay." *Human Nature* 12(4): 273–298.

———. 2004. "To give and to give not: The behavioral ecology of human food transfers." *Behavioral and Brain Sciences* 27: 543–583.

Gurven, Michael, and Kim Hill. 2009. "Why do men hunt? A reevaluation of "man the hunter" and the sexual division of labor." *Current Anthropology* 50(1): 51–74.

Gurven, M., K. Hill, and H. Kaplan. 2002. "From forest to reservation: Transitions in food sharing behavior among the Ache of Paraguay." *Journal of Anthropological Research* 58(1): 91–118.

Gurven, Michael, Wesley Allen-Arave, Kim Hill, and Magdalena Hurtado. 2001. "Reservation food sharing among the Ache of Paraguay." *Human Nature* 12(4): 273–297.

Gurven, Michael, Kim Hill, Hillard Kaplan, Ana Hurtado, and Lyle Lyle. 2000. "Food transfers among Hiwi foragers of Venezuela: Tests of reciprocity." *Human Ecology* 28(2): 171–218.

Haarmann, Claudia. 2009. *Making the difference! The BIG in Namibia.* Windhoek, Namibia: NANGOF.

Hames, Raymond, and Carl McCabe. 2007. "Meal sharing among the Ye'kwana." *Human Nature* 18: 1–21.

Hart, Keith. 2000. *The memory bank: Money in an unequal world.* London: Profile Books.

Hawkes, Kristen. 1993. "Why hunter-gatherers work: An ancient version of the problem of public goods." *Current Anthropology* 34(4): 341–361.

Hawkes, Kristen, Kim Hill, and James O'Connell. 1982. "Why hunters gather: Optimal foraging and the Ache of Eastern Paraguay." *American Ethnologist* 9(2): 379–398.

Hawkes, Kristen, James O'Connell, Kim Hill, and Eric Charnov. 1985. "How much is enough? Hunters and limited needs." *Ethology and Sociobiology* 6: 3–15.

Hayden, Brian. 1994. "Competition, labor, and complex hunter-gatherers." In Ernest Burch and Linda Ellanna eds. *Key issues in hunter-gatherer research.* pp. 223–239 Oxford: Berg.

Henrich, Joseph, Steven Heine, and Ara Norenzayan. 2010. "The weirdest people in the world?" *Behavioral and Brain Sciences* 33: 61–135.

Henrich, Joseph et al 2005. ""Economic man" in cross-cultural perspective: Behavioral experiments in 15 small-scale societies." *Behavioral and Brain Sciences* 28: 795–855.

Hewlett, Barry, Michael Lamb, Birgit Leyendecker, and Axel Schölmerich. 2000. "Internal working models, trust, and sharing among foragers." *Current Anthropology* 41(2): 287–297.

Hill, Kim. 2002. "Altruistic cooperation during foraging by the Ache, and the evolved human predisposition to cooperate." *Human Nature* 13(1): 105–128.

Holland, Maximilian. 2012. *Social bonding and nurture kinship: Compatibility between cultural and biological approaches.* [North Charleston]: Createspace Independent Publishing.

Hoymann, Gertie. 2010. "Questions and responses in =Akhoe Hai//om." *Journal of Pragmatics* 42(10): 2726–2740.

Hunt, Robert C. 2000. "Forager food sharing economy: Transfers and exchanges." In George Wenzel, Greta Hovelsrud-Broda, and Nobuhiro Kishigami eds. *The social economy of sharing: Resources allocation and modern hunter gatherers,* pp. 7–26. Osaka: National Museum of Ethnology.

Hutchinson, Sharon. 1997. "The cattle of money and the cattle of girls among the Nuer." In Roy R. Grinker, Stephen C. Lubkemann and Christopher B. Steiner, eds *Perspectives on Africa. A reader in culture, history, and representation.* pp. 190–210. Oxford: Blackwell.

Hyndman, David. 1985. "Comment on H. Kaplan and K. Hill, Food Sharing among Ache foragers." *Current Anthropology* 26(2): 240.

Ichikawa, Mitsuo. 2005. "Food sharing and ownership among Central African hunter-gatherers: An evolutionary perspective." In Thomas Widlok and Wolde Gossa Tadesse eds. *Property and equality. Volume 1: Ritualisation, sharing, egalitarianism.* pp. 151–164. New York: Berghahn.

Ingold, Tim. 1983. "The significance of storage in hunting societies." *Man (New Series)* 18(3): 553–571.

——. 1986. *The appropriation of nature: Essays on human ecology and social relations.* Manchester: Manchester University Press.

——. 1999. "On the social relations of the hunter-gatherer band." In Richard B. Lee and Richard H. Daly eds. *The Cambridge encyclopedia of hunters and gatherers.* pp. 399–410. Cambridge, U.K., New York, NY: Cambridge University Press.

——. 2000. *The perception of the environment: Essays on livelihood, dwelling & skill.* New York: Routledge.

——. 2005. "Time, Memory and Property." In *Property and equality. Volume 1: Ritualisation, sharing, egalitarianism. ed.* Thomas Widlok and Wolde Gossa Tadesse, 165–174. New York: Berghahn.

——. 2007. *Lines: A brief history*. London: Routledge.

——. 2011. *Being alive: Essays on movement, knowledge and description*. London: Routledge.

Ingold, Tim, David Riches, and James Woodburn, eds. 1988. *Hunters and gatherers*. Oxford: Berg.

Jaeggi, Adrian, and Carel van Schaik. 2011. "The evolution of food sharing in primates." *Behavioral Ecology and Sociobiology* 65: 2125-2140.

Jaeggi, Adrian V., and Michael Gurven. 2013. "Natural cooperators: Food sharing in humans and other primates." *Evolutionary Anthropology* 22: 186–195.

John, Nicholas. 2012. "Sharing and Web 2.0: The emergence of a keyword." *New Media and Society* 15(2): 167–182.

Kantorowicz, Ernst. 1957. *The King's two bodies*. Princeton, NJ: Princeton University Press.

Kaplan, Hillard, and Kim Hill. 1985. "Food sharing among Ache foragers: Tests of explanatory hypothese." *Current Anthropology* 26: 223–246.

Kästner, Sibylle. 2012. *Jagende Sammlerinnen und sammelnde Jägerinnen: Wie australische Aborigines-Frauen Tiere erbeuten*. Münster: Lit-Verl.

Keeffe, Kevin. 2003. *Paddy's road: Life stories of Patrick Dodson*. Canberra: Aboriginal Studies Press.

Keen, Ian. 2000. "A bundle of sticks: The debate over Yolngu clans." *Journal of the Royal Anthropological Institute* 6 (3): 419–436.

Kelly, Robert L. 1995. *The foraging spectrum: Diversity in hunter-gatherer lifeways*. Washington: Smithsonian.

Kempen, Jonathan. 2016. *"Sharing is over!" A case study on sharing norms in the Namibian resettlement projects of Skoonheid and Drimiopsis*. Köln: Cologne African Studies Centre.

Kent, Susan. 1993. "Sharing in an egalitarian Kalahari community." Man (New Series) 28(3): 479–514.

Kishigami, Nobuhiro. 2004. "A new typology of food-sharing practices among hunter-gatherers, with a special focus on Inuit examples." *Journal of Anthropological Research* 60 (3): 341–358.

Klocke-Daffa, Sabine. 2001. *"Wenn du hast, mußt du geben": Soziale Sicherung im Ritus und im Alltag bei den Nama von Berseba/Namibia*. Münster: Lit.

——. 2012. *Is BIG big enough? Basic Income Grant in Namibia: An anthropological enquiry* Report. Tübingen: University of Tübingen. Department of Social and Cultural Anthropology.

Köhler, Axel, and Jerome Lewis. 2002. "Putting hunter-gatherer and farmer relations in perspective: A Commentary from Central Africa." In Susan Kent ed. *Ethnicity, hunter-gatherers, and the "other". Association and assimilation in Africa.* pp. 276–305. Washington: Smithsonian.

Kopytoff, Igor. 1971. *Ancestors as elders in Africa*. Indianapolis: Bobbs-Merrill.

——. 1998. "The cultural biography of things: Commoditization as process." *Economic anthropology:* 426–453.

Koster, Jeremy. 2011. "Inter-household meat sharing among Mayangna and Miskito horticulturalists in Nicaragua." *Human Nature* 22: 394–415.

Koster, Jeremy, and George Leckie. 2014. "Food sharing networks in lowland Nicaragua: an application of the social relations model to count data." *Social Networks* 38: 100–110.

Kropotkin, Pëtr A. 1995. *The conquest of bread and other writings*. Cambridge: Cambridge University Press.

LaRose, Robert, Ying Ju Lai, Ryan Lange, Bradley Love, and Yuehua Wu. 2006. "Sharing or piracy? An exploration of downloading behavior." *Journal of Computer-Mediated Communication* 11: 1–21.

Lave, Jean. 2011. *Apprenticeship in critical ethnographic practice*. Chicago: University of Chicago Press.

Lave, Jean, and Etienne Wenger. 1991. *Situated learning: Legitimate peripheral participation*. Cambridge: Cambridge University Press.

Layton, Robert. 2000. *Anthropology and history in Franche-Comté: A critique of social theory*. Oxford: Oxford University Press.

Ledenena, Alena, ed. 1998. *Russia's economy of favors. Blat, networking and informal exchange*. Cambridge: Cambridge University Press.

Lee, Richard B. 1968. "What hunters do for a living, or, how to make out on scarce resources." In Richard Lee and Irvine DeVore eds. *Man the hunter:* pp. 30–48. Aldine: Transaction Publishers.

——. 1988. "Reflections on primitive communism." In Tim Ingold, David Riches and James Woodburn eds. *Hunters and gatherers.* pp. 252–268. Oxford: Berg.

——. 1993. *The Dobe Ju/'hoansi*. Fort Worth: Harcourt Brace College Publishers.

Lee, Richard B., and Richard Daly, eds. 1999. *The Cambridge encyclopedia of hunters and gatherers*. Cambridge: Cambridge University Press.

Lee, Richard B., and Irven DeVore. 1968. "Problems in the study of hunters and gatherers." In Richard Lee and Irvine DeVore eds. *Man the hunter*, pp. 3–12. Aldine: Transaction Publishers.

Leggewie, Claus, Darius Zifonun, Anne Lang, Marcel Siepmann, and Johanna Hoppen. 2012. *Schlüsselwerke der Kulturwissenschaften*. Bielefeld: Transcript-Verl.

Lévi-Strauss, Claude. 1949. *Les structures élémentaires de la parenté*. Paris: Presses Universitaires de France.

——. 1965. *La pensée sauvage*. Paris: Plon.

Lewis, Jerome. 2005. "Whose forest is it anyway? Mbendjele Yaka Pygmies, the Ndoki Forest and the wider world." In Thomas Widlok and Wolde Tadesse, eds. *Property and equality:* Vol. 2. Encapsulation, Commercialisation, Discrimination, pp. 56–78. New York: Berghahn.

——. 2008. "Managing abundance, not chasing scarcity: The real challenge for the 21st century." *Radical Anthropology* 2(9): 11–19.

Leyshon, Andrew, Peter Webb, Shaun French, Nigel Thrift, and Louise Crewe. 2005. "On the reproduction of the musical economy after the internet." *Media, Culture & Society* 27(2): 177–209.

Liberman, Kenneth. 1985. *Understanding interaction in central Australia: An ethnomethodological study of Australian Aboriginal people*. Boston, MA: Routledge & Paul.

Lief, Jacob 2015. *I am because you are. How the spirit of Ubuntu inspired an unlikely friendship and transformed a community*. New York: Rodale.

Løgstrup, K. E. 1997. *The ethical demand*. Notre Dame, Ind.: University of Notre Dame Press.

Lowe, Pat, and Jimmy Pike. 1997. *Jimmy and Pat meet the Queen*. Broome, W.A.: Backroom Press.

Lüdtke, Nico. 2009. "Die (biologische) Natur des Menschen: Soziobiologie - Philosophische Anthropologie - Soziologie." Ralf Becker, Joachim Fischer and Matthias Schloßberger, eds. In *Philosophische Anthropologie im Aufbruch. Max Scheler und Helmuth Plessner im Vergleich*. pp. 343–355. Berlin: Akademie Verlag Berlin.

Lye, Tuck-Po. 2004. *Changing pathways: Forest degradation and the Batek of Pahang, Malaysia*. Lanham: Lexington Books.

Macdonald, Gaynor. 2000. "Economies and personhood: Demand sharing among the Wiradjuri of New South Wales." In George W. Wenzel, Grete Hovelsrud-Broda and

Nobuhiro Kishigami eds. *The social economy of sharing. Resource allocation and modern hunter-gatherers*. pp. 87–111. Osaka: National Museum of Ethnology.

Mantziaris, Christos, and David Martin. 2000. *Native title corporations: A legal and anthropological analysis*. Sydney: Federation Press.

Marlowe, Frank W. 2004. "What explains Hadza food sharing?" *Socioeconomic aspects of human behavioral ecology. Research in economic anthropology* 23: 69–88.

Marshall, Lorna. 1961. "Sharing, talking, and giving: Relief of social tensions among the !Kung bushmen." *Journal of the International African Institute* 31(3): 231–249.

——. 1976. *The !Kung of Nyae Nyae*. Cambridge, MA: Harvard University Press.

Marten, Rainer. 1987. *Der menschliche Tod: Eine philosophische Revision*. Paderborn: Schöningh.

——. 1993. *Lebenskunst*. München: Fink.

——. 2009. *Masslosigkeit: Zur Notwendigkeit des Unnötigen*. Freiburg, Br., München: Alber.

——. 2013. *Endlichkeit: Zum Drama von Leben und Tod*. Freiburg, Br., München: Alber.

Mathew, Sarah, Robert Boyd, and Matthijs Van Veelen. 2013. "Human cooperation among kin and close associates may require enforcement of norms by third parties." In Peter J. Richerson and Morten H. Christiansen eds. *Cultural evolution. Society, technology, language, and religion*. pp. 45–60. Cambridge, Mass.: MIT Press.

Mauss, Marcel. 2002. *Essai sur le don: Forme et raison de l'échange dans les sociétés archaïques:* Edition électronique.

Mechlenburg, Gustav. *Monde entfernt*. http://www.textem.de/index.php?id=998.

Menestrey Schwieger, Diego A. 2012. *Institutions and conflict: An ethnographic study of communal water management in North-West Namibia*. Master thesis Köln: Inst. für Ethnologie. Univ. zu Köln.

——. 2015. *The pump keeps on running: On the emergence of water management institutions between state decentralisation and local practices in northern Kunene*. PhD dissertation Inst. fur Ethnologie. Univ.zu Köln.

Michéa, Jean-Claude. 2007. *L'empire du moindre mal: Essai sur la civilisation libérale*. Paris: Climats.

Miller, Daniel, ed. 2001. *Car cultures*. Oxford: Berg.

Mitani, John, and David Watts. 2001. "Why do chimpanzees hunt and share meat." *Animal Behaviour* 61: 915–924.

Moizo, Bernard R. 1991. *We all one mob but different: Groups, grouping and identity in a Kimberley Aboriginal village*. PhD dissertation Australian National University. Canberra.

Morel, Petronella, and Helen Ross. 1993. *Housing design assessment for bush communities*. Alice Springs: Tangentyere Council.

Morell, Mayo. 2011. "The unethics of sharing: Wikiwashing." *International Review of Information Ethics* 15: 9–16.

Morris, Brian. 1987. *Anthropological studies of religion: An introductory text*. Cambridge: Cambridge University Press.

Musharbash, Yasmine. 2008. *Yuendumu everyday: Contemporary life in remote Aboriginal Australia*. Canberra: Aboriginal Studies Press.

Myers, Fred R. 1988. "Burning the truck and holding the country: Property, time, and the negotiation identity among Pintupi Aborigines." In Tim Ingold, David Riches and James Woodburn eds. *Hunters and Gatherers. Vol. 2. Property, Power and Ideology*. pp. 52–94. Oxford: Berg.

Nadasdy, Paul. 2007. "The gift in the animal: The ontology of hunting and human-animal sociality." *American Ethnologist* 34(1): 25–43.

Nolin, David. 2010. "Food-sharing networks in Lamalera, Indonesia." *Human Nature,* 21: 243–268.

——. 2012. "Food-sharing networks in Lamalera, Indonesia: status, sharing, and signaling." *Evolution and Human Behavior,* 33: 334–345.

Nuttall, Mark. 2000. "Choosing kin: Sharing and subsistence in a Greenlandic hunting community In Peter Schweltzer ed." *Dividends of kinship: meanings and uses of social relatedness:* pp. 33–60. London: Routledge.

Obeyesekere, Gananath. 1992. *The apotheosis of captain Cook: European mythmaking in the Pacific.* Princeton NJ: Princeton University Press.

Packer, Craig, and Anne E. Pusey. 1997. *La cooperacion en las leones.* Barcelona, España: Prensa Cientifica.

Pelto, Pertti J. 1973. *The snowmobile revolution: Technology and social change in the Arctic.* Menlo Park, CA: Cummings.

Peristiany, Jean G. 1939. *The social institutions of the Kipsigis.* London: Routledge.

Peterson, Nicolas. 1993. "Demand sharing: Reciprocity and the pressure for generosity among foragers." *American Anthropologist* 95(4): 860–874.

——. 2002. *From mode of production to moral economy: Kinship and sharing in fourth world social orders.* Paper delivered at the ninth national conference on hunting and gathering societies, 9-13 September 2002, Edinburgh.

——. 2013. "On the persistence of sharing: Personhood, asymmetrical reciprocity, and demand sharing in the indigenous Australian domestic moral economy." *The Australian Journal of Anthropology:* 24(2): 166–176.

Polanyi, Karl. 1944. *The great transformation.* New York NY: Rinehart.

Price, John A. 1975. "Sharing: The integration of intimate economies." *Anthropologica* 17 (1): 3–27.

Pryor, Frederic and Nelson Graburn. 1980. "The Myth of Reciprocity." In Kenneth J. Gergen, Martin S. Greenberg and Richard H. Willis eds. *Social exchange.* Advances in theory and research. pp. 215–237. New York: Plenum Press.

Rapold, Christian. 2011. "Semantics of Khoekhoe reciprocal constructions." In Nicholas Evans ed. *Reciprocals and semantic typology.* pp. 61–74. Amsterdam, Philadelphia: John Benjamins.

Read, Peter. 2000. *Settlement: A history of Australian indigenous housing.* Canberra: Aboriginal Studies Press.

Richerson, Peter and Morten Christiansen. 2013. "Introduction." In Peter J. Richerson and Morten H. Christiansen eds. *Cultural evolution. Society, technology, language, and religion.* pp. 1–21. Cambridge, MA: MIT Press.

Riches, David. 2000. "The holistic person; or, the ideology of egalitarianism." *Journal of the Royal Anthropological Institute* 6: 669–685.

Rifkin, Jeremy. 2014. *The zero marginal cost society: The internet of things, the collaborative commons, and the eclipse of capitalism.* New York NY: Palgrave Macmillan.

Rio, Knut. 2007. "Denying the gift: Aspects of ceremonial exchange and sacrifice on Ambrym Island, Vanuatu." *Anthropological Theory* 7(4): 449–470.

Rival, Laura. 2000. "Marginality with a difference, or How the Huaorani preserve their sharing relations and naturalize outside powers." In Peter Schweitzer, Megan Biesele, and Hitchcock Robert eds. *Hunters and gatherers in the modern context: Conflict, resistance and self-determination.* pp. 244–260. Oxford: Berghahn.

Robertson, A. F. 2001. *Greed: Gut feelings, growth, and history.* Cambridge: Polity.

Ross, Helen. 1987. *Just for living: Aboriginal perceptions of housing in northwest Australia.* Canberra: Aboriginal Studies Press.

Rousseau, Jean-Jacques. 1994. *Discourse on the origin of inequality.* Oxford, New York: Oxford University Press.

Ruskola, Teemu. 2005. "Home economics: What is the difference between a family and a corporation?" In Martha M. Ertman and Joan Williams eds. *Rethinking commodification. Cases and readings in law and culture.* pp. 324–344. New York: New York University Press.

Sahlins, Marshall. 1985. *Islands of history.* London: Tavistock.

——. 1988. *Stone age economics.* London: Routledge.

Saul, John R. 1997. *The unconscious civilization.* Concord, Ontario: Anansi Press.

Schäfer, Marie. *Cultural variation in children's development of resource sharing and fairness.* PhD dissertation. Leipzig University.

Schäfers, Manfred. *Transferzahlungen.* www.faz.net/-gqe-we69.

Schmidt, Mario. 2014. *"It will always be with us" – Corruption as an ontological fact among Kenyan Luo.* Global Cooperation Research Papers 7. Duisburg.

Schnegg, Michael. 2006. "'Give me some sugar!' Rhythm and structure of sharing in a Namibian community." *soFid Methoden und Instrumente der Sozialwissenschaften* 2: 11–21.

——. 2015. "Reciprocity on demand: Sharing and exchanging food in northwestern Namibia." *Human Nature* 26(3): 313-330.

Schor, Juliet. 2010. *Plenitude: The new economics of true wealth.* New York: Penguin Press.

Schweitzer, Peter P., ed. 2000. *Dividends of kinship: Meanings and uses of social relatedness.* London, New York: Routledge.

Schweizer, Thomas. 1996. "Reconsidering social networks: Reciprocal gift exchange among the !Kung." *Journal of Quantitative Anthropology* 6: 147–170.

——. 1997. "Embeddedness of ethnographic cases: A social networks perspective." *Current Anthropology* 38(5): 739–760.

Sigrist, Christian. 1979. *Regulierte Anarchie: Unters. zum Fehlen und zur Entstehung politischer Herrschaft in segmentären Gesellschaften Afrikas.* Frankfurt a.M.: Syndikat.

Smith, Erica A. 1988. "Risk and uncertainty in the 'original affluent society': Evolutionary ecology of resource-sharing and land tenure." In Tim Ingold, David Riches and James Woodburn eds. *Hunters and gatherers:* pp. 222–251. Oxford: Berg.

Ssorin-Chaikov, Nikolai. 2006. "On heterochrony: birthday gifts to Stalin, 1949." *Journal of the Royal Anthropological Institute* 12(2): 355–375.

Stack, Carol B. 1974. *All our kin: Strategies for survival in a Black community.* New York: Harper & Row.

Stalder, Felix, and Wolfgang Sützl. 2011. "Ethics of sharing." *International Review of Information Ethics* 15: 2.

Stotz, Gertrude. 1993. *"Kurdungurlu got to drive Toyota": Differential colonizing process among the Warlpiri.* PhD dissertation, Deakin University Melbourne.

——. 2001. "The colonizing vehicle." In Daniel Miller, ed. *Car Cultures.* pp. 223–244. Oxford: Berg.

——. 2015. *Rights and obligations in a hunter-gatherer economy amongst Warlpiri in central Australia.* Paper held at the 11th Conference for Hunting and Gathering Societies (CHAGS 11) Wien.

Strathern, Marilyn. 1988. *The gender of the gift: Problems with women and problems with society in Melanesia.* Berkeley: University of California Press.

——. 2011. "Sharing, stealing and borrowing simultaneously." In Veronica Strang and Mark Busse eds. *Ownership and appropriation.* pp. 23–42. Oxford: Berg.

Strecker, Ivo. 1988. *The social practice of symbolization. An anthropological analysis.* London: Athlone.

Sugawara, Kazuyoshi. 2001. "Cognitive space concerning habitual thought and practice toward animals among the Central San (Gui and Gana): Deictic/indirect cognition and prospective/retrospective intention." *African Study Monographs* 27: 61–98.

——. 2005a. "Body configuration as resource in the experience of 'the hunter and the hunted': Narratives of the /Gui Bushmen." In Kazuyoshi Sugawara ed. *Construction and distribution of body resources. Correlations between ecological, symbolic, and medical systems.* pp. 56–78. Tokyo: Research Institute for Languages and Cultures of Asia and Africa, Tokyo University of Foreign Studies.

——. 2005b. *Construction and distribution of body resources: Correlations between ecological, symbolic, and medical systems.* Tokyo: Research Institute for Languages and Cultures of Asia and Africa, Tokyo University of Foreign Studies.

——. 2005c. "Possession, equality and gender relations in /Gui discourse." In Thomas Widlok and Wolde Gossa Tadesse eds. *Property and Equality. Volume 1: Ritualisation, Sharing, Egalitarianism.* pp. 105–129. New York: Berghahn.

Szalay, Miklós, ed. 2002. *Der Mond als Schuh: Zeichnungen der San ; Zeichnungen und Aquarelle von Diä!kwain, /Han kass'o, !Nanni, Tamme, /Uma und Da; The Moon as shoe.* Zürich: Scheidegger und Spiess.

Tax, Sol. 1975. *Families as corporations: A proposal* Unpublished. No place.

Taylor, Christopher C. 1997. "Sacrifice as terror: The Rwandan genocide of 1994." In Roy R. Grinker and Christopher B. Steiner eds. *Perspectives on Africa. A reader in culture, history, and representation.* pp. 555–568. Oxford: Blackwell.

Testart, Alain. 1987. "Game sharing systems and kinship systems among hunter-gatherers." *Man* 22(2): 287–304.

Tsuru, Daisaku. 2001. "Generation and transaction processes in the spirit ritual of the Baka Pygmies in Southeast Cameroon." In Thomas Widlok and Kazuyoshi Sugawara eds. *Symbolic categories and ritual practice in hunter-gatherer experience.* pp. 103–123. Kyoto: Center for African Area Studies.

Turner, David H. 1999. *Genesis regained: Aboriginal forms of renunciation in Judeo-Christian scriptures and other major traditions.* New York: P. Lang.

Turner, Victor W. 1969. *The ritual process: Structure and anti-structure.* London: Routledge & Kegan Paul.

Valeri, Valerio. 1994. "Buying women but not selling them: Gift and commodity exchange in Hualulu alliance." *Man* 29(1):1–26.

van der Sluys, Cornelia. 2000. "Gifts from the immortal ancestors: Cosmology and ideology of Jahai sharing." In Megan Biesele, Robert Hitchcock and Peter Schweitzer eds. *Hunters and gatherers in the modern world: Conflict, resistance and self-determination.* pp. 429–454. Oxford: Berghahn.

Venbrux, Eric, Janneke Peelen, and Marga Altena. (2009). "Mortuary rituals in the Netherlands." *Mortality* 29(2) 97-101.

Voland, Eckart. 2007. *Die Natur des Menschen: Grundkurs Soziobiologie.* München: Beck.

Waal, Frans de, and Michelle Berger. 2000. "Payment for labour in monkeys: Capuchins will voluntarily share treats with other monkeys that helped to secure them." *Nature* 404: 563.

Wagner, Roy. 1975. *The invention of culture.* Englewood Cliffs: Prentice-Hall.

——. 1991. "The fractal person." In Maurice Godelier and Marilyn Strathern eds. *Big men and great men. Personifications of power in Melanesia.* pp. 159–173. Cambridge: Cambridge Univ. Press.

Wasko, Molly, and Samer Faraj. 2005. "Why should I share? Examining social capital and knowledge contribution in electronic networks of practice." *MIS Quarterly* 29(1): 35–57.

Weber, Max. 1985. *Wirtschaft und Gesellschaft: Grundriß der verstehenden Soziologie.* Tübingen: Mohr.

Weber, Thomas P. 2003. *Soziobiologie*. Frankfurt am Main: Fischer.

Weig, Dörte. 2013. *Motility and relational mobility of the Baka in North-Eastern Gabon*. Köln: PhD dissertation. Köln Universität zu Köln. Universitäts- und Stadtbibliothek Köln.

Weiner, Annette B. 1992. *Inalienable possessions: The paradox of keeping-while-giving*. Berkeley, CA: University of California Press.

Wenzel, George W. 2000. "Sharing, Money, and Modern Inuit Subsistence: Obligation and Reciprocity at Clyde River, Nunavut." In George Wenzel, Grete Hovelsrud-Broda and Nabuhiro Kishigami, eds. *The social economy of sharing: Resource allocation and modern hunter-gatherers*. pp. 61–85. Osaka: National Museum of Ethnology.

Wenzel, George W., Grete Hovelsrud-Broda, and Nobuhiro Kishigami, eds. 2000. *The social economy of sharing: Resource allocation and modern hunter-gatherers*. Osaka: National Museum of Ethnology.

Whitehouse, Harvey. 2013. "Rethinking proximate causation and development in religious evolution." In Peter J. Richerson and Morten H. Christiansen eds. *Cultural evolution. Society, technology, language, and religion*. pp. 349–363. Cambridge, MA: MIT Press.

Widlok, Thomas. forthcoming. *Storage and Sharing*; Wiley International Encyclopedia of Anthropology ed. by H. Callan.

——. in press a. "Hunter-gatherer situations." *Hunter Gatherer Research*

——. in press b. "Making persons accountable: The impact of identification technology and of legal incorporation on notions of the person." *Zeitschrift für Ethnologie*.

——. 1992 "Practice, politics and ideology of the "travelling business" in Aboriginal religion." *Oceania* 63: 114–136.

——. 1998. "Unearthing culture. Khoisan funerals and social change." *Anthropos* 93: 115–126.

——. 1999. *Living on Mangetti. 'Bushman' autonomy and Namibian independence*. Oxford: Oxford University Press.

——. 2000. "Names that escape the state: Hai//om naming practices versus domination and isolation. In Peter Schweitzer, Megan Biesele, Robert Hitchcock, eds." *Hunters and gatherers in the modern world:* pp. 361–379. Oxford: Berghahn.

——. 2001a. "The illusion of a future? Medicine dance rituals for the civil society of tomorrow." In Thomas Widlok and Kazuyoshi Sugawara eds. *Symbolic categories and ritual practice in hunter-gatherer experiences*. African Study Monographs Supplementary Issue. pp. 165–183. Kyoto: The Center for African Area Studies.

——. 2001b. "Equality, group rights, and corporate ownership of land." *Max Planck Institute for Social Anthropology working papers* 21.

——. 2004. "Sharing by default? Outline of an anthropology of virtue." *Anthropological Theory* 4(1): 53–70.

——. 2005. "Introduction." In Thomas Widlok and Wolde Gossa Tadesse eds. *Property and equality. Volume 1: Ritualisation, sharing, egalitarianism*. pp. 1–17. New York: Berghahn.

——. 2006. "Two ways of looking at a Mangetti grove." In Junko Maruyama et al. eds. *Crossing disciplinary boundaries and re-visioning area studies: Perspectives from Asia and Africa*. pp. 11–20. Kyoto: Graduate School of Asian and African Area Studies, Kyoto University.

——. 2009a. "Norm and spontaneity: Elicitation with moral dilemma scenarios." In Monica Heintz ed. *The anthropology of moralities*. pp. 20–45. New York: Berghahn.

——. 2009b. "Where settlements and the landscape merge: Towards an integrated approach to the spatial dimension of social relations." In Michael Bollig and Olaf Bubenzer eds. *African landscapes. Interdisciplinary approaches*. pp. 407–427. New York, NY: Springer.

——. 2010. "Sharing as a cultural innovation." In Marion Benz, ed. *The principle of sharing. Segregation and construction of social identities at the transition from foraging to farming*; proceedings of a symposium held on 29 - 31 January 2009 at the Albert-Ludwigs-University of Freiburg. pp. 91–104. Berlin: Ex Oriente.

———. 2012. "Virtue." In Didier Fassin ed. *A companion to moral anthropology.* pp. 186–203. Malden, MA: Wiley-Blackwell.

———. 2013. "Sharing: Allowing others to take what is valued." *HAU: Journal of Ethnographic Theory* 3(2): 11–31.

———. 2016. Small words – big issues: The Anthropological relevance of Khoesan interjections", *African Study Monographs*, Suppl. 50: 25–41.

Widlok, Thomas, and Niclas Burenhult. 2014. "Sehen, riechen, orientieren." *Spektrum der Wissenschaft* (7): 76–81.

Widlok, Thomas, and Keith Stenning. forthcoming "Seeking common cause between cognitive science and ethnography: alternative logic in cooperative action." To appear in the *Journal of Cognition and Culture.*

Widlok, Thomas, and Kazuyoshi Sugawara, eds. 2001. *Symbolic categories and ritual practice in hunter-gatherer experience.* Kyoto: Center for African Area Studies.

Widlok, Thomas, and Wolde Gossa Tadesse, eds. 2005. *Property and equality. Volume 1: Ritualisation, sharing, egalitarianism.* New York: Berghahn.

Wiessner, Polly. 1982. "Risk, reciprocity and social influences on !Kung San economies." In Eleanor Leacock and Richard Lee eds. *Politics and history in band societies.* pp. 61–84. Cambridge: Cambridge University Press.

———. 1998. "On network analysis: The potential for understanding (and misunderstanding) !Kung Hxaro." *Current Anthropology* 39(4): 514–519.

Willerslev, Rane. 2007. *Soul hunters: Hunting, animism, and personhood among the Siberian Yukaghirs.* Berkeley: University of California Press.

———. 2015. *"The dark side of sharing" - egalitarianism, hunter and violence among the Ik of northern Uganda.* Paper held at the 11th Conference for Hunting and Gathering Societies (CHAGS 11). Wien.

Wilson, Peter J. 1988. *The domestication of the human species.* New Haven: Yale University Press.

Winterhalder, Bruce. 1996. "Social foraging and the behavioral ecology of intra-group resource transfers." *Evolutionary Anthropology* 5: 46–57.

———. 1997. "Gifts given, gifts taken: The behavioral ecology of nonmarket, intragroup exchange." *Journal of Archaeological Research* 5: 121–168.

Wittel, Andreas. 2011. "Qualities of sharing and their transformations in the digital age." *International Review of Information Ethics* 15: 3–8.

Wittgenstein, Ludwig, 1993. *Philosophical occasions, 1912 - 1951.* Indianapolis, Ind.: Hackett.

Wood, Brian, and Frank Marlowe. 2013. "Household and kin provisioning by Hadza men." *Human Nature* 24: 280–317.

Woodburn, James. 1982. "Egalitarian societies." *Man* 17(3): 431–451.

———. 1982. "Social dimension of death in four African hunting and gathering societies." In Maurice Bloch and Jonathan Parry eds. *Death and the regeneration of life.* pp 187–210 Cambridge: Cambridge University Press.

———. 1998. "'Sharing is not a form of exchange': An analysis of property-sharing in immediate-return hunter-gatherer societies." In Chris Hann ed. *Property relations. Renewing the anthropological tradition.* pp. 48–63. Cambridge: Cambridge University Press.

———. 2005. "Egalitarian Societies Revisited." In Thomas Widlok and Wolde Gossa Tadesse eds. *Property and equality. Volume 1: Ritualisation, sharing, egalitarianism.* pp. 18–31. New York: Berghahn.

Yan, Yunxiang. 1996. *The flow of gifts: Reciprocity and social networks in a Chinese village.* Stanford, CA: Stanford University Press.

Young, Diana. 2011. "Mutable things: Colours as material practice in the northwest of South Australia." *Journal of the Royal Anthropological Institute* 17(2): 356–376.

Zeitlyn, David. 2003. "Gift economies on the development of open source software: Anthropological reflections." *Research policy: A journal devoted to research policy, research management and planning* 32(7): 1287–1291.

Zhu, Haiyi, Robert Kraut, and Aniket Kittur. 2012. "Effectiveness of shared leadership in online communities." *The proceedings of the ACM conference on computer supported cooperative work:* 407–416.

Ziker, John. 2014. "Sharing, subsistence, and social norms in Northern Siberia." In J. Ensminger and J. P. Henrich eds. *Experimenting with social norms: fairness and punishment in cross-cultural perspective.* pp. 337–356. New York: Sage.

Ziker, John, and Michael Schnegg. 2005. "Food sharing at meals: Kinship, reciprocity, and clustering in the Taimyr Autonomous Okrug, Northern Russia." *Human Nature* 16(2): 178–210.

Zips-Mairitsch, Manuela. 2013. *Lost lands? (Land) rights of the San in Botswana and the legal concept of indigeneity in Africa.* Wien.: Lit-Verl.

INDEX